triumphlearning™

Mathematics 7

Coach®

Table of Contents

Domain 1: Diagnostic Assessment for Lessons 1–8

1. Mr. Brooks is buying a television set for $850. The sales tax is 6%. What will be the total amount he will pay for the television set after sales tax is included?

   A. $799

   B. $861

   C. $901

   D. $1,360

2. The temperature in the morning was $-2°F$. By the afternoon, the temperature had risen $9°F$. What was the afternoon temperature?

   A. $-11°F$

   B. $-7°F$

   C. $7°F$

   D. $11°F$

3. Which fraction can be expressed as a repeating decimal?

   A. $\frac{1}{10}$

   B. $\frac{1}{2}$

   C. $\frac{3}{5}$

   D. $\frac{7}{9}$

4. At a school dance, $\frac{3}{8}$ of the students were seventh graders. Which decimal is equivalent to $\frac{3}{8}$?

   A. 0.375

   B. 0.38

   C. 3.75

   D. 3.8

5. What is the sum of $-35 + 12$?

   A. -47

   B. -23

   C. 23

   D. 47

6. There are 180 students registered in a soccer camp. Of those registered, 35% are seventh graders. How many of the students registered are in the seventh grade?

   A. 54

   B. 63

   C. 117

   D. 145

7. Divide.

$$-448 \div 28 = \boxed{}$$

   A. -16

   B. -15

   C. 15

   D. 16

8. Subtract.

$$\frac{7}{8} - \frac{2}{3} = \boxed{}$$

   A. $\dfrac{5}{5}$

   B. $\dfrac{9}{11}$

   C. $\dfrac{9}{24}$

   D. $\dfrac{5}{24}$

9. A diver at -60 feet stops every 5 feet before reaching the surface. How many stops will the diver make before reaching the surface?

_____

10. Laila had $350 in her checking account. She made 5 deposits of $46.75 each. She also wrote 3 checks for $28.50 each.

   A. Write a decimal number to represent the total deposits Laila made and another decimal number to represent the total amount of the checks Laila wrote. Show your work.

   _____

   _____

   B. How much money is in Laila's account now? Show your work.

   _____

   _____

Relate Fractions, Decimals, and Percents

Getting the Idea

Rational numbers are numbers that can be expressed in the form $\frac{a}{b}$, where a and b are **integers** and $b \neq 0$. **Fractions, decimals**, and **percents** are rational numbers that can be used to show parts of a whole. Percent means *per hundred*. For example, 70% of a number means $\frac{70}{100}$ times the quantity. The symbol for percent is %.

You can convert rational numbers to different forms. To convert a percent to a fraction, write the percent as the **numerator** over a **denominator** of 100. Then write the fraction in **simplest form** using the **greatest common factor (GCF)**.

Example 1

Write 72% as a fraction in simplest form.

Strategy   **Write the percent as a fraction with a denominator of 100. Simplify.**

Step 1   Remove the percent sign. Write the percent as the numerator and 100 as the denominator.

$$72\% \longrightarrow \frac{72}{100}$$

Step 2   Simplify the fraction using the GCF.

The GCF of 72 and 100 is 4.

Divide the numerator and denominator by 4.

$$\frac{72}{100} = \frac{72 \div 4}{100 \div 4} = \frac{18}{25}$$

Solution $72\% = \frac{18}{25}$

Example 2

What is 84% written as a decimal?

Strategy   **Remove the percent sign and move the decimal point two places to the left.**

$$84\% \longrightarrow 84. \longrightarrow 0.84$$

Solution $84\% = 0.84$

Example 3

What is $\frac{2}{5}$ written as a decimal?

Strategy   **Write an equivalent fraction with a denominator of 10.**

Step 1   Find a fraction equivalent to $\frac{2}{5}$ that has a denominator of 10.

Since $5 \times 2 = 10$, multiply the numerator and denominator by 2.

$$\frac{2}{5} = \frac{2 \times 2}{5 \times 2} = \frac{4}{10}$$

Step 2   Write the decimal equivalent of $\frac{4}{10}$.

$\frac{4}{10}$ is read "four tenths."

$$\frac{4}{10} = 0.4$$

Solution $\frac{2}{5} = 0.4$

Example 4

Write 0.65 as a fraction in simplest form.

Strategy   **Write the digits after the decimal point as the numerator.**
The denominator is the place value of the last digit. Simplify.

Step 1   Write the digits 65 as the numerator of the fraction.

The denominator is 100 because the last digit, 5, is in the hundredths place.

$$0.65 = \frac{65}{100}$$

Step 2   Simplify using the GCF.

The GCF of 65 and 100 is 5.

$$\frac{65}{100} = \frac{65 \div 5}{100 \div 5} = \frac{13}{20}$$

Solution $0.65 = \frac{13}{20}$

To convert a decimal to a percent, multiply the decimal by 100 and insert a percent sign. Multiplying a decimal by 100 is the same as moving the decimal point 2 places to the right.

Example 5

What is 0.875 written as a percent?

Strategy   **Multiply the decimal by 100.**

Move the decimal point two places to the right.

$0.875 \times 100 = 87.5$

Insert a percent sign.

87.5%

Solution   **0.875 = 87.5%**

Example 6

Write $\frac{16}{25}$ as a percent.

Strategy   **Write an equivalent fraction.**

Step 1   Percent means per hundred, so write an equivalent fraction with a denominator of 100.

$25 \times 4 = 100$, so multiply the numerator and denominator by 4.

$\frac{16}{25} = \frac{16 \times 4}{25 \times 4} = \frac{64}{100}$

Step 2   Insert a percent sign next to the numerator.

$\frac{64}{100} \longrightarrow 64\%$

Solution $\frac{16}{25} = 64\%$

If the denominator is not a factor of 100, convert the fraction to a decimal.

Then convert the decimal to a percent. Some decimals, such as $\frac{1}{3}$, are repeating decimals.

To write a repeating decimal as a percent, write the percent and the part that repeats as a fraction.

Example 7

What is $\frac{2}{3}$ written as a percent?

Strategy   **Convert the fraction to a decimal. Then convert the decimal to a percent.**

| Step 1 | Divide the numerator by the denominator. |

$$\frac{2}{3} = 2 \div 3 = 0.\overline{6}$$

| Step 2 | Multiply the decimal by 100. |

$$0.\overline{6} \times 100 = 66.\overline{6}$$

Insert a percent sign.

$66.\overline{6}\%$ or $66\frac{2}{3}\%$

Solution $\frac{2}{3} = 66\frac{2}{3}\%$

Coached Example

Maria received 55% of the vote in a student council election. What decimal and fraction, written in simplest form, are equivalent to the percentage of the vote Maria received?

To convert a percent to a decimal, remove the percent sign and move the decimal point 2 places to the _____.

The decimal _____ is equivalent to 55%.

To convert a percent to a fraction, write the percent as the numerator over a denominator of _____.

What is the GCF of the numerator and denominator? _____

Divide the numerator and denominator by _____.

Simplify. _____

55% written as a decimal is _____. 55% written as a fraction is _____.

Lesson Practice • Part 1

Choose the correct answer.

1. About 60.7% of eligible voters voted in the election. Which decimal is equivalent to 60.7%?

   A. 0.0607

   B. 0.607

   C. 6.07

   D. 60.7

2. In a survey of patients, Dr. Molar found that 8% of his patients floss daily. Which fraction is equivalent to 8%?

   A. $\frac{4}{5}$

   B. $\frac{2}{5}$

   C. $\frac{4}{25}$

   D. $\frac{2}{25}$

3. Kristen made $\frac{3}{8}$ of her free throws for the season. Which percent is equivalent to $\frac{3}{8}$?

   A. 37.5%

   B. 38%

   C. 38.5%

   D. 375%

4. Tomas correctly spelled 18 out of 20 words on his last spelling quiz. What decimal represents the portion of the words that Tomas spelled correctly?

   A. 0.18

   B. 0.36

   C. 0.8

   D. 0.9

5. Which fraction is equivalent to 48%?

   A. $\frac{4}{5}$

   B. $\frac{4}{8}$

   C. $\frac{12}{25}$

   D. $\frac{8}{25}$

6. Sales at Cycle Time increased by 370% this year. Which of the following is equivalent to 370%?

   A. $\frac{37}{100}$

   B. 3.7

   C. $3\frac{7}{100}$

   D. 37

7. Which rational number is **not** equivalent to the others?

   A. 75%

   B. $\frac{3}{4}$

   C. 0.75

   D. $\frac{7}{50}$

8. Which of the following shows a set of equivalent rational numbers?

   A. $\frac{2}{5}$ 0.4   25%

   B. $\frac{2}{3}$ 0.6   66%

   C. $\frac{3}{10}$ 0.3   30%

   D. $\frac{73}{100}$ 0.73   730%

9. The Lions won 35 out of 40 games this season.

   A. What fraction of games played did the Lions win? Write your answer in simplest form.

   _____

   B. Write a decimal and a percent equivalent to the fraction of games the Lions won. Show your work.

   _____

   _____

Lesson Practice • Part 2

Choose the correct answer.

1. Which describes how to rename a percent as a decimal?

   A. divide the percent by 100 and remove the percent sign

   B. divide the percent by 10 and remove the percent sign

   C. multiply the percent by 10 and remove the percent sign

   D. multiply the percent by 100 and remove the percent sign

2. A baseball team won $\frac{5}{9}$ of its games this season. Which percent is equivalent to $\frac{5}{9}$?

   A. 55%

   B. 55.5%

   C. $55\frac{5}{9}$%

   D. 59%

3. Of the 360 pages in a book, 72 have diagrams. Which decimal represents the part of the pages that have diagrams?

   A. 0.15

   B. 0.2

   C. 0.25

   D. 0.3

4. Of the songs on a playlist, 72% are country songs. Which fraction is equivalent to 72%?

   A. $\frac{3}{4}$

   B. $\frac{11}{16}$

   C. $\frac{13}{18}$

   D. $\frac{18}{25}$

5. Once he figured out how to play a computer game, Dinesh's score improved by 275%. Which decimal is equivalent to 275%?

   A. 0.275

   B. 2.75

   C. 27.5

   D. 275

6. Which rational number has a different value than the others?

   A. 44%

   B. $\frac{22}{50}$

   C. 0.44

   D. $\frac{4}{9}$

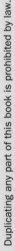

7. Of the students at Fillmore Middle School, 0.5625 are bused to school. Which percent is equivalent to 0.5625?

 A. 0.5625%

 B. 5.625%

 C. 56.25%

 D. 562.5%

8. Interest rates have risen by $\frac{1}{4}$%. Which decimal is equivalent to $\frac{1}{4}$%?

 A. 0.0025

 B. 0.025

 C. 0.25

 D. 2.5

9. Ximena made 26 out of 32 penalty kicks with her brother as the goalie.

 A. In simplest form, what fraction of the penalty kicks did Ximena make?

 _____

 B. Write a decimal and a percent equivalent to the fraction of the penalty kicks that Ximena made. Show your work.

 _____

10. Victor correctly answered 18 of the 20 questions on his math quiz. Circle the fraction that makes the statement true.

The fraction of questions that Victor answered correctly is

$$\frac{4}{5}$$

$$\frac{9}{10}$$

$$\frac{7}{15}$$

$$\frac{3}{25}$$

.

11. Which shows a set of equivalent rational numbers? Circle all that apply.

    A. $\frac{4}{5}$, 0.8, 80%

    B. $\frac{3}{4}$, 0.75, 75%

    C. $\frac{3}{1}$, 0.3, 3%

    D. $\frac{5}{8}$, 0.625, 6.25%

12. Draw a line from each fraction or decimal to its equivalent percent.

    A. $\frac{1}{8}$ •   • 87.5%

    B. $\frac{1}{5}$ •   • 30%

    C. 0.875 •   • 20%

    D. 0.3 •   • 12.5%

    E. 0.05 •   • 5%

13. Look at each equation. Are the numbers equivalent? Select Yes or No.

    A. $\frac{2}{5} = 0.4$ ○ Yes ○ No

    B. 0.329 = 3.29%   ○ Yes ○ No

    C. $\frac{1}{8} = 12.5\%$ ○ Yes ○ No

    D. 0.1 = 10%   ○ Yes ○ No

14. Write each number under its equivalent number in the table.

| $\frac{7}{10}$ | 40% | 0.4 | 55% | 0.7 | $\frac{11}{20}$ |

70%	$\frac{2}{5}$	0.55

15. Antonia ate $\frac{3}{8}$ of a bunch of grapes. Circle the percent that makes the statement true.

Antonia ate

| 3.8% |
| 37.5% |
| 38% |
| 375% |

of the bunch of grapes.

16. Brent read 56 pages of his 64-page book. Which value represents the part of the book that Brent read? Circle all that apply.

A. 0.875

B. $\frac{7}{8}$

C. 0.0875

D. 87.5%

E. $\frac{5}{6}$

F. 8.75%

Solve Problems with Percents

Getting the Idea

Percents are used for many things, such as the sale price of an item, the sales tax you pay on an item, and the interest earned on a bank deposit. Sometimes it is necessary to change a percent to a fraction or a decimal to solve a percent problem.

Example 1

What is 8% of 214?

Strategy   **Change the percent to a decimal. Then multiply.**

Step 1	Change the percent to a decimal.

Remove the percent symbol and divide by 100.

$$8\% \longrightarrow .08. \longrightarrow 0.08$$

Step 2	Multiply the decimal by 214.

$$0.08 \times 214 = 17.12$$

Solution   **8% of 214 is 17.12.**

A **discount** is the amount of money that is taken off the original price of an item.

The **sale price** is the cost of the item after the discount has been applied.

Example 2

Debbie sees a pair of jeans that was originally priced at $36. The jeans are on sale for 25% off. What is the sale price of the jeans?

Strategy   **Change the percent to a fraction. Then multiply to find the discount.**

Step 1	Write an expression to represent the discount.

Find 25% of $36.

Step 2	Rename 25% as a fraction in simplest form.

$$25\% = \frac{25}{100} = \frac{1}{4}$$

Step 3   Find $\frac{1}{4}$ of $36, the amount of the discount.

$$\frac{1}{4} \times \$36 = \frac{1}{\underset{1}{\cancel{4}}} \times \frac{\overset{9}{\cancel{36}}}{1} = \frac{9}{1} = \$9$$

So, the amount of the discount is $9.

Step 4   Subtract the discount from the original price.

$36 − $9 = $27

Solution   **The sale price of the jeans is $27.**

Sales tax is a tax based on the cost of an item. You can find sales tax in the same way you find the percent of a number.

Example 3

A DVD costs $19.80. The sales tax is 7%. What is the cost of the DVD, with tax included?

Strategy   **Find the amount of sales tax. Then add the tax to the cost of the DVD.**

Step 1   Change 7% to a decimal.

7% = 0.07

Step 2   Multiply the decimal by the cost of the DVD.

0.07 × $19.80 = $1.386

Round $1.386 to $1.39.

So, the tax is $1.39.

Step 3   Add the sales tax to the cost of the DVD.

$19.80 + $1.39 = $21.19

Solution   **The cost of the DVD, with tax included, is $21.19.**

Interest is the amount of money the bank pays you for its use of the money in a savings account. Interest could also be the amount of money you pay a lender for the use of borrowed money.

The amount of money in your savings account or the amount you borrow is the **principal**. One type of interest is **simple interest**. To calculate simple interest, use the formula $I = prt$, where I represents simple interest, p represents the principal, r represents the rate of interest, and t represents time, in years.

Example 4

Jen deposited $750 in her savings account. She had the money in the account for 18 months without making any deposits or withdrawals. The account earns 2% annual simple interest. How much money did Jen earn in simple interest?

Strategy   Use the formula $I = prt$.

Step 1   Convert the time to years and the rate to a decimal.

18 months $= 1\frac{1}{2}$ years $= 1.5$ years

$2\% \longrightarrow 0.02$

Step 2   Substitute the known values into the formula.

$I = prt$

$I = \$750 \times 0.02 \times 1.5$

Step 3   Multiply.

$I = \$750 \times (0.02 \times 1.5)$

$= \$750 \times 0.03$

$= \$22.50$

Solution   Jen earned $22.50 in simple interest.

To find the percent increase or the percent decrease, write the difference in amounts as the numerator of a fraction with the original amount as the denominator. For prices, a percent of increase is a markup and a percent of decrease is a markdown. Then change the fraction to a percent.

Example 5

A computer game that originally cost $40 is on sale for $28. What is the percent decrease in the price of the game?

Strategy   **Write a fraction to represent the decrease.**

Step 1   Write and simplify a fraction.

$$\frac{\text{original price} - \text{sale price}}{\text{original price}} = \frac{\$40 - \$28}{\$40} = \frac{12}{40} = \frac{3}{10}$$

Step 2   Convert the fraction to a percent.

$$\frac{3}{10} = \frac{30}{100} = 30\%$$

Solution   **The percent decrease in the price of the game is 30%.**

Example 6

A basketball team won 15 games during the 2008–2009 season. In the 2009–2010 season, the team won 21 games. What was the percent of increase in games won?

Strategy   **Write a fraction to represent the increase.**

Step 1   Write and simplify a fraction.

$$\frac{\text{games won in 2009–2010} - \text{games won in 2008–2009}}{\text{games won in 2008–2009}} = \frac{21 - 15}{15} = \frac{6}{15} = \frac{2}{5}$$

Step 2   Convert the fraction to a percent.

$$\frac{2}{5} = 0.4 = 40\%$$

Solution   **The percent of increase in games won is 40%.**

A **percent error** measures how far off an estimate is to the actual value. The percent error is the **absolute value** of the difference between an estimate and the actual value, divided by the actual value. Multiply by 100 to express the error as a percent.

Example 7

Johnny used mental math to estimate that 11×5 is approximately 50.

What is his percent error?

Strategy   **Find the actual value. Then calculate the percent error.**

Step 1   Find the actual value of 11×5.

$11 \times 5 = 55$

Step 2   Find the difference between the estimate and the actual value.

$55 - 50 = 5$

Step 3   Divide the difference by the actual value. Round to the nearest hundredth.

$\frac{5}{55} \approx 0.09$

Step 4   Convert the decimal to a percent.

$0.09 \longrightarrow 9\%$

Solution   **Johnny's percent error is about 9%.**

Coached Example

Angela and Sadie had dinner at a restaurant. Their bill was $24.50. They left a 15% tip for their server. How much money did Angela and Sadie spend for their bill and tip?

To solve this problem, add the amount of the _____ and the amount of the _____.

The bill was $_____.

To find the amount of the tip, first change _____ to a decimal.

_____% ⟶ _____

Then multiply the decimal by the amount of the _____.

_____ × $_____ = $_____

Round the amount of the tip to the nearest cent. $_____

Add the amount of the _____ and the amount of the _____.

$_____ + $_____ = $_____

Angela and Sadie spent $_____ for their bill and tip.

Lesson Practice • Part 1

Choose the correct answer.

1. What is 72% of 175?

   A.   1.26

   B.   12.6

   C.   126

   D.   1,260

2. A computer that originally cost $850 is on sale for 15% off. What is the sale price of the computer?

   A. $127.50

   B. $722.50

   C. $835.00

   D. $977.50

3. There were 60 seventh-grade students who signed up for soccer tryouts last year. This year, 48 seventh-grade students signed up for tryouts. What is the percent decrease in the number of students from last year to this year?

   A.   18%

   B.   20%

   C.   25%

   D.   80%

4. Pablo put $1,260 into a savings account that earns 3% simple interest per year. He does not make any deposits or withdrawals. How much money will be in Pablo's account after 2 years?

   A. $75.60

   B. $1,297.80

   C. $1,335.60

   D. $8,820.00

5. Mrs. Blake's bill at a restaurant was $42.75. She wants to leave the waiter an 18% tip. How much will she pay in all, including the tip?

   A. $6.41

   B. $7.70

   C. $49.14

   D. $50.45

6. Mr. Chung stayed four nights at a hotel. His bill was $725 before the sales tax of 6% was added. How much was the sales tax?

   A. $43.50

   B. $45.00

   C. $46.50

   D. $49.00

7. In September, there were 16 members in the Music Club. In October, the number of members was 24. What was the percent increase from September to October?

   A. 20%

   B. 30%

   C. $33\frac{1}{3}$%

   D. 50%

8. There are 120 students in the seventh grade. Seventy percent of these students are involved in extracurricular activities. How many seventh-grade students are **not** involved in an extracurricular activity?

   A. 36

   B. 50

   C. 70

   D. 84

9. Isme estimated that there are 50 students in the seventh-grade class. There are actually 40 students in the seventh-grade class.

   A. What is Isme's percent error? Show your work.

   _____

   _____

   B. Out of the 40 students in the seventh-grade class, 60% of the students carry a cell phone. What fraction of the students in the seventh-grade class carry a cell phone? How many students in the seventh-grade class carry a cell phone? Show your work.

   _____

   _____

Lesson Practice • Part 2

Choose the correct answer.

1. Noah bought a computer cartridge for $28.50. Sales tax on the cartridge was 6.5%. What was the total amount that Noah paid for the cartridge?

   A. $26.65
   B. $30.35
   C. $35.00
   D. $47.03

2. A realtor earns 1.25% commission on the price of any home that she sells. Last month she sold two homes for a total of $750,000. How much money in commissions did the realtor earn last month?

   A. $9,055
   B. $9,375
   C. $90,550
   D. $93,750

3. Alexa put $850 into a savings account that earns 0.75% annual simple interest. If Alexa does not make any deposits or withdrawals for 18 months, how much money will be in her account?

   A. $859.56
   B. $945.63
   C. $964.75
   D. $977.50

4. A computer normally costs $640. This week that same computer is on sale for $480. What is the markdown on the price of the computer?

   A. 25%
   B. $33\frac{1}{3}$%
   C. $66\frac{2}{3}$%
   D. 75%

5. Sebastian said he could hit a golf ball 160 yards on his first drive. He hit the ball 152 yards. To the nearest tenth, what was Sebastian's percent error on his prediction?

   A. 95%
   B. 94.7%
   C. 5.3%
   D. 5%

6. Luke bought a jacket that was 30% off the cost. He paid sales tax of 6% after the discount had been applied. If the jacket had a price tag of $75, what was the actual amount that Luke paid including tax?

   A. $48.00
   B. $55.65
   C. $91.65
   D. $102.00

7. Each T-shirt that Just Tees produces costs $1.50 to make. They sell their T-shirts for $15 at events. What is the markup on the T-shirts?

A. 90%

B. 100%

C. 900%

D. 1,000%

8. What sentence about markdowns and markups is true?

A. Markdowns and markups have no limit.

B. A markdown has no limit, but a markup is limited to 100% or less.

C. A markup has no limit, but a markdown is limited to 100% or less.

D. Markdowns and markups are limited to 100% or less.

9. There were 20 members in the running club in September. The membership increased to 25 in October. The membership decreased back to 20 in November.

A. What was the percent increase from September to October? Show your work.

_____

B. What was the percent decrease from October to November? Show your work.

_____

10. Use numbers from the box to complete each equation.

35% of 120 = _____

12% of 50 = _____

55% of 40 = _____

| 6 |
| 22 |
| 30 |
| 42 |
| 110 |

11. Read each word problem and its stated solution. Is the solution correct? Select Yes or No.

    A. Jing scored 21 points during her seventh-grade basketball   ○ Yes   ○ No
        season and 30 points during her eighth-grade basketball
        season. The percent of increase is 9%.

    B. Austin bought a trampoline for $180 that originally cost   ○ Yes   ○ No
        $300. The percent of decrease is 40%.

    C. Margery guessed that she read 24 pages in a book. She   ○ Yes   ○ No
        actually read 30 pages in the book. The percent of error
        was 20%.

12. Draw a line from each expression to its solution.

    A. 22% of 60   ●   ● 32

    B. 40% of 80   ●   ● 28.75

    C. 25% of 115   ●   ● 13.2

13. Conner deposited $450 into his savings account. He had the money in the account for 24 months without making any withdrawals or deposits. The account earns 3% simple interest. Circle the amount of simple interest that Conner earned.

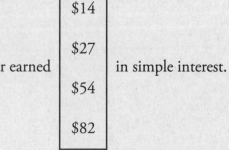

Conner earned
$14

$27

$54

$82
   in simple interest.

14. Helena's family went to dinner and the bill was $75.80. The restaurant charged a mandatory tip of 15% of the bill. Which is a true statement? Circle all that apply.

    A. The amount of the tip was $11.37.

    B. The amount of the tip was $27.90.

    C. The total amount that they paid, including the tip, was $87.17.

    D. The total amount that they paid, including the tip, was $103.70.

15. There are 80 members of the show choir. For a fund-raiser, 95% of the members raised money. Circle the number that makes the statement true.

4
15
55
74

members did **not** raise money for the fund-raiser.

16. Select True or False for each statement.

A. A purse costs $35.60 with sales tax of 5%. The total cost of the purchase is $37.38.   ○ True   ○ False

B. A bicycle costs $75.80 with sales tax of 6.5%. The total cost of the purchase is $91.25.   ○ True   ○ False

C. A hat costs $25.50 with sales tax of 6%. The total cost of the purchase is $27.03.   ○ True   ○ False

D. A table costs $198.20 with sales tax of 7%. The total cost of the purchase is $336.94.   ○ True   ○ False

Terminating and Repeating Decimals

Getting the Idea

Terminating and repeating decimals are also rational numbers. A **terminating decimal** ends. A **repeating decimal** does not end. Instead, it repeats a digit or pattern of digits over and over.

To determine whether a fraction can be expressed as a terminating or repeating decimal, convert the fraction to a decimal using long division. The **quotient** will terminate or repeat.

Example 1

Can the fraction $\frac{1}{3}$ be expressed as a terminating or repeating decimal?

Strategy   **Divide the numerator by the denominator. Analyze the quotient.**

Step 1   Divide the numerator by the denominator.

$$
\begin{array}{r}
0.333\ldots \\
3\overline{)1.000} \\
\underline{-9} \\
10 \\
\underline{-9} \\
10 \\
\underline{-9} \\
1
\end{array}
$$

Step 2   Does the decimal end?

No, the decimal does not end, so it is not terminating.

Step 3   Does one digit or a pattern of digits in the decimal repeat?

Yes, the digit 3 repeats.

So, the decimal is repeating.

Solution   **The fraction $\frac{1}{3}$ can be expressed as a repeating decimal.**

To indicate the numbers that repeat in a repeating decimal, draw a bar over the repeating digit or digits. The repeating decimal 0.333 … can be written as $0.\overline{3}$.

Example 2

Can the fraction $\frac{7}{8}$ be expressed as a terminating or repeating decimal?

Strategy   **Divide the numerator by the denominator. Analyze the quotient.**

Step 1   Divide the numerator by the denominator.

$$
\begin{array}{r}
0.875 \\
8{\overline{\smash{\big)}\,7.000}} \\
\underline{-6\ 4} \\
60 \\
\underline{-56} \\
40 \\
\underline{-40} \\
0
\end{array}
$$

Step 2   Does the decimal end?

Yes, the decimal ends.

So, the decimal is terminating.

Solution   **The fraction $\frac{7}{8}$ can be expressed as a terminating decimal.**

Coached Example

Can the fraction $\frac{3}{8}$ be expressed as a terminating or repeating decimal?

Divide the _____ by the _____.

$$8{\overline{\smash{\big)}\,3}}$$

Does the decimal end? _____

The fraction $\frac{7}{8}$ can be expressed as a _____ decimal.

Lesson Practice • Part 1

Choose the correct answer.

1. Which fraction can be expressed as a terminating decimal?

    A. $\frac{1}{9}$

    B. $\frac{3}{11}$

    C. $\frac{5}{8}$

    D. $\frac{2}{3}$

2. Which fraction can be expressed as a repeating decimal?

    A. $\frac{1}{10}$

    B. $\frac{1}{4}$

    C. $\frac{3}{5}$

    D. $\frac{7}{9}$

3. Which fraction **cannot** be expressed as a terminating decimal?

    A. $\frac{1}{15}$

    B. $\frac{3}{10}$

    C. $\frac{2}{5}$

    D. $\frac{7}{8}$

4. Which fraction **cannot** be expressed as a repeating decimal?

    A. $\frac{8}{9}$

    B. $\frac{3}{4}$

    C. $\frac{13}{18}$

    D. $\frac{1}{7}$

5. Which numbers repeat in the decimal form of $\frac{5}{11}$?

    A. 4

    B. 45

    C. 444

    D. 454

6. Which shows the fraction $\frac{2}{9}$ as a decimal?

    A. $0.\overline{2}$

    B. 0.22

    C. $0.2\overline{9}$

    D. $0.\overline{29}$

7. Which shows the fraction $\frac{7}{12}$ as a decimal?

    A. 7.12

    B. $0.71\overline{2}$

    C. $0.58\overline{3}$

    D. $0.\overline{58}$

8. Which shows the fraction $\frac{1}{8}$ as a decimal?

    A. $0.12\overline{5}$

    B. 0.125

    C. 0.18

    D. $0.\overline{18}$

9. George wrote the division expression $2 \div 5$.

    A. Can George's expression be expressed as a rational number? Explain your answer.

    _____

    _____

    B. Can George's expression be expressed as a terminating or repeating decimal? Explain.

    _____

    _____

Lesson Practice • Part 2

Choose the correct answer.

1. The denominator of a fraction is 7. The numerator is a whole number greater than 0 and less than 7. Which sentence about when the fraction is expressed as a decimal is true?

   A. All of the numerators will result in a repeating decimal.

   B. All of the numerators will result in a terminating decimal.

   C. The majority of the numerators, but not all, will result in a repeating decimal.

   D. The majority of the numerators, but not all, will result in a terminating decimal.

2. Which shows $\frac{11}{18}$ as a decimal?

   A. 0.61

   B. $0.6\overline{1}$

   C. $0.\overline{61}$

   D. $0.61\overline{1}$

3. Which fraction can be expressed as a terminating decimal?

   A. $\frac{4}{11}$

   B. $\frac{5}{13}$

   C. $\frac{6}{15}$

   D. $\frac{7}{17}$

4. The denominator of a fraction is 12. The numerator is a whole number greater than 0 and less than 12. Which sentence about when the fraction is expressed as a decimal is true?

   A. All of the numerators will result in a repeating decimal.

   B. All of the numerators will result in a terminating decimal.

   C. The majority of the numerators, but not all, will result in a repeating decimal.

   D. The majority of the numerators, but not all, will result in a terminating decimal.

5. Which shows $\frac{4}{15}$ as a decimal?

   A. 0.26

   B. $0.\overline{26}$

   C. $0.2\overline{6}$

   D. $0.26\overline{}$

6. Which fraction can be expressed as a repeating decimal?

   A. $\frac{3}{6}$

   B. $\frac{5}{8}$

   C. $\frac{7}{10}$

   D. $\frac{11}{12}$

7. The denominator of a fraction is 16. The numerator is a whole number greater than 0 and less than 16. Which sentence about when the fraction is expressed as a decimal is true?

    A. All of the numerators will result in a repeating decimal.

    B. All of the numerators will result in a terminating decimal.

    C. The majority of the numerators, but not all, will result in a repeating decimal.

    D. The majority of the numerators, but not all, will result in a terminating decimal.

8. Which numerator completes a fraction that can be expressed as a repeating decimal?

$$\frac{x}{24}$$

    A. 6   **C.** 12

    B. 10   **D.** 18

9. Which shows $\frac{4}{25}$ as a decimal?

    A. 0.16

    B. $0.\overline{1}6$

    C. $0.1\overline{6}$

    D. $0.16\overline{}$

10. The numerator of a fraction is 1 less than the denominator.

    A. Which fractions with this rule for denominators from 3 to 10 repeat? Write each as a decimal.

_____

    B. Which fractions with this rule for denominators from 3 to 10 terminate? Write each as a decimal.

_____

11. Select True or False for each statement.

    A. $\frac{3}{5}$ can be expressed as a terminating decimal.   ○ True   ○ False

    B. $\frac{5}{6}$ can be expressed as a terminating decimal.   ○ True   ○ False

    C. $\frac{4}{11}$ can be expressed as a repeating decimal.   ○ True   ○ False

    D. $\frac{9}{10}$ can be expressed as a repeating decimal.   ○ True   ○ False

12. Use numbers from the box to complete each sentence.

0.27

$0.\overline{27}$

$0.2\overline{7}$

$0.\overline{27}$

$0.\overline{027}$

The fraction $\frac{3}{11}$ is equivalent to _____.

The fraction $\frac{1}{37}$ is equivalent to _____.

13. Look at each fraction. Can it be expressed as a repeating decimal? Select Yes or No.

A. $\frac{5}{6}$ ⃝ Yes ⃝ No

B. $\frac{3}{8}$ ⃝ Yes ⃝ No

C. $\frac{3}{13}$ ⃝ Yes ⃝ No

D. $\frac{3}{5}$ ⃝ Yes ⃝ No

14. Draw a line from each fraction to its equivalent decimal.

A. $\frac{1}{12}$ •   • 0.75

B. $\frac{3}{4}$ •   • $0.\overline{45}$

C. $\frac{1}{25}$ •   • 0.04

D. $\frac{5}{11}$ •   • $0.08\overline{3}$

15. Determine if each fraction can be expressed as a terminating decimal or a repeating decimal. Write each fraction in the correct box.

| $\frac{1}{3}$ | $\frac{7}{12}$ | $\frac{1}{5}$ | $\frac{5}{8}$ | $\frac{2}{9}$ |

Terminating Decimal	Repeating Decimal

16. Which fraction **cannot** be represented by a terminating decimal? Circle all that apply.

A. $\frac{3}{4}$

B. $\frac{6}{11}$

C. $\frac{2}{3}$

D. $\frac{1}{5}$

E. $\frac{7}{9}$

17. Circle the equivalent decimal for each fraction.

$\frac{1}{9} =$

| 0.1 |
| 0.$\overline{1}$ |
| 0.9 |
| 0.$\overline{9}$ |

$\frac{5}{6} =$

| 0.83 |
| 0.8$\overline{3}$ |
| 0.$\overline{83}$ |
| $\overline{0.83}$ |

Divide Fractions

Getting the Idea

To divide fractions, first find the **reciprocal** of the **divisor**. Then multiply the **dividend** by the reciprocal of the divisor. Reciprocals are two numbers whose **product** is 1.

You can find the reciprocal of a fraction or whole number by switching the numerator and the denominator. For example, $\frac{3}{8}$ and $\frac{8}{3}$ are reciprocals because $\frac{3}{8} \times \frac{8}{3} = \frac{24}{24} = 1$.

Example 1

Divide.

$$\frac{3}{5} \div \frac{2}{3} = \boxed{}$$

Strategy   **Multiply the dividend by the reciprocal of the divisor.**

Step 1   Rewrite as a multiplication problem, using the reciprocal of the divisor.

The reciprocal of $\frac{2}{3}$ is $\frac{3}{2}$.

$$\frac{3}{5} \div \frac{2}{3} = \frac{3}{5} \times \frac{3}{2}$$

Step 2   Multiply.

$$\frac{3}{5} \times \frac{3}{2} = \frac{9}{10}$$

$\frac{9}{10}$ is in simplest form.

Solution $\frac{3}{5} \div \frac{2}{3} = \frac{9}{10}$

A **complex fraction** is a fraction in which the numerator and/or denominator contains a fraction. Recall that a fraction represents a quotient. The quotient is the numerator divided by the denominator (where the denominator is not equal to 0). For example, $\frac{3}{4} = 3 \div 4$.

The division expression in Example 1 can be written as a complex fraction: $\frac{\frac{3}{5}}{\frac{2}{3}}$.

The numerator of the complex fraction is $\frac{3}{5}$ and the denominator is $\frac{2}{3}$.

The complex fraction and the division expression are equivalent: $\frac{\frac{3}{5}}{\frac{2}{3}} = \frac{3}{5} \div \frac{2}{3}$.

Simplifying a complex fraction is the same as dividing its numerator by its denominator.

Example 2

Simplify.

$$\dfrac{\frac{1}{4}}{\frac{1}{12}} = \boxed{}$$

Strategy   **Multiply the numerator by the reciprocal of the denominator.**

Step 1   Rewrite as a multiplication problem using the reciprocal of the denominator.

The reciprocal of $\frac{1}{12}$ is $\frac{12}{1}$.

$$\frac{1}{4} \div \frac{1}{12} = \frac{1}{4} \times \frac{12}{1}$$

Step 2   Multiply.

$$\frac{1}{4} \times \frac{12}{1} = \frac{12}{4}$$

Step 3   Write the answer in simplest form.

$$\frac{12 \div 4}{4 \div 4} = \frac{3}{1} = 3$$

Solution $\dfrac{\frac{1}{4}}{\frac{1}{12}} = 3$

Example 3

Simplify.

$$\dfrac{\frac{5}{8}}{\frac{2}{3}} = \boxed{}$$

Strategy   **Multiply the numerator by the reciprocal of the denominator.**

Step 1   Rewrite as a multiplication problem using the reciprocal of the denominator.

$$\frac{5}{8} \div \frac{2}{3} = \frac{5}{8} \times \frac{3}{2}$$

Step 2   Multiply.

$$\frac{5}{8} \times \frac{3}{2} = \frac{15}{16}$$

Solution $\dfrac{\frac{5}{8}}{\frac{2}{3}} = \frac{15}{16}$

To divide **mixed numbers**, first rewrite the mixed numbers as **improper fractions**. Then follow the rules for dividing fractions.

Example 4

Jamie divided $5\frac{1}{4}$ pounds of apples into baskets that hold $1\frac{3}{4}$ pounds each.

How many baskets did she use?

Strategy   **Rewrite the mixed numbers as improper fractions. Then divide.**

| Step 1 | Write an expression to represent the problem. |

Find $5\frac{1}{4} \div 1\frac{3}{4}$.

| Step 2 | Rewrite the mixed numbers as improper fractions. |

$$5\frac{1}{4} \longrightarrow \frac{(5 \times 4) + 1}{4} = \frac{21}{4}$$

$$1\frac{3}{4} \longrightarrow \frac{(1 \times 4) + 3}{4} = \frac{7}{4}$$

$$5\frac{1}{4} \div 1\frac{3}{4} = \frac{21}{4} \div \frac{7}{4}$$

| Step 3 | Rewrite as a multiplication problem using the reciprocal of the divisor. |

The reciprocal of $\frac{7}{4}$ is $\frac{4}{7}$.

$$\frac{21}{4} \div \frac{7}{4} = \frac{21}{4} \times \frac{4}{7}$$

| Step 4 | Simplify the factors and multiply. |

$$\overset{3}{\underset{1}{\cancel{\frac{21}{4}}}} \times \overset{1}{\underset{1}{\cancel{\frac{4}{7}}}} = \frac{3 \times 1}{1 \times 1} = \frac{3}{1}$$

| Step 5 | Simplify. |

$$\frac{3}{1} = 3$$

Solution   **Jamie used 3 baskets.**

Any whole number can be expressed as a fraction. For example, $4 = \frac{4}{1}$. So, the reciprocal of a whole number divisor is a unit fraction. For example, the reciprocal of 4 is $\frac{1}{4}$.

Example 5

Divide.

$$6\frac{5}{8} \div 3 = \boxed{}$$

Strategy   **Rewrite the whole number as a fraction. Then find the reciprocal.**

Step 1 Rewrite $6\frac{5}{8}$ as an improper fraction. Write the reciprocal of 3.

$$6\frac{5}{8} \longrightarrow \frac{(6 \times 8) + 5}{8} = \frac{53}{8}$$

The reciprocal of 3 is $\frac{1}{3}$.

Step 2 Rewrite as a multiplication problem and solve.

$$6\frac{5}{8} \div 3 = \frac{53}{8} \times \frac{1}{3}$$

Step 3 Multiply.

$$\frac{53}{8} \times \frac{1}{3} = \frac{53 \times 1}{8 \times 3} = \frac{53}{24}$$

Step 4 Simplify the product.

$$\frac{53}{24} = 2\frac{5}{24}$$

Solution $6\frac{5}{8} \div 3 = 2\frac{5}{24}$

Coached Example

Mr. Camara cuts a 15-foot wooden board into pieces that are each $1\frac{2}{3}$ feet long. How many pieces of wood does he have?

Let w represent the number of pieces of wood.

Write a number sentence to represent this problem. _____

Rewrite 15 as an improper fraction. _____

Rewrite $1\frac{2}{3}$ as an improper fraction. _____

Rewrite the number sentence using improper fractions. _____

To divide fractions, multiply the dividend by the _____ of the divisor.

The reciprocal of the divisor is _____.

Rewrite as a multiplication problem using the reciprocal of the divisor.

_____ ÷ _____ = _____ × _____

Multiply.

_____

Simplify the product. _____

Mr. Camara has _____ pieces of wood.

Lesson Practice • Part 1

Choose the correct answer.

1. Divide.

   $\frac{1}{3} \div \frac{1}{8} = \boxed{}$

   A. $\frac{1}{24}$

   B. $\frac{3}{8}$

   C. $2\frac{2}{3}$

   D. 24

2. Mrs. Chapman made vests for cast members of the school play. She used $\frac{3}{4}$ yard of material for each vest. She used 6 yards in all. How many vests did she make?

   A. 1

   B. 4

   C. 6

   D. 8

3. Divide.

   $\frac{7}{16} \div 2\frac{3}{8} = \boxed{}$

   A. $\frac{7}{46}$

   B. $\frac{7}{38}$

   C. $1\frac{5}{128}$

   D. $2\frac{4}{7}$

4. Simplify.

   $\dfrac{\frac{3}{8}}{\frac{7}{10}}$

   A. $\frac{21}{80}$

   B. $\frac{15}{28}$

   C. $1\frac{13}{15}$

   D. $3\frac{17}{21}$

5. Kelly had a ribbon that was $5\frac{1}{3}$ feet long. Each piece she cut was $1\frac{1}{3}$ feet long. How many pieces of ribbon did she cut?

   A. 1

   B. 4

   C. 8

   D. 12

6. Divide.

   $2\frac{1}{5} \div \frac{1}{10} = \boxed{}$

   A. 11

   B. 21

   C. 22

   D. 221

7. What is the value of the following expression?

$$\frac{1}{2} \div \frac{1}{12}$$

A. 3

B. 6

C. 9

D. 24

8. Which quotient is less than 1?

A. $\frac{5}{8} \div \frac{2}{3}$

B. $\frac{7}{10} \div \frac{3}{5}$

C. $\frac{3}{4} \div \frac{1}{3}$

D. $\frac{7}{8} \div \frac{7}{9}$

9. In math class, Ms. Kuramoto wrote the following complex fraction on the board: $\frac{\frac{5}{6}}{\frac{4}{9}}$.

A. Rewrite the complex fraction as a division expression.

_____

_____

B. Show the complex fraction $\frac{\frac{5}{6}}{\frac{4}{9}}$ in simplest form. Show your work.

_____

_____

_____

Lesson Practice • Part 2

Choose the correct answer.

1. A recipe calls for $\frac{3}{4}$ cup of milk. It makes 6 servings. How much milk is there in each serving?

   A. $\frac{1}{8}$ cup

   B. $\frac{2}{9}$ cup

   C. $2\frac{1}{4}$ cups

   D. $4\frac{1}{2}$ cups

2. Rich jogged $2\frac{1}{2}$ miles around a park. Each lap is $\frac{4}{5}$ mile. How many laps did Rich jog around the park?

   A. $1\frac{7}{10}$

   B. 2

   C. $3\frac{1}{8}$

   D. $3\frac{3}{10}$

3. Which describes how to tell if a complex fraction is less than 1?

   A. The numerator is greater than the denominator.

   B. The numerator is less than the denominator.

   C. The numerator in the numerator is greater than the numerator in the denominator.

   D. The denominator in the numerator is less than the denominator in the denominator.

4. Divide.

   $$3\frac{2}{5} \div 2\frac{7}{8} = \boxed{}$$

   A. $\frac{40}{391}$

   B. $\frac{115}{136}$

   C. $1\frac{21}{115}$

   D. $9\frac{31}{40}$

5. Aubrey completed a miniseries that lasted $10\frac{1}{2}$ hours. Each episode lasted $1\frac{3}{4}$ hours. How many episodes were in the miniseries?

   A. 7

   B. 6

   C. 5

   D. 4

6. Joe wants to pour $4\frac{1}{2}$ cups of water into a pot. He only has a $\frac{1}{4}$-cup measuring cup. How many times must he fill the $\frac{1}{4}$-cup measuring cup?

   A. $1\frac{1}{8}$

   B. $4\frac{1}{4}$

   C. 9

   D. 18

7. Simplify.

$$\dfrac{\frac{5}{12}}{\frac{7}{8}}$$

A. $\dfrac{10}{21}$

B. $\dfrac{35}{96}$

C. $2\frac{1}{10}$

D. $2\frac{26}{35}$

8. A recipe for 8 servings calls for $1\frac{1}{2}$ cups of water. If the number of servings are cut to 2, how much water is needed?

A. $\dfrac{3}{16}$ cup

B. $\dfrac{3}{8}$ cup

C. $\dfrac{3}{4}$ cup

D. $1\frac{1}{8}$ cups

9. Berry Boulevard is $4\frac{4}{5}$ miles long. There are sets of 2 traffic lights on Berry Boulevard every $\frac{2}{5}$ mile after the street begins. There are 2 stop signs every $1\frac{3}{5}$ miles.

A. How many traffic lights are there on Berry Boulevard? Show your work.

_____

B. How many stop signs are there on Berry Boulevard? Show your work.

_____

10. Look at each equation. Is the equation true? Select Yes or No.

A. $\dfrac{2}{3} \div \dfrac{1}{9} = 6$ ○ Yes   ○ No

B. $2\frac{1}{10} \div \dfrac{3}{10} = 7$ ○ Yes   ○ No

C. $3\frac{3}{5} \div \dfrac{4}{5} = 5\frac{1}{4}$ ○ Yes   ○ No

D. $\dfrac{7}{9} \div \dfrac{1}{3} = \dfrac{3}{7}$ ○ Yes   ○ No

11. Select True or False for each equation.

   A. $\frac{9}{16} \div \frac{1}{4} = 2\frac{1}{4}$ ○ True   ○ False

   B. $2\frac{1}{2} \div 1\frac{2}{3} = 1\frac{1}{2}$ ○ True   ○ False

   C. $\frac{9}{10} \div \frac{1}{6} = \frac{3}{20}$ ○ True   ○ False

   D. $\frac{7}{8} \div 1\frac{1}{2} = \frac{7}{12}$ ○ True   ○ False

12. Which equations are correct? Circle all that apply.

   A. $\dfrac{\frac{3}{4}}{\frac{7}{8}} = \frac{21}{32}$

   B. $\dfrac{\frac{5}{6}}{\frac{2}{3}} = 1\frac{1}{4}$

   C. $\dfrac{\frac{2}{5}}{\frac{3}{7}} = \frac{14}{15}$

   D. $\dfrac{\frac{9}{10}}{\frac{5}{8}} = \frac{9}{16}$

   E. $\dfrac{\frac{3}{10}}{\frac{2}{5}} = 1\frac{1}{3}$

   F. $\dfrac{\frac{7}{9}}{\frac{2}{15}} = 5\frac{5}{6}$

13. Emanuel had $2\frac{1}{4}$ gallons of paint. He used $\frac{3}{4}$ gallon of paint for each room. Circle the number of rooms that Emanuel painted.

Emanuel painted
$$\boxed{\begin{array}{c} 2 \\[4pt] 3 \\[4pt] 4 \\[4pt] 6 \end{array}}$$
rooms.

14. Simplify each complex fraction. Write each complex fraction in the correct box.

$$\dfrac{\frac{1}{2}}{\frac{3}{4}} \qquad \dfrac{\frac{1}{4}}{\frac{1}{2}} \qquad \dfrac{\frac{3}{2}}{3} \qquad \dfrac{\frac{4}{5}}{\frac{6}{5}}$$

Equal to $\frac{2}{3}$	Equal to $\frac{1}{2}$

15. Use numbers from the box to complete each equation.

$$\frac{7}{8} \div \underline{\hspace{1.5cm}} = 3\frac{1}{2}$$

$$\frac{1}{16} \div \frac{5}{8} = \underline{\hspace{1.5cm}}$$

$$2\frac{2}{5} \div \underline{\hspace{1.5cm}} = 4\frac{4}{5}$$

$$\frac{1}{3} \div \frac{2}{3} = \underline{\hspace{1.5cm}}$$

$$4\frac{1}{2} \div \underline{\hspace{1.5cm}} = 45$$

$$\frac{1}{10} \qquad \frac{1}{4} \qquad \frac{1}{2}$$

Add and Subtract Integers

Getting the Idea

You can use a number line to add integers. Start at the point that represents the first integer. To add a positive integer, move to the right. To add a negative integer, move to the left.

Example 1

Find the sum of 3 and its additive inverse.

Strategy	Use a number line.
Step 1	Write an addition expression for the sum.
	The additive inverse of 3 is -3.
	Find $3 + (-3)$.
Step 2	Use a number line to add.
	Start at 3. Since you are adding a negative integer, move 3 units to the left.

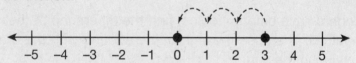

The sum is 0.

Solution	**The sum of 3 and its additive inverse is 0.**

$3 + (-3) = 0$ is an example of the **existence of the additive inverse property**. It states that the sum of a number and its **additive inverse** is 0.

In Example 1, the sum of $3 + (-3)$ is 0, located a distance of 3 units to the left of 3. So, $(-3) + 3$ will also have the sum of 0 because it is located 3 units to the right of -3.

Let a and b represent two integers. To find the sum of $a + b$ on a number line, start at a and move a distance of $|b|$. Move to the right of a if b is positive and to the left of a if b is negative. The sign of the sum depends upon the direction and the number of units moved from a.

Example 2

Find the sum.

$$-4 + 3 = \boxed{}$$

Strategy   **Use a number line to add the two integers.**

Start at -4.

Since you are adding a positive integer, move 3 units to the right.

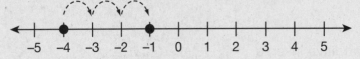

The sum is -1.

Solution $-4 + 3 = -1$

You can use the following rules to add integers.

Rules for Adding Two Integers

- When integers have the same sign, add the absolute values and use the sign of the addends in the sum.

- When integers have different signs, find the difference of their absolute values. Then use the sign of the addend with the greater absolute value in the sum.

Example 3

Add.

$$-11 + (-8) = \boxed{}$$

Strategy   **Apply the rules for adding two integers.**

The integers have the same sign, so add the absolute values. The sum will be negative.

$$|-11| = 11$$
$$|-8| = 8$$
$$11 + 8 = 19$$

Solution $-11 + (-8) = -19$

You can also use the properties of addition to add integers.

Example 4

Add.

$$24 + (-10) = \boxed{}$$

Strategy   **Use the properties of addition.**

Step 1   Rewrite 24 as a sum with an addend of 10.

$$24 = (14 + 10)$$

Step 2   Rewrite the problem using the new form of 24.

$$24 + (-10) = (14 + 10) + (-10)$$

Step 3   Use the associative property of addition.

$$(14 + 10) + (-10) = 14 + (10 + (-10))$$
$$= 14 + 0 \quad \longleftarrow \text{The sum of a number and its additive inverse is 0.}$$
$$= 14$$

Solution $24 + (-10) = 14$

A number line can also be used to subtract integers. To subtract a positive integer, move to the left. To subtract a negative integer, move to the right.

Example 5

Find the difference.

$$3 - 7 = \boxed{}$$

Strategy   **Use a number line to subtract two integers.**

Start at 3.

Since you are subtracting a positive integer, move 7 units to the left.

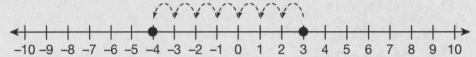

Solution $3 - 7 = -4$

Use these rules to subtract integers.

> **Rules for Subtracting Two Integers**
>
> - Write the additive inverse (opposite) of the number to be subtracted (the **subtrahend**).
>
> - Change the minus sign to a plus sign.
>
> - Apply the rules for adding two integers.

Example 6

Subtract.

$$-5 - 4 = \boxed{}$$

Strategy   **Add the opposite of the subtrahend.**

Step 1   Find the opposite of the number to be subtracted.

The subtrahend is 4.

The opposite of 4 is -4.

Step 2   Add the opposite of the subtrahend to the minuend.

$$-5 - 4 = -5 + (-4)$$

Both integers being added have a negative sign. The sum will be negative.

Step 3   Add the absolute values of the integers.

$$|-5| = 5 \text{ and } |-4| = 4$$

$$5 + 4 = 9$$

Solution $-5 - 4 = -9$

Example 7

Subtract.

$2 - (-8) = \boxed{}$

Strategy	**Add the opposite of the subtrahend.**

Step 1   Find the opposite of the number to be subtracted.

The subtrahend is -8.

The opposite of -8 is 8.

Step 2   Add the opposite of the subtrahend to the minuend.

$2 - (-8) = 2 + 8$

Both integers being added are positive.

Step 3   Add the integers.

$2 + 8 = 10$

Since both integers are positive, the sum will also be positive.

Solution $2 - (-8) = 10$

The properties of addition and subtraction can be used to show that $a - (b + c) = a - b - c$ if a, b, and c are integers.

$a - (b + c) = a + -(b + c)$ Add the opposite.

$\qquad\qquad = a + (-b) + (-c)$ Rewrite the sum using the distributive property.

$\qquad\qquad = a - b - c$ Use the properties of subtraction.

You can use the rules for adding and subtracting integers to solve problems.

Example 8

Carly has $50 in a bank account. She writes a check for $60 from the account. How much money does Carly have in her account after writing the check?

Strategy	**Write a number sentence for the problem. Then solve.**

Step 1   Write a number sentence for the problem.

Let m represent the amount Carly has in her account after writing the check.

$\$50 - \$60 = m$

Step 2 Add the opposite of the number to be subtracted.

$50 − $60 = $50 + (−$60)$

The integers being added have different signs.

Step 3 Find the difference of the absolute values of the integers.

$|50| = 50$

$|−60| = 60$

$60 − 50 = 10$

Step 4 Use the sign of the addend with the greater absolute value.

$|−60| > |50|$, so the sum is negative.

$50 + (−$60) = −10

Solution **Carly has −$10 in her account after writing the check.**

Coached Example

The record low temperature for Albany, New York, was −28°F in January 1971. The lowest temperature in U.S. history is 52°F lower than Albany's record low temperature. What is the lowest temperature in U.S. history?

Let *l* represent the lowest temperature in U.S. history.

Write a number sentence to represent the problem. _____

Is the subtrahend positive or negative? _____

Find the opposite of the subtrahend. _____

Add the opposite of the subtrahend to the minuend. _____

Both integers being added have a _____ sign.

Apply the rules for adding two integers.

Find the absolute value of the first addend. _____

Find the absolute value of the second addend. _____

Add the absolute values. _____

Use the sign of the addends in the sum. The sign for the sum is _____.

The lowest temperature in U.S. history is _____°F.

Lesson Practice • Part 1

Choose the correct answer.

1. Subtract.

   $$3 - (-6) = \boxed{}$$

   A. -9

   B. -3

   C. 3

   D. 9

2. Add.

   $$9 + (-16) = \boxed{}$$

   A. 25

   B. 7

   C. -7

   D. -25

3. Subtract.

   $$-10 - 4 = \boxed{}$$

   A. -14

   B. -6

   C. 6

   D. 14

4. The temperature one morning in Shasta was $-12°$F. By the afternoon, the temperature had risen $8°$F. What was the temperature in the afternoon?

   A. $20°$F

   B. $4°$F

   C. $-4°$F

   D. $-20°$F

5. Find the sum.

   $$-4 + (-2) = \boxed{}$$

   A. -6

   B. -2

   C. 2

   D. 6

6. Find the difference.

   $$6 - 11 = \boxed{}$$

   A. -17

   B. -5

   C. 5

   D. 17

7. A submarine at -28 feet dives 40 feet. What is the submarine's elevation after the dive?

   A.   68 feet

   B.   12 feet

   C. -12 feet

   D. -68 feet

8. The Panthers lost 6 yards on their first play and lost another 8 yards on their next play. What was their net result in yards after these two plays?

   A. -14 yards

   B. -2 yards

   C.   2 yards

   D.   14 yards

9. The temperature at the base of a mountain was $14°F$. The temperature at the summit was $16°F$ lower than at the base.

   A. Write a subtraction expression to represent the temperature at the summit.

      _____

   B. What was the temperature at the summit? Show your work.

      _____

      _____

      _____

Lesson Practice • Part 2

Choose the correct answer.

1. Madison's checking account had a balance of −$12. Then she wrote a check for $15. Which represents Madison's account balance now?

   A. −$27

   B. −$3

   C. $3

   D. $27

2. Which is the sum of −4 and its additive inverse?

   A. −8

   B. −4

   C. 0

   D. 8

3. Ellie and Stella played miniature golf. Ellie's score was 2. Stella's score was 5 less than Ellie's. What was Stella's score?

   A. −7

   B. −3

   C. 3

   D. 7

4. Nolan is a running back on his football team. He gained 3 yards on his first carry. He lost 6 yards on his second carry and he gained 4 yards on his third carry. How many total yards did Nolan carry the ball?

   A. −13 yards

   B. −1 yard

   C. 1 yard

   D. 13 yards

5. Which shows another way to write 6 − 9?

   A. 9 − 6

   B. 9 − (−6)

   C. 6 + 9

   D. 6 + (−9)

6. Which describes a situation in which two quantities must have a sum of 0?

   A. a temperature above 0°F and another temperature that is below 0°F

   B. an elevator this is below the lobby and then is above the lobby

   C. an element that has the same number of electrons as protons

   D. a golfer who plays two rounds and has one above par and one below par

7. Subtract.

$$-8 - (-4) = \boxed{}$$

   A. -12

   B. -4

   C. 4

   D. 12

8. Which will never result in a positive number?

   A. negative + positive

   B. positive + negative

   C. negative − negative

   D. negative − positive

9. The normal mean temperature in Barrow, Alaska is $-2°F$ in November.

   A. The normal mean temperature in October is 19°F warmer than in November. What is the normal mean temperature in October? Show your work.

   B. The normal mean temperature in December is 6°F cooler than in November. What is the normal mean temperature in December? Show your work.

   C. The normal minimum temperature in January is 12°F cooler than the normal mean temperature in December. What is the normal minimum temperature in January? Show your work.

10. Which word problem has the solution of -4? Circle all that apply.

   A. Earl jogged 5 yards forward and then jogged 9 yards backward. What was his final position compared to his starting point?

   B. A rainbow trout was swimming at -2 feet. It swam downward 4 more feet. What was the new depth of the trout?

   C. Clarissa had $49 in her checking account. She spent $53 on a pair of shoes. What was the new balance of her account?

11. Simplify each expression. Write each expression in the correct box.

| $8 + (-2)$ | $-6 - 4$ | $2 - 4$ | $-13 + 3$ | $4 - (-2)$ |

−10	6	−2

12. A scuba diver is at −4 feet. He dives down 7 more feet to a coral reef. Circle the elevation of the top of the coral reef.

The elevation of the top of the coral reef is
11
3
−3
−11
feet.

13. Select True or False for each equation.

A. $4 - (-6) = 10$ ○ True ○ False

B. $5 + (-11) = -6$ ○ True ○ False

C. $-7 + (-3) = 10$ ○ True ○ False

D. $2 - 9 = -7$ ○ True ○ False

14. Use numbers from the box to complete each equation.

$-21 + 34 = $ _____

_____ $+ (-8) = 26$

$17 - (-38) = $ _____

$64 - $ _____ $= 30$

$-5 - (-18) = $ _____

13
34
55

15. Draw a line from each expression to its equivalent value.

A. $-3 + (-5)$ •   • 8
B. $14 - 6$ •   • -8
C. $-5 - 8$ •   • 13
D. $4 - (-9)$ •   • -13

16. The temperature at noon was 72°F. The temperature dropped 16°F by 9:00 P.M. Circle the temperature at 9:00 P.M.

The temperature at 9:00 P.M. was

37
56
88

°F.

Multiply and Divide Integers

Getting the Idea

Use these rules to multiply two integers.

> **Rules for Multiplying Two Integers**
>
> Multiply the two integers as positive numbers.
>
> Then find the sign of the product using these rules.
>
> - If the signs of the two numbers are the same, the product is positive.
>
> - If the signs of the two numbers are different, the product is negative.

Example 1

Multiply.

$(-25) \cdot (-3) = \boxed{}$

Strategy   **Apply the rules for multiplying two integers.**

Step 1   Multiply the two integers as positive numbers.

$25 \cdot 3 = 75$

Step 2   Find the sign of the product.

The signs of the two numbers are the same, so the product is positive.

$(-) \cdot (-) = (+)$

The product is $+75$.

Solution $(-25) \cdot (-3) = 75$

Example 2

Marshall has $12 automatically deducted from his checking account each month as a charitable donation. What is the total amount deducted from his account after 1 year?

Strategy   **Write an expression for the problem. Then solve.**

Step 1   Write an expression to represent the problem.

The amount deducted each month can be represented by $-\$12$.

There are 12 months in 1 year.

So, find $-\$12 \cdot 12$.

Step 2 Multiply the two integers as positive numbers.

$$12 \cdot 12 = 144$$

Step 3 Find the sign of the product.

The signs of the two numbers are different, so the product is negative.

$$(-) \cdot (+) = (-)$$

The product is -144.

Solution **The total amount deducted from Marshall's account is $144.**

The **distributive property** applies the rules for multiplying and adding signed numbers. The work below shows that $-(a + b) = -a - b$.

$$-(a + b) = -1(a + b)$$

$$= -1 \cdot (a + b) \qquad \text{Apply the distributive property.}$$

$$= -1 \cdot (a) + -1 \cdot (b) \qquad \text{Multiply each addend by } -1.$$

$$= -a + (-b) \qquad \text{Apply the rules for adding integers.}$$

$$= -a - b$$

Example 3

Write $-(a - b)$ as a sum.

Strategy **Use the distributive property.**

Step 1 Rewrite the expression to show the multiplication.

$$-(a - b) = -1 \cdot (a - b)$$

Step 2 Apply the distributive property.

$$-1 \cdot (a - b) = -1 \cdot (a) - (-1) \cdot (b)$$

Step 3 Multiply each addend by -1.

$$-1 \cdot (a) - (-1) \cdot (b) = -a - (-b)$$

Step 4 Apply the rules for subtracting two integers.

The additive inverse of $-b$ is b.

$$-a - (-b) = -a + b$$

Solution $-(a - b) = -a + b$

Use these rules to divide two integers.

> ### Rules for Dividing Two Integers
>
> Divide the two integers as positive numbers.
>
> Then find the sign of the quotient using these rules.
>
> - If the signs of the two numbers are the same, the quotient is positive.
> - If the signs of the two numbers are different, the quotient is negative.

All integers can be divided as long as the divisor is not zero.

Example 4

Divide.

$$(-32) \div (-8) = \boxed{}$$

Strategy   **Apply the rules for dividing two integers.**

Step 1   Divide the two integers as positive numbers.

$$32 \div 8 = 4$$

Step 2   Find the sign of the quotient.

The signs of the two numbers are the same, so the quotient is positive.

$$(-) \div (-) = (+)$$

The quotient is $+4$.

Solution $(-32) \div (-8) = 4$

Example 5

The temperature fell 18°F in 3 hours. The temperature fell at the same rate every hour. How much did the temperature change each hour?

Strategy   **Write an expression for the problem. Then solve.**

Step 1   Write an expression to represent the problem.

The temperature changed −18°F.

$\frac{(-18)}{3}$ or −18 ÷ 3 represents the temperature change per hour.

Step 2   Divide the two integers as positive numbers.

18 ÷ 3 = 6

Step 3   Find the sign of the product.

The signs of the two numbers are different, so the product is negative.

(−) ÷ (+) = (−)

The quotient is −6°.

Solution   **The temperature changed −6°F each hour.**

Instead of using a multiplication sign, sometimes multiplication is shown by putting the factors in parentheses. For example, (−3)(2) = −3 × 2.

Coached Example

What is the value of (−5)(4)(−1)(−2)?

Will the product of the first two integers be positive or negative? _____

−5 · 4 = _____

When you multiply this product by the third integer, −1, will the product be positive or negative? _____

Multiply the product of the first two integers by the third integer, −1.

_____ · (−1) = _____

When you multiply this product by the fourth integer, −2, will the product be positive or negative? _____

_____ · (−2) = _____

The value of (−5)(4)(−1)(−2) is _____.

Lesson Practice • Part 1

Choose the correct answer.

1. Multiply.

   $29 \cdot (-5) = \boxed{}$

   A. -145

   B. -105

   C. 105

   D. 145

2. Divide.

   $378 \div (-7) = \boxed{}$

   A. -54

   B. -45

   C. 45

   D. 54

3. Multiply.

   $-72 \cdot (-6) = \boxed{}$

   A. -442

   B. -432

   C. 432

   D. 442

4. The temperature fell 36°F in 9 hours. If the temperature fell at the same rate every hour, which represents the change in temperature each hour?

   A. $-324°F$

   B. $-27°F$

   C. $-4°F$

   D. $45°F$

5. Divide.

   $-385 \div 77 = \boxed{}$

   A. -15

   B. -5

   C. 5

   D. 15

6. What is the value of $(-3)(5)(-4)$?

   A. -60

   B. -12

   C. 12

   D. 60

7. A shoreline is changing -3 centimeters each year due to erosion. What is the change in the shoreline over 6 years?

   A. -18 cm

   B. -9 cm

   C. -3 cm

   D. -2 cm

8. The price of a stock rose $2 yesterday. If the stock continues to change at the same rate each day, what will be the total change over 10 days?

   A. $-\$20$

   B. $-\$5$

   C. $\$5$

   D. $\$20$

9. Evan withdrew a total of $160 from an ATM machine over a 4-day period. He withdrew the same amount of money each day.

   A. Write an expression to represent the total amount that Evan's account changed each day.

   _____

   B. What integer represents the total amount that Evan's account changed each day? Show your work.

   _____

   _____

Lesson Practice • Part 2

Choose the correct answer.

1. Which quotient is positive?

   A. $-24 \div 6$

   B. $42 \div -7$

   C. $-35 \div -5$

   D. $28 \div -4$

2. Gavin is going to multiply -1 by itself a number of times. Which expression results in a product of 1?

   A. $-1 \cdot -1 \cdot -1$

   B. $-1 \cdot -1 \cdot -1 \cdot -1$

   C. $-1 \cdot -1 \cdot -1 \cdot -1 \cdot -1$

   D. $-1 \cdot -1 \cdot -1 \cdot -1 \cdot -1 \cdot -1 \cdot -1$

3. TDC, Inc.'s net profits were $-\$2,000$ each month last year. What was TDC's net profits for the year?

   A. $-\$24,000$

   B. $-\$14,000$

   C. $\$10,000$

   D. $\$24,000$

4. What is the value of $8 \times -6 \div -2$?

   A. -96

   B. -24

   C. 24

   D. 96

5. Naomi was watching a game show where a contestant had 20 points and then had 5 turns where he scored -10 points on each turn. Then she stopped watching. What was the contestant's score when Naomi stopped watching the show?

   A. -50

   B. -30

   C. 50

   D. 70

6. A hiker in California was at an elevation of -45 feet. He increased his elevation by 12 feet each minute for 5 minutes. What was his elevation after 5 minutes?

   A. -900 feet

   B. -105 feet

   C. -60 feet

   D. 15 feet

7. What is the value of $(-4)(-4)(-4)$?

   A. -64

   B. -12

   C. 12

   D. 64

8. A golfer shot 2 rounds of −4 each and then shot 2 rounds of 2 each. What was the golfer's composite score?

- **A.** −12
- **B.** −4
- **C.** 4
- **D.** 12

9. Divide.

$$-120 \div -5 = \boxed{}$$

- **A.** −24
- **B.** −22
- **C.** 22
- **D.** 24

10. Cooper is the quarterback for his football team. He was sacked 5 times for a loss of 9 yards each time. What was the total result of the sacks?

- **A.** 45 yards
- **B.** 14 yards
- **C.** −14 yards
- **D.** −45 yards

11. Multiply.

$$-15 \times 6 = \boxed{}$$

- **A.** −90
- **B.** −80
- **C.** 80
- **D.** 90

12. For an experiment a specimen was kept at a temperature of 10°C. Each hour for 5 hours the temperature of the specimen dropped by 4°C. After 5 hours, the temperature was raised 8°C each hour for 4 hours?

- **A.** What was the temperature of the specimen after 2 hours?

  _____

- **B.** What was the temperature of the specimen after 5 hours?

  _____

- **C.** What was the temperature of the specimen after 9 hours?

  _____

13. Draw a line from each expression to its equivalent value.

- **A.** -14×5 •
- **B.** $-7 \times (-10)$ •
- **C.** $-81 \div 3$ •
- **D.** $-162 \div (-6)$ •

• −70
• −27
• 27
• 70

14. Savannah's dog lost 2 pounds each week for 4 weeks. Circle the weight change after 4 weeks.

The dog's weight change after 4 weeks was

8
6
−6
−8

pounds.

15. Is each equation correct? Select True or False.

    A. $15 \times (-6) = 90$ ○ True   ○ False

    B. $-494 \div 26 = -19$ ○ True   ○ False

    C. $(-2)(6)(-7) = 84$ ○ True   ○ False

    D. $-63 \div (-9) = -7$ ○ True   ○ False

16. Evaluate each expression. Write each expression in the correct box.

-2×6	$-4 \times (-3)$	$-24 \div (-2)$	$48 \div (-4)$	-6×2

−12	12

17. Use numbers from the box to make each equation true.

$-2 \times 5 =$ _____

$6 \div (-2) =$ _____

$-2 \times$ _____ $= 14$

$80 \div (-8) =$ _____

$-28 \div 4 =$ _____

-3
-7
-10

18. A plant grew 4 inches each month for a year. The rate of growth was constant. Circle the amount that the plant had grown after 7 months.

The growth of the plant after 7 months was

-28
-11
28
11

inches.

19. Which expression is equivalent to -6? Circle all that apply.

A. $-18 \div 3$

B. -2×3

C. $-24 \div 4$

D. -6×-1

E. $36 \div (-6)$

Add and Subtract Rational Numbers

Getting the Idea

You can use the rules for adding and subtracting positive and negative integers to add and subtract other positive and negative rational numbers.

Rules for Adding Two Rational Numbers

- When rational numbers have the same sign, add the absolute values and use the sign of the addends in the sum.

- When rational numbers have different signs, find the difference of their absolute values. Then use the sign of the addend with the greater absolute value in the sum.

Example 1

Add.

$2.5 + (-5) = \boxed{}$

Strategy   **Use a number line to add.**

Start at 2.5. Move 5 places to the left.

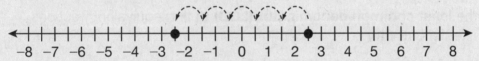

Solution $2.5 + (-5) = -2.5$

In real-world situations involving rational numbers, you may find the amount of money in a savings or checking account or net earnings. The **net** is the amount that remains after deductions and adjustments have been made.

Example 2

Elena had $267.35 in her checking account when a check for $280.50 was cashed. What is the balance in her account now?

Strategy   **Write an expression for the problem. Then solve.**

Step 1   Write an expression to represent the problem.

The problem can be represented as $267.35 − $280.50 or as $267.35 + (−$280.50).

Step 2   Find the absolute value of the two decimals.

$|267.35| = 267.35$

$|-280.50| = 280.50$

Step 3   Subtract the lesser absolute value from the greater absolute value.

$280.5 − 267.35 = 13.15$

Step 4   The difference should have the same sign as the decimal with the greater absolute value.

−280.50 has the greater absolute value, so the account has a negative balance.

Solution   **The balance in the account is −$13.15.**

To add or subtract fractions or mixed numbers with unlike denominators:

- Use the **least common denominator (LCD)** to find equivalent fractions with like denominators.

- Add or subtract, regrouping as needed.

- Write the answer in simplest form. You may need to rename an improper fraction as a mixed number.

Example 3

Add.

$$-\frac{5}{6} + \left(-\frac{4}{9}\right) = \square$$

Strategy   **Write equivalent rational numbers using the LCD. Then add.**

Step 1   Determine the LCD of the fractions.

The LCD of $\frac{5}{6}$ and $\frac{4}{9}$ is 18.

Step 2   Write equivalent fractions with a denominator of 18.

$$-\frac{5}{6} \times \frac{3}{3} = -\frac{15}{18}$$

$$-\frac{4}{9} \times \frac{2}{2} = -\frac{8}{18}$$

Step 3   Add.

$$-\frac{15}{18} + \left(-\frac{8}{18}\right) = -\frac{23}{18}$$

Step 4   Rename the sum as a mixed number.

$$-\frac{23}{18} = -1\frac{5}{18}$$

Solution $-\frac{5}{6} + \left(-\frac{4}{9}\right) = -1\frac{5}{18}$

You can use a number line to subtract rational numbers.

Example 4

Subtract.

$$-3\frac{1}{5} - 2\frac{3}{5} = \square$$

Strategy   **Rename as addition and use a number line.**

Step 1   Rewrite as addition.

$$-3\frac{1}{5} - 2\frac{3}{5} = -3\frac{1}{5} + \left(-2\frac{3}{5}\right)$$

Step 2   Use a number line to add.

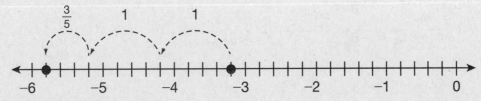

Solution $-3\frac{1}{5} - 2\frac{3}{5} = -5\frac{4}{5}$

Example 5

Subtract.

$$-0.7 - (-1.6) = \boxed{}$$

Strategy   **Rename as addition and use a number line.**

Step 1   Rewrite as addition.

$$-0.7 - (-1.6) = -0.7 + 1.6$$

Step 2   Use a number line to add.

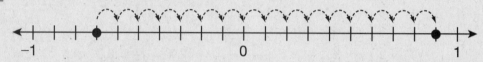

Solution $-0.7 - (-1.6) = 0.9$

Example 6

Subtract.

$$-4\frac{1}{4} - 1\frac{7}{8} = \boxed{}$$

Strategy   **Rename the fractional parts of the mixed numbers.**

Step 1   Rewrite as addition.

$$-4\frac{1}{4} - 1\frac{7}{8} = -4\frac{1}{4} + \left(-1\frac{7}{8}\right)$$

Step 2   Determine the LCD of the fractional parts.

The LCD of $\frac{1}{4}$ and $\frac{7}{8}$ is 8.

Step 3   Rename $-4\frac{1}{4}$ as a mixed number with 8 as the denominator.

$$\frac{1}{4} \times \frac{2}{2} = \frac{2}{8}, \text{ so } -4\frac{1}{4} = -4\frac{2}{8}$$

Step 4   Add.

$$-4\frac{2}{8} + \left(-1\frac{7}{8}\right) = -5\frac{9}{8}$$

$$-5\frac{9}{8} = -6\frac{1}{8}$$

Solution $-4\frac{1}{4} - 1\frac{7}{8} = -6\frac{1}{8}$

Coached Example

Genesis walked $2\frac{1}{4}$ miles south and then $1\frac{1}{2}$ miles north. Describe Genesis's location from her starting point.

Think of a number line. South is represented by _____ numbers and north is represented by _____ numbers.

Write a rational number to represent $2\frac{1}{4}$ miles south. _____

Write a rational number to represent $1\frac{1}{2}$ miles north. _____

Let f represent Genesis's location.

Write an addition equation to represent Genesis's location.

_____

Which addend has a greater absolute value? _____

The sum has the sign of the _____ absolute value.

Is Genesis north or south from her starting location? _____

Solve your equation.

Genesis's location is _____ from her starting point.

Lesson Practice • Part 1

Choose the correct answer.

1. Andre uses $\frac{3}{4}$ teaspoon of oregano and $\frac{3}{8}$ teaspoon of rosemary in a recipe. How much oregano and rosemary does Andre use in all?

    A. $\frac{1}{2}$ teaspoon

    B. $\frac{8}{9}$ teaspoon

    C. $1\frac{1}{8}$ teaspoons

    D. $1\frac{3}{8}$ teaspoons

Use this information for questions 2 and 3.

Sharon's house, the library, and Lisa's house are all on the same straight road. Sharon has to ride her bike $1\frac{3}{5}$ miles to get from her house to the library and another $2\frac{3}{4}$ miles to get from the library to Lisa's house.

2. How far does Sharon live from Lisa?

    A. $4\frac{1}{4}$ miles   **C.** $4\frac{7}{20}$ miles

    B. $4\frac{3}{10}$ miles   **D.** $4\frac{2}{5}$ miles

3. How much closer to the library does Sharon live than Lisa?

    A. $\frac{17}{20}$ mile   **C.** $1\frac{1}{5}$ miles

    B. $1\frac{3}{20}$ miles   **D.** $1\frac{1}{4}$ miles

4. Add.

    $$3.65 + (-4.7) = \boxed{}$$

    A. -8.35

    B. -1.05

    C. 1.05

    D. 8.35

5. Paul owes his father $10.75. He borrows $5.50 more from his father. Which of the following best represents Paul's debt to his father?

    A. $-\$16.25$

    B. $-\$15.25$

    C. $-\$5.25$

    D. $\$5.25$

6. Subtract.

    $$2\frac{1}{2} - 4\frac{1}{4} = \boxed{}$$

    A. $-2\frac{1}{4}$

    B. $-1\frac{3}{4}$

    C. $1\frac{3}{4}$

    D. $7\frac{3}{4}$

7. Subtract.

$$-\frac{2}{3} - \left(-\frac{7}{8}\right) = \boxed{}$$

A. $-1\frac{13}{24}$

B. $-\frac{5}{24}$

C. $\frac{5}{24}$

D. $1\frac{13}{24}$

8. Max walked $1\frac{3}{4}$ miles east and then he walked $2\frac{7}{10}$ miles west. Which describes Max's location from his original starting point?

A. $4\frac{9}{20}$ miles east

B. $4\frac{9}{20}$ miles west

C. $\frac{19}{20}$ mile east

D. $\frac{19}{20}$ mile west

9. Add.

$$-3\frac{1}{5} + \left(-2\frac{3}{4}\right) = \boxed{}$$

A. $-5\frac{19}{20}$

B. $-5\frac{4}{9}$

C. $-1\frac{11}{20}$

D. $-\frac{9}{20}$

10. Which has the least result?

A. $\frac{3}{4} - \frac{3}{4}$

B. $\frac{3}{4} + \frac{3}{4}$

C. $-\frac{3}{4} + \frac{3}{4}$

D. $-\frac{3}{4} - \frac{3}{4}$

11. The outside temperature was 4.2°F at 8:30 P.M. By 12 midnight, the temperature had fallen 9.5°F. Let m represent the temperature at 12 midnight.

A. Write a subtraction equation to represent how to find m, the temperature at 12 midnight.

_____

B. Write an addition equation to represent how to find m, the temperature at 12 midnight.

_____

C. What was the temperature at 12 midnight?

_____

Lesson Practice • Part 2

Choose the correct answer.

1. Add.

$$-\frac{7}{8} + \left(-1\frac{3}{5}\right) = \square$$

A. $-2\frac{17}{40}$

B. $-\frac{29}{40}$

C. $\frac{29}{40}$

D. $2\frac{17}{40}$

2. Carter's checking account had a balance of $-\$12.75$. He deposited a check for $22.40 into his account. What is Carter's account balance now?

A. $-\$35.15$

B. $-\$9.65$

C. $\$9.65$

D. $\$35.15$

3. Before going out of business, Just DVDs had net profits of $-\$6.25$ million one year and $-\$8.4$ million the next year. What was Just DVDs net profits the last two years of its business?

A. $-\$14.65$ million

B. $-\$14.29$ million

C. $-\$2.15$ million

D. $\$2.15$ million

4. Subtract.

$$2\frac{7}{10} - 5\frac{1}{5} = \square$$

A. $-7\frac{9}{10}$

B. $-2\frac{1}{2}$

C. $2\frac{1}{2}$

D. $7\frac{9}{10}$

5. The seventh-grade class at Van Buren Middle School spent $225.98 on supplies for a car wash. The day of the car wash it rained and they only earned $82.75. What were the net earnings of the car wash?

A. $-\$308.73$

B. $-\$143.23$

C. $\$143.23$

D. $\$308.73$

6. Cora walked $\frac{3}{5}$ mile east and then $1\frac{1}{4}$ miles west. Which describes Cora's location from her original location?

A. $1\frac{17}{20}$ miles east

B. $1\frac{17}{20}$ miles west

C. $\frac{13}{20}$ mile east

D. $\frac{13}{20}$ mile west

7. Which does **not** give the same result as
   $-2.34 + 5.2$?

   A. $5.2 - 2.34$

   B. $5.2 + (-2.34)$

   C. $-2.34 - (-5.2)$

   D. $5.2 - (-2.34)$

8. Add.

   $$-6.475 + 4.9 = \boxed{}$$

   A. -11.375

   B. -1.575

   C. 1.575

   D. 11.375

9. Which gives the same result as
   $-3\frac{1}{2} - \left(-2\frac{3}{5}\right)$?

   A. $-3\frac{1}{2} - 2\frac{3}{5}$

   B. $-3\frac{1}{2} + \left(-2\frac{3}{5}\right)$

   C. $-3\frac{1}{2} + 2\frac{3}{5}$

   D. $-2\frac{3}{5} - 3\frac{1}{2}$

10. Subtract.

    $$-4.2 - (-6.9) = \boxed{}$$

    A. -11.1

    B. -2.7

    C. 2.7

    D. 11.1

11. A movie cost $7.5 million to make. The film earned $2.65 million the first week and $2.1 million the second week.

    A. Let p represent the net profits, in millions of dollars, that the movie made. Write an equation to represent the net profits, in millions of dollars, of the movie after 2 weeks.

    _____

    B. What are the net profits, in millions of dollars, of the movie after 2 weeks?

    _____

12. Which will result in 0? Circle all that apply.

A. $-\frac{2}{3} - \left(-\frac{2}{3}\right)$

B. $-\frac{2}{3} - \frac{2}{3}$

C. $-\frac{2}{3} + \frac{2}{3}$

D. $-\frac{2}{3} + \left(-\frac{2}{3}\right)$

E. $\frac{2}{3} - \left(-\frac{2}{3}\right)$

F. $\frac{2}{3} + \left(-\frac{2}{3}\right)$

G. $\frac{2}{3} - \frac{2}{3}$

13. Ming took two horses to the State Fair. The first horse weighed 955.65 pounds and the second horse weighed 1,164.7 pounds. Circle the number that makes the statement true.

The total weight of Ming's horses is

| 209.05 |
| 1,567.35 |
| 2,120.35 |

pounds.

14. Look at each equation. Is the equation true? Select Yes or No.

A. $-2\frac{4}{5} + 1\frac{7}{10} = -1\frac{1}{10}$ ◯ Yes   ◯ No

B. $-3.62 - 2.48 = -1.14$ ◯ Yes   ◯ No

C. $4\frac{1}{2} - \left(-2\frac{1}{8}\right) = 2\frac{3}{8}$ ◯ Yes   ◯ No

D. $5.92 + (-7.4) = -1.48$ ◯ Yes   ◯ No

15. Use numbers from the box to complete each equation.

$$3\frac{2}{5} + \left(-2\frac{1}{2}\right) = \underline{\hspace{1cm}}$$

$$-4\frac{1}{2} - \left(-2\frac{3}{5}\right) = \underline{\hspace{1cm}}$$

$$2\frac{7}{10} - 4\frac{1}{5} = \underline{\hspace{1cm}}$$

$$-1\frac{9}{10}$$

$$-1\frac{1}{2}$$

$$-\frac{9}{10}$$

16. Select True of False for each statement.

A. Opposites that are added always have a sum of 0. ○ True ○ False

B. A negative subtracted from a negative is always negative. ○ True ○ False

C. A positive subtracted from a negative is always negative. ○ True ○ False

D. A positive subtracted from a positive is always positive. ○ True ○ False

17. Draw a line from each expression to its solution.

A. $5.43 - 3.427$ •   • 7.044

B. $2.834 + 4.21$ •   • 5.585

C. $2.375 + 3.21$ •   • 3.337

D. $6.283 - 2.946$ •   • 2.003

18. Gretchen used $2\frac{3}{4}$ cups of flour and $\frac{1}{3}$ cup of brown sugar for a recipe. Circle the number that makes the sentence true.

$$2\frac{5}{12}$$

Gretchen used $3\frac{1}{12}$ more cups of flour than brown sugar.

$$4\frac{4}{7}$$

Multiply and Divide Rational Numbers

Getting the Idea

Use these rules to help you multiply decimals:

- Multiply as you would with whole numbers.
- Count the total number of decimal places in the factors. The sum is the number of decimal places in the product.

Use these rules when multiplying two rational numbers.

- When both numbers have the same sign, the product is positive.
- When the numbers have different signs, the product is negative.

You can use the distributive property to break numbers into lesser numbers to compute with.

Example 1

Multiply.

$$-3.98 \times 20.5 = \boxed{}$$

Strategy   **Use the distributive property.**

Step 1   Use the distributive property.
$$-3.98 \times 20.5 = (-3.98 \times 20) + (-3.98 \times 0.5)$$

Step 2   Find the partial products.
$$-3.98 \times 20 = -79.6$$
$$-3.98 \times 0.5 = -1.99$$

Step 3   Add the partial products.
$$-79.6 + (-1.99) = -81.59$$

Solution   **$-3.98 \times 20.5 = -81.59$**

To divide a decimal by a whole number, place the decimal point in the quotient above the decimal point in the quotient. Then divide as you would with whole numbers.

Example 2

Divide.

$$-41.12 \div (-16) = \boxed{}$$

Strategy   **Determine the sign of the quotient and divide.**

Step 1   Determine the sign of the quotient.

Both signs are negative, so the quotient will be positive.

You can now ignore the signs.

Step 2   Place the decimal point in the quotient above the decimal point in the dividend. Divide.

```
        2.57
   16)41.12
      -32
        91
       -80
        112
       -112
          0
```

Solution   **−41.12 ÷ (−16) = 2.57**

Use these rules to divide a decimal by a decimal:

- Multiply the divisor by a **power of 10**, such as 10 or 100, to make it a whole number. Then multiply the dividend by the same power of 10.

- Divide as you would divide whole numbers.

Example 3

Kaz is competing in a 13.5-kilometer race. There will be water stops every 0.75-kilometer, including at the end of the race. How many water stops will there be in all?

Strategy   **Multiply the divisor and the dividend by the same power of 10. Then divide.**

Step 1   Multiply the dividend and divisor by the same power of 10, so the divisor becomes a whole number.

The divisor 0.75 is in hundredths so multiply by 100.

$0.75 \times 100 = 75$

$13.5 \times 100 = 1{,}350$

Divide $1{,}350 \div 75$.

Step 2   Divide.

$$
\begin{array}{r}
18 \\
75\overline{)1350} \\
-75 \\
\hline
600 \\
-600 \\
\hline
0
\end{array}
$$

Solution   **There will be 18 water stops in all.**

Sometimes, you will divide until the decimal terminates. Other times, it will be necessary to interpret a remainder.

Example 4

It costs $0.36 to buy an eraser. Ms. Cole wants to buy as many erasers as she can for $5.00. How many erasers can Ms. Cole buy?

Strategy   **Multiply the divisor and the dividend by the same power of 10. Then divide.**

Step 1   Multiply the dividend and divisor by the same power of 10, so the divisor becomes a whole number.

The divisor 0.36 is in hundredths so multiply by 100.

$0.36 \times 100 = 36$

$\$5 \times 100 = \$500$

Divide $\$500 \div 36$

Step 2	Divide.

$$13R32$$
$$36\overline{)500}$$
$$\underline{-36}$$
$$140$$
$$\underline{-108}$$
$$32$$

Step 3	Interpret the remainder.

The quotient is 13 R32, or $13\frac{32}{36}$.

Since it is not possible to buy $\frac{32}{36}$ of an eraser, ignore the remainder.

Solution   **Ms. Cole can buy 13 erasers with $5.00.**

Use these rules to multiply fractions or mixed numbers.

- To multiply fractions, multiply the numerators. Then multiply the denominators. Write the answer in simplest form.

- To multiply mixed numbers, first rename them as improper fractions.

Example 5

Multiply.

$$-\frac{2}{3} \times \left(-\frac{7}{8}\right) = \boxed{}$$

Strategy   **Determine the sign of the product. Then multiply.**

Step 1	Determine the sign of the product.

Both signs are negative, so the product will be positive.

You can now ignore the signs.

Step 2	Cancel like terms and multiply

$$\frac{\overset{1}{\cancel{2}}}{3} \times \frac{7}{\underset{4}{\cancel{8}}} = \frac{7}{12}$$

Solution $-\frac{2}{3} \times \left(-\frac{7}{8}\right) = \frac{7}{12}$

Example 6

Multiply.

$$-4\frac{2}{3} \times 1\frac{5}{7} = \boxed{}$$

Strategy   **Rename the mixed numbers as improper fractions. Multiply.**

Step 1   Determine the sign of the product.

The signs are different, so the product will be negative.

You can ignore the signs for now.

Step 2   Rename the mixed numbers as improper fractions.

$$4\frac{2}{3} = \frac{4 \times 3 + 2}{3} = \frac{14}{3}$$

$$1\frac{5}{7} = \frac{1 \times 7 + 5}{7} = \frac{12}{7}$$

Step 3   Cancel like terms and multiply.

$$\frac{\overset{2}{\cancel{14}}}{\underset{1}{\cancel{3}}} \times \frac{\overset{4}{\cancel{12}}}{\underset{1}{\cancel{7}}} = \frac{8}{1} = 8$$

Step 4   Remember to put the negative sign back in the product.

Solution $-4\frac{2}{3} \times 1\frac{5}{7} = -8$

Use these rules when dividing two rational numbers.

- When both numbers have the same sign, the quotient is positive.

- When the numbers have difference signs, the quotient is negative.

Example 7

Divide.

$$-3\frac{1}{2} \div -4\frac{4}{5} = \boxed{}$$

Strategy   **Rename the mixed numbers as improper fractions. Multiply.**

Step 1   Determine the sign of the quotient.

The signs are the same, so the quotient will be positive.

You can ignore the signs for now.

Step 2   Rename the mixed numbers as improper fractions.

$$3\frac{1}{2} = \frac{3 \times 2 + 1}{2} = \frac{7}{2}$$

$$4\frac{4}{5} = \frac{4 \times 5 + 4}{5} = \frac{24}{5}$$

Step 3   Multiply by the reciprocal of the dividend.

There are no like terms to cancel.

$$\frac{7}{2} \div \frac{24}{5} = \frac{7}{2} \times \frac{5}{24} = \frac{35}{48}$$

Solution $-3\frac{1}{2} \div -4\frac{4}{5} = \frac{35}{48}$

Coached Example

Mr. Livio earns an hourly wage for every hour he works. Last week, he earned $663.85 and worked for 35.5 hours. How much money does Mr. Livio earn per hour?

To solve the problem, divide 663.85 by _____ to find the amount of money Mr. Livio earns per hour.

Multiply the divisor, 35.5, by _____ to make it a whole number: _____

Multiply the dividend, 663.85, by that same power of 10: _____

Divide as you would with whole numbers.

$$355\overline{)6{,}638.5}$$

Place a dollar sign and a decimal point in the quotient.

The answer is an amount of money, so be sure to give it two decimal places.

Mr. Livio earns _____ per hour.

Lesson Practice • Part 1

Choose the correct answer.

1. Multiply.

    $$-3.8 \times 4.7 = \square$$

    A. -17.86

    B. -17.36

    C. 17.36

    D. 17.86

2. Each lap around Spring Reservoir is $2\frac{3}{8}$ miles long. Terrence walked $2\frac{1}{2}$ laps around the reservoir. How many miles did Terrence walk?

    A. $4\frac{3}{16}$ miles

    B. $5\frac{1}{4}$ miles

    C. $5\frac{3}{8}$ miles

    D. $5\frac{15}{16}$ miles

3. Pens are on sale for $0.79 each. Tamira is going to buy as many pens as she can for $13.50 for the upcoming school year. How many pens can Tamira buy?

    A. 15

    B. 16

    C. 17

    D. 18

4. Jamal found 32 shells at the beach. Hayes found $\frac{7}{8}$ as many shells as Jamal found. How many shells did Hayes find?

    A. 24

    B. 28

    C. 30

    D. 39

5. Divide.

    $$-21.92 \div (-3.2) = \square$$

    A. -6.85

    B. -6.225

    C. 6.225

    D. 6.85

6. The temperature dropped 1.8°C each hour for $4\frac{1}{2}$ hours starting from 8 P.M. If the temperature was 4.6°C at 8 P.M., what was the temperature at 12:30 A.M.?

    A. $-8.1°C$

    B. $-3.5°C$

    C. $-3.1°C$

    D. $12.7°C$

7. Divide.

$$-4\frac{5}{8} \div 1\frac{1}{2} = \boxed{}$$

A. $-3\frac{2}{3}$

B. $-3\frac{1}{12}$

C. $3\frac{1}{12}$

D. $3\frac{2}{3}$

8. Multiply.

$$-\frac{3}{4} \times -1\frac{1}{5} = \boxed{}$$

A. $-\frac{9}{10}$

B. $-\frac{3}{4}$

C. $\frac{3}{4}$

D. $\frac{9}{10}$

9. Last year at Roberts Middle School, $\frac{11}{30}$ of the books in the library were more than 50 years old. At the end of the year, $\frac{1}{10}$ of those books were given to charity.

A. What fraction of all the books was given to charity? Show your work.

_____

_____

B. This year, the school library plans to increase its total of 1,210 books by a factor of 1.1. How many books will the library have? Show your work.

_____

_____

Lesson Practice • Part 2

Choose the correct answer.

1. Multiply.

   $$-47.3 \times 2.6 = \boxed{}$$

   A. -122.98

   B. -111.88

   C. 111.88

   D. 122.98

2. Property taxes on homes decreased this year by an average of $75.90 in Silvertown. There are 270 homes in Silvertown. Which describes the change in Silvertown's revenue from last year to this year?

   A. $-\$21{,}093$

   B. $-\$20{,}493$

   C. $\$20{,}493$

   D. $\$21{,}093$

3. Before it went out of business, Just DVDs had net profits of $-\$8.64$ million in its last 36 months. What was Just DVDs's net profits per month for its last 3 years?

   A. $-\$2.4$ million per month

   B. $-\$0.24$ million per month

   C. $\$0.24$ million per month

   D. $\$2.4$ million per month

4. Which describes how to use powers of 10 to divide $-3.82 \div 0.027$?

   A. multiply the dividend by 100 and the divisor by 1,000

   B. multiply the dividend by 1,000 and the divisor by 100

   C. multiply the dividend and divisor by 100

   D. multiply the dividend and divisor by 1,000

5. Alice was given $15.5 \div 0.25$ to divide. Alice said she knows a way that she can find the quotient without even dividing. Is Alice correct?

   A. Alice is incorrect. She has to multiply the dividend and divisor by 100 before dividing.

   B. Alice is incorrect. She has to multiply the divided and divisor by 10 before dividing.

   C. Alice is correct. If she multiplies the dividend and divisor by 4, the divisor becomes 1.

   D. Alice is correct. If she multiplies the dividend and divisor by 25, the divisor becomes 1.

6. Multiply.

$$-\frac{5}{6} \times -\frac{4}{5} = \boxed{}$$

A. $-\frac{9}{11}$

B. $-\frac{2}{3}$

C. $\frac{2}{3}$

D. $\frac{9}{11}$

7. Mike bought 8 shares of stock for $57.50 each, hoping that the value would increase. When he sold the shares it was only for $42.75 per share. Which describes Mike's net profits?

A. −$342

B. −$118

C. $118

D. $342

8. Divide.

$$-2\frac{3}{8} \div \left(-\frac{2}{3}\right) = \boxed{}$$

A. $-3\frac{9}{16}$

B. $-1\frac{7}{12}$

C. $1\frac{7}{12}$

D. $3\frac{9}{16}$

9. As a cold front moved in, the temperature dropped 3°F each hour for 6 hours. What was the total temperature change after the 6 hours?

A. −18°F

B. −9°F

C. −3°F

D. −2°F

10. The temperature at 9 A.M. was 13.6°C. The temperature at 9 P.M. was 6.4°C. The temperature at 3 A.M. was −3.5°C.

A. What was the average change in temperature from 9 A.M. to 9 P.M.? Show your work.

_____

B. What was the average change in temperature from 9 A.M. to 3 A.M.? Show your work.

_____

11. Use numbers from the box to complete each equation.

$$-7\frac{2}{3} \div 2\frac{1}{2} = \underline{}$$

$$-1\frac{2}{3} \times \left(-1\frac{3}{5}\right) = \underline{}$$

$$3\frac{2}{5} \times \left(-\frac{5}{6}\right) = \underline{}$$

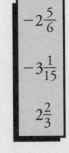

$$-2\frac{5}{6}$$

$$-3\frac{1}{15}$$

$$2\frac{2}{3}$$

12. Libby pays $22.75 for each hour of private dance lessons. She completed 25.5 hours of lessons last month. Circle the total amount that Libby paid for dance lessons last month.

Libby paid

$580.13
$225.65
$48.25

for private dance lessons.

13. Which expressions have products greater than 1 or less than -1? Circle all that apply.

A. $-\frac{2}{5} \times 1\frac{1}{2}$

B. $-1\frac{3}{8} \times \frac{4}{5}$

C. $1\frac{1}{3} \times \frac{5}{6}$

D. $-\frac{3}{4} \times \left(-1\frac{1}{8}\right)$

14. Milo had $5.20 to spend. He bought packs of gum for $0.65 per pack. Circle the number of packs of gum that Milo bought.

Milo bought

8
9
10

packs of gum.

15. Read each word problem and its stated solution. Is the solution correct? Select True or False.

A. Raj used $4\frac{3}{4}$ cups of sugar for each batch of muffins. ○ True ○ False
He made $3\frac{1}{2}$ batches. Raj used $16\frac{5}{8}$ cups of sugar
altogether.

B. Bessie added $1\frac{2}{3}$ cups of fertilizer to each bag of ○ True ○ False
topsoil. She used $7\frac{5}{8}$ bags of topsoil. Bessie used
$12\frac{17}{24}$ cups of fertilizer altogether.

C. Greg had $27\frac{3}{8}$ cups of popcorn. He divided the ○ True ○ False
popcorn evenly among 3 friends. Each friend got
$9\frac{1}{2}$ cups of popcorn.

16. Use numbers from the box to complete each equation.

$-0.75 \div 0.2 =$ _____

$-0.7 \times 4.5 =$ _____

$-9.75 \div -3 =$ _____

$$-3.15$$
$$3.25$$
$$-3.75$$

17. Draw a line from each expression to its solution.

A. 3.6×0.7 • • 2.52
B. $9.66 \div 2.1$ • • 3.7
C. $5.92 \div 1.6$ • • 4.6
D. 5.2×1.4 • • 7.28

Domain 1: Cumulative Assessment for Lessons 1–8

1. A computer that originally cost $899 is on sale for 15% off. What is the sale price of the computer?

   A. $134.85

   B. $764.15

   C. $884.00

   D. $1,033.85

2. The temperature on Mars may reach a high of 70°F at the equator in the summer. It may reach a low of −225°F at the poles. Which expression gives the difference between those temperatures?

   A. 225°F − 70°F

   B. −70°F + 225°F

   C. 70°F − 225°F

   D. 70°F − (−225°F)

3. Which fraction can be expressed as a terminating decimal?

   A. $\frac{7}{8}$

   B. $\frac{1}{3}$

   C. $\frac{2}{9}$

   D. $\frac{1}{7}$

4. Ms. Peters said that $\frac{5}{8}$ of her dance students prefer ballet. Which percent is equivalent to $\frac{5}{8}$?

   A. 58%

   B. 62.5%

   C. 580%

   D. 625%

5. What is the sum of 63 + (−81)?

   A. −144

   B. −18

   C. 18

   D. 144

6. Val scored 85% on a test with 60 multiple-choice problems. How many problems did Val answer correctly?

   A. 51

   B. 45

   C. 33

   D. 25

7. Divide.

   $$-960 \div (-8) = \boxed{}$$

   A. −968

   B. −120

   C. 12

   D. 120

8. Subtract.

$$2\frac{4}{5} - 1\frac{1}{2} = \boxed{}$$

A. $6\frac{1}{3}$

B. $2\frac{3}{5}$

C. $1\frac{3}{10}$

D. $1\frac{1}{5}$

9. In an experiment, the temperature fell 48°F in 8 minutes. If the temperature fell at the same rate every minute, how many degrees did it change each minute?

_____

10. Broderick had $420 in his checking account. He made 6 deposits of $35.50 each. He needs to write 4 checks for $310.75 each.

A. Write an integer to represent the total deposits Broderick made and another integer to represent the total amount Broderick needs from his checking account to cover the checks.

Show your work.

_____

_____

B. How much money does Broderick need to add to his account to cover his checks?

Show your work.

_____

_____

Domain 2

Ratios and Proportional Relationships

Domain 2: Diagnostic Assessment for Lessons 9–12

Domain 2: Cumulative Assessment for Lessons 9–12

Domain 2: Diagnostic Assessment for Lessons 9–12

1. Ramon drove 145 miles in 2.5 hours. What was his speed in miles per hour?

   A. 48 miles per hour

   B. 52 miles per hour

   C. 58 miles per hour

   D. 362.5 miles per hour

2. What value of x makes this proportion true?

   $$\frac{7.5}{x} = \frac{18}{28.8}$$

   A. 10.8   C. 21.8

   B. 12   D. 69.12

3. A recipe for applesauce calls for $\frac{1}{3}$ cup of honey. The recipe makes 8 servings. How many cups of honey are needed to make 20 servings?

   A. $\frac{5}{6}$ cup   C. $1\frac{1}{3}$ cups

   B. $1\frac{1}{6}$ cups   D. $2\frac{2}{3}$ cups

4. It takes Bill $\frac{1}{10}$ hour to walk a $\frac{1}{6}$-mile park loop. What is Bill's unit rate, in miles per hour?

   A. $\frac{1}{10}$ mile per hour

   B. $1\frac{2}{3}$ miles per hour

   C. 6 miles per hour

   D. 60 miles per hour

5. What value of y makes this proportion true?

   $$\frac{15}{35} = \frac{y}{84}$$

   A. $y = 21$ C. $y = 36$

   B. $y = 28$ D. $y = 49$

6. Nina types 126 words in 3 minutes. Which equation shows the relationship between the number of words, w, and the time, in minutes, m, that she types?

   A. $w = 3m$ C. $w = 126m$

   B. $w = 42m$ D. $w = 378m$

7. The function table shows the relationship between the cost and the number of ham sandwiches purchased at a deli.

Number of Sandwiches, n	Cost, C (in dollars)
1	4
2	8
3	12
4	16
5	20

   Which equation shows the relationship between the cost and the number of sandwiches purchased?

   A. $C = n + 4$

   B. $C = 4n$

   C. $C = \frac{1}{4}n$

   D. $C = 4n + 4$

8. Daniel bought 2 pounds of mixed nuts for $7.18. Which ratio is proportional to 2 pounds at $7.18?

A. $\dfrac{\$10.77}{3 \text{ pounds}}$

B. $\dfrac{\$10.83}{3 \text{ pounds}}$

C. $\dfrac{\$11.18}{4 \text{ pounds}}$

D. $\dfrac{\$14.20}{4 \text{ pounds}}$

9. Sondra's room is 15 feet long by 8 feet wide. She is putting carpet in the room. It costs $3.75 per square foot. How much will it cost to carpet Sondra's room?

_____

10. Mason earns $10 for each lawn he mows. How much will he earn if he mows 6 lawns?

A. Write and solve an equation to solve the problem. Show your work.

_____

_____

B. Make a graph to display the relationship.

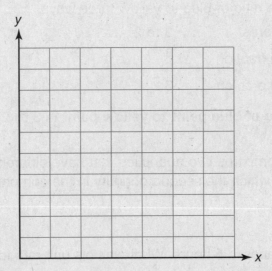

Ratios and Rates

Getting the Idea

A **ratio** is a comparison of two numbers. Ratios can be written to compare a part to a part, a part to the whole, or the whole to a part. Each number in a ratio is called a **term**.

You can write a ratio in three ways:

1. in words   5 to 6

2. as a fraction $\frac{5}{6}$

3. using a colon   5:6

Example 1

For a certain shade of green paint, the paint store mixes 3 parts blue paint to 2 parts yellow paint. What is the ratio of blue paint to yellow paint?

Strategy   **Compare the number of blue parts to the number of yellow parts.**

    Step 1   Break down the paint mix.

               blue = 3

               yellow = 2

    Step 2   Write the ratio of blue to yellow three ways.

               In words   3 to 2

               As a fraction $\frac{3}{2}$

               With a colon   3:2

Solution   **The ratio of blue paint to yellow paint is 3 to 2, $\frac{3}{2}$, or 3:2.**

A **rate** is a ratio that compares two quantities that have different units of measure. A **unit rate** is a rate in which the second quantity in the comparison is 1 unit.

Example 2

Lazlo built 30 toy airplanes in 5 hours. What was his unit rate for building the airplanes?

Strategy   **Divide to find the unit rate.**

    Step 1   Write the rate as a fraction.

               $\frac{30 \text{ airplanes}}{5 \text{ hours}}$

Step 2	Divide to find the unit rate.
	$30 \div 5 = 6$

Solution   **Lazlo's unit rate was 6 toy airplanes per hour.**

Example 3

Jen works for a florist. She worked 15 hours last week and earned $112.50. At that rate, how much will she earn if she works for 10 hours?

Strategy   **Find the unit rate. Then multiply.**

Step 1	Write the rate as a fraction.
	$\dfrac{\$112.50}{15 \text{ hours}}$

Step 2	Divide to find the unit rate.
	$112.50 \div 15 = 7.5$
	Jen earns $7.50 per hour.

Step 3	Multiply the unit rate by 10 hours.
	$7.50 per hour $\times$ 10 hours = $75.00

Solution   **Jen will earn $75.00 if she works 10 hours.**

Example 4

One lap around the path in a park is $\frac{1}{4}$ mile. It takes Andy $\frac{1}{6}$ hour to walk one lap. What is Andy's unit rate around the park?

Strategy   **Find the unit rate.**

Step 1	Write the rate as a fraction.
	In this case the rate is a complex fraction.
	$\dfrac{\frac{1}{4}\text{ mi}}{\frac{1}{6}\text{ hr}}$

Step 2	Simplify the complex fraction.
	$\dfrac{\frac{1}{4}}{\frac{1}{6}} = \frac{1}{4} \div \frac{1}{6}$

Step 3	Divide to find the unit rate.
	Multiply by the reciprocal and simplify.
	$\frac{1}{4} \div \frac{1}{6} = \frac{1}{\underset{2}{\cancel{4}}} \times \frac{\overset{3}{\cancel{6}}}{1} = \frac{3}{2} = 1\frac{1}{2}$

Solution   **Andy's unit rate is $1\frac{1}{2}$ miles per hour.**

Example 5

Holly's room is 12 feet long by 9 feet wide. The carpet she wants to put in the room costs $4.50 per square foot. How much will it cost to carpet Holly's room?

Strategy   **Multiply the area by the unit rate.**

> Step 1   Find the area of the room.
>
> Use the formula for the area of a rectangle: Area = length × width.
>
> A = length × width
>
>   = 12 ft × 9 ft = 108 sq ft

> Step 2   Multiply the area by the unit rate.
>
>   108 × $4.50 = $486.00

Solution   **It will cost $486.00 to carpet Holly's room.**

Coached Example

If 5 tomatoes cost $2.00, what is the unit price of the tomatoes? How much will a dozen tomatoes cost?

Write a ratio that compares the total cost to the number of tomatoes. _____

Divide to find the unit price. _____

To find the cost of a dozen tomatoes, multiply the unit price by _____.

_____ × _____ = _____

The unit price of the tomatoes is _____ per tomato.

One dozen tomatoes will cost $_____.

Lesson Practice • Part 1

Choose the correct answer.

1. The cost of a tent rental is $160 for 5 days. At this rate, how much does it cost to rent the tent for one day?

   A. $25

   B. $30

   C. $32

   D. $35

2. There are 3 counselors for every 45 students enrolled in a camp. What is the maximum number of students allowed if there are 10 counselors?

   A. 15

   B. 135

   C. 150

   D. 300

3. A recipe for rice pudding calls for $2\frac{1}{2}$ cups of milk. The recipe makes 5 servings. How many cups of milk are needed to make 8 servings?

   A. $3\frac{1}{2}$ cups

   B. 4 cups

   C. $4\frac{1}{2}$ cups

   D. $7\frac{1}{2}$ cups

4. Camille bought 3 pounds of nuts for $10.35. What is the unit price per pound?

   A. $3.45

   B. $4.65

   C. $6.65

   D. $7.35

5. Derek's car averages 30 miles per gallon. Which is closest to the amount of gas he will use traveling 454.5 miles?

   A. 10 gallons

   B. 12 gallons

   C. 13 gallons

   D. 15 gallons

6. Ms. Carson drove 96 miles in 1.5 hours. What was her speed in miles per hour?

   A. 48 miles per hour

   B. 54 miles per hour

   C. 64 miles per hour

   D. 144 miles per hour

7. Which of the following shows the least expensive unit price?

   A. 3 oranges for $1.02
   B. 4 oranges for $1.52
   C. 5 oranges for $1.75
   D. 6 oranges for $2.46

8. It takes Eduardo $\frac{1}{20}$ hour to run $\frac{1}{4}$ mile. What is Eduardo's unit rate, in miles per hour, when he runs?

   A. 3 miles per hour
   B. 4 miles per hour
   C. 5 miles per hour
   D. 6 miles per hour

9. Whitney earns $206.25 for 25 hours of work.

   A. How much does Whitney earn per hour? Show your work.

   _____

   _____

   B. At this rate, how much will Whitney earn in 30 hours? Show your work.

   _____

   _____

Lesson Practice • Part 2

Choose the correct answer.

1. A recipe calls for $\frac{1}{2}$ teaspoon of crushed red pepper and $\frac{3}{4}$ teaspoon of thyme leaves. What is the unit rate of teaspoons of crushed pepper to 1 teaspoon of thyme leaves?

   A. $\frac{1}{4}$ teaspoon

   B. $\frac{3}{8}$ teaspoon

   C. $\frac{2}{3}$ teaspoon

   D. $\frac{3}{4}$ teaspoon

2. Miguel scored 74 points in his first 5 games this season. How many points has he scored per game?

   A. 13.8

   B. 14.2

   C. 14.8

   D. 15.2

3. Ayden read 84 pages in 2 hours. At that rate, how many pages can he read in 5 hours?

   A. 168

   B. 210

   C. 378

   D. 420

4. Mr. Hanson bought 8 ounces of smoked salmon for $12.24. What is the unit rate per ounce?

   A. $1.53

   B. $4.44

   C. $20.24

   D. $24.48

5. Mrs. Ellis wants to tile a rectangular room that is 16 feet long and 12 feet wide with square tiles. Each square floor tile is 2 feet. The tiles cost $0.84 per tile. What is the cost to tile the room not including labor?

   A. $40.32

   B. $47.04

   C. $80.64

   D. $161.28

6. A 6-pack of bottled water costs $2.40. An 8-pack of bottled water costs $3.20. Which is the better deal?

   A. The 6-pack is the better deal because it is less expensive.

   B. The 8-pack is the better deal because there are more bottles.

   C. The two packages have the same unit price, so neither is the better deal.

   D. The capacities of the bottles are unknown, so it is not possible to determine the better deal.

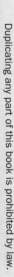

7. A set of 3 pens costs $1.68. At that unit price, how much would 10 pens cost?

    A. $5.04

    B. $5.60

    C. $6.16

    D. $6.72

8. It takes Layla $\frac{2}{5}$ hour to swim $\frac{1}{2}$ mile. What is the unit rate of miles that Layla can swim per hour?

    A. $\frac{1}{5}$ mile per hour

    B. $\frac{4}{5}$ mile per hour

    C. $1\frac{1}{4}$ miles per hour

    D. $1\frac{1}{2}$ miles per hour

9. Bryson bought $2\frac{3}{4}$ pounds of veggie burgers for $8.80.

    A. What is the unit price per pound of the veggies burgers? Show your work.

    _____

    B. There are 16 ounces in a pound. What is the unit price per ounce of the veggie burgers?

    _____

    C. At that unit price, what is the price for $4\frac{1}{2}$ pounds of veggie burgers? Show your work.

    _____

10. It rained 15 millimeters in 12 hours. Select True or False for each statement.

    A. The unit rate is $1\frac{1}{4}$ millimeters of rain per hour.   ○ True   ○ False

    B. The ratio of millimeters of rain to hours of rain is 5:4.   ○ True   ○ False

    C. At the same rate, it would take 8 hours to rain 10 millimeters.   ○ True   ○ False

    D. At the same rate, it would rain 36 millimeters in 45 hours.   ○ True   ○ False

11. Eighty people can ride on a certain Ferris wheel in 20 minutes. Circle the number that makes the statement true.

At that rate,
| 160 |
| 240 |
| 320 |
people can ride the Ferris wheel in 1 hour.

12. A recipe uses $\frac{1}{2}$ cup of flour for every $\frac{1}{4}$ cup of sugar. Which is a true statement? Circle all that apply.

A. The unit rate of flour to sugar is 1 to 2.

B. The unit rate of flour to sugar is 2 to 1.

C. If you used 12 cups of flour, you used 24 cups of sugar.

D. If you used 6 cups of sugar, you used 12 cups of flour.

E. If you had 6 cups of sugar and used 20 cups of flour, you would need 4 more cups of sugar.

13. A bakery makes 500 bagels in 3 hours. Write each number in the correct box.

| 1,000 | 1,200 | 1,400 | 835 | 900 | 1,150 |

Number of Bagels Made in Less Than 7 Hours	Number of Bagels Made in More Than 7 Hours

14. At the grocery store, 5 pounds of apples costs $4.60. At the same rate, could you buy each given number of pounds of apples for the stated price? Select Yes or No.

A. 6 pounds for $5.52   ○ Yes ○ No

B. 3 pounds for $2.76   ○ Yes ○ No

C. 8 pounds for $7.39   ○ Yes ○ No

D. 2 pounds for $1.80   ○ Yes ○ No

E. 9 pounds for $8.28   ○ Yes ○ No

15. Edward drove 434 miles in 7 hours. Use numbers from the box to complete each statement.

4	186
8	248
9	310

At the same rate, Edward would drive _____ miles in 3 hours.

At the same rate, Edward would drive 558 miles in _____ hours.

At the same rate, Edward would drive _____ miles in _____ hours.

16. Draw a line from each sentence to its unit rate.

A. Darlene ran $\frac{1}{2}$ mile in $\frac{1}{10}$ hour. •

B. Hector made 22 necklaces in 4 hours. •

C. Lucas paid $82.50 for 5 shirts. •

D. Karen drove 403 miles using 26 gallons of gas. •

• 5.5 to 1

• 5 to 1

• 15.5 to 1

• 16.5 to 1

Proportions

Getting the Idea

A **proportion** is an equation that shows that two ratios are equivalent. For example, $\frac{1}{2} = \frac{5}{10}$ is a proportion. To tell if two ratios form a proportion, write each ratio in simplest form or use another common denominator. A common denominator can always be found by multiplying the denominators. If the ratios are equal, a proportion is formed.

Example 1

Determine if $\frac{10}{16}$ and $\frac{18}{28}$ forms a proportion.

Strategy   **Write each ratio in simplest form.**

$$\frac{10}{16} \div \frac{2}{2} = \frac{5}{8}$$

$$\frac{18}{28} \div \frac{2}{2} = \frac{9}{14}$$

$$\frac{5}{8} \neq \frac{9}{14}$$

Solution   **The ratios $\frac{10}{16}$ and $\frac{18}{28}$ do not form a proportion.**

A proportion can be solved by writing both ratios with a common denominator. This can be done by multiplying the denominators and then writing equivalent fractions. If one denominator is a factor of the other denominator, simply rename the fraction with the lesser denominator.

Example 2

Solve the proportion by using a common denominator.

$$\frac{a}{16} = \frac{21}{28}$$

Strategy   **Write equivalent fractions using like denominators.**

Step 1   Multiply the denominators to find a common denominator.

$16 \times 28 = 448$

Step 2   Write equivalent fractions with 448 as the denominator.

$$\frac{a}{16} \times \frac{28}{28} = \frac{28a}{448}$$

$$\frac{21}{28} \times \frac{16}{16} = \frac{336}{448}$$

So, $28a = 336$.

Step 3   Divide to solve for a.

$$\frac{28a}{28} = \frac{336}{28}$$

$$a = 12$$

Solution   The solution is $a = 12$.

You can use **cross multiplication** to solve a proportion. To cross multiply is to multiply the numerator of one fraction by the denominator of the other.

Example 3

Solve the proportion.

$$\frac{8}{12} = \frac{6}{x}$$

Strategy   **Cross multiply to solve for x.**

Step 1   Multiply each numerator by the other denominator to find the cross products.

$$8 \times x = 12 \times 6$$

$$8x = 72$$

Step 2   Divide to solve for x.

$$\frac{8x}{8} = \frac{72}{8}$$

$$x = 9$$

Solution   **The solution is $x = 9$.**

Example 4

What value of y makes this proportion true?

$$\frac{0.4}{y} = \frac{3.4}{10.2}$$

Strategy   **Cross multiply to solve for y.**

Step 1   Multiply to find the cross products.

$$3.4 \times y = 0.4 \times 10.2$$

$$3.4y = 4.08$$

Step 2   Divide to solve for y.

$$\frac{3.4y}{3.4} = \frac{4.08}{3.4}$$

$$y = 1.2$$

Solution   **The solution is $y = 1.2$.**

Coached Example

What value of x makes this proportion true?

$$\frac{72}{90} = \frac{x}{25}$$

To cross multiply, multiply the _____ of each fraction by the

_____ of the other fraction.

Write the factors for the cross products.

_____ × _____ = _____ × _____

Multiply to find the cross products.

_____ = _____

Divide both sides by _____ to solve for x.

$$x = \underline{\hspace{2cm}}$$

Substituting the value _____ for x makes the proportion $\frac{72}{90} = \frac{x}{25}$ true.

Lesson Practice • Part 1

Choose the correct answer.

1. What value of x makes this proportion true?

   $$\frac{14}{20} = \frac{56}{x}$$

   A. $x = 62$

   B. $x = 70$

   C. $x = 80$

   D. $x = 100$

2. What value of d makes this proportion true?

   $$\frac{6}{16} = \frac{d}{12}$$

   A. $d = 3.2$

   B. $d = 4.5$

   C. $d = 8$

   D. $d = 8.5$

3. What value of y makes this proportion true?

   $$\frac{15}{35} = \frac{y}{224}$$

   A. $y = 90$

   B. $y = 93$

   C. $y = 96$

   D. $y = 99$

4. Which pair of ratios does **not** form a proportion?

   A. 8:14 and 20:35

   B. 6 to 10 and 15 to 25

   C. $\frac{9}{4}$ and $\frac{36}{16}$

   D. 12:15 and 30:40

5. What value of n makes this proportion true?

   $$\frac{8}{18} = \frac{n}{45}$$

   A. $n = 16$

   B. $n = 18$

   C. $n = 20$

   D. $n = 25$

6. What value of w makes this proportion true?

   $$\frac{0.6}{1.6} = \frac{w}{1.2}$$

   A. $w = 0.45$

   B. $w = 0.8$

   C. $w = 1.6$

   D. $w = 3.2$

7. Which pair of ratios forms a proportion?

 A. 6:16 and 9:25

 B. 8:18 and 22:50

 C. 9:21 and 15:36

 D. 12:27 and 20:45

8. Solve this proportion.

$$\frac{2.1}{c} = \frac{1.5}{1.4}$$

 A. $c = 0.6$

 B. $c = 1.96$

 C. $c = 2.25$

 D. $c = 2.94$

9. Gina wants to solve the following proportion.

$$\frac{a}{\frac{5}{8}} = \frac{\frac{3}{5}}{\frac{2}{3}}$$

 A. Explain how to solve the proportion.

 _____

 _____

 _____

 B. Solve the proportion. Show your work.

 _____

 _____

 _____

 _____

Lesson Practice • Part 2

Choose the correct answer.

1. Which pair of ratios forms a proportion?

   A. 8:14 and 22:40

   B. 10:18 and 25:45

   C. 12:20 and 25:40

   D. 14:30 and 22:45

2. What value of a makes this proportion true?

   $$\frac{4}{12} = \frac{a}{27}$$

   A. $a = 9$

   B. $a = 10$

   C. $a = 12$

   D. $a = 19$

3. What value of b makes this proportion true?

   $$\frac{12}{16} = \frac{21}{b}$$

   A. $b = 25$

   B. $b = 27$

   C. $b = 28$

   D. $b = 30$

4. Which pair of ratios forms a proportion?

   A. $\frac{14}{8}$ and $\frac{10}{6}$

   B. $\frac{16}{9}$ and $\frac{36}{21}$

   C. $\frac{18}{10}$ and $\frac{44}{20}$

   D. $\frac{24}{9}$ and $\frac{40}{15}$

5. Which is **not** a way to determine if two ratios are proportional?

   A. cross multiply to see if the cross products are equal

   B. write each ratio in simplest form to see if the fractions are equal

   C. write equivalent fractions using a common denominator to see if the fractions are equal

   D. add the same fraction to both ratios to see if the fractions are equal

6. What value of c makes this proportion true?

   $$\frac{1.6}{c} = \frac{2.4}{6.3}$$

   A. $c = 3.84$

   B. $c = 4.2$

   C. $c = 5.5$

   D. $c = 10.08$

7. Which value of d makes this proportion true?

$$\frac{d}{3.6} = \frac{3.5}{9}$$

A. $d = 1.6$

B. $d = 1.5$

C. $d = 1.4$

D. $d = 1.2$

8. Which value of e makes this proportion true?

$$\frac{33}{45} = \frac{77}{e}$$

A. $e = 90$

B. $e = 105$

C. $e = 120$

D. $e = 135$

9. The following proportions were written on the board by Ms. Warren.

$$\frac{3.6}{5.7} = \frac{f}{9.5}$$

$$\frac{3.6}{5.7} = \frac{16.2}{g}$$

A. What is the value of f? Show your work.

_____

B. What is the value of g? Show your work.

_____

10. Select True or False for each statement.

A. If $\frac{x}{6} = \frac{8}{3}$, then $x = 14$. ○ True ○ False

B. If $\frac{2}{13} = \frac{8}{d}$, then $d = 52$. ○ True ○ False

C. If $\frac{z}{11} = \frac{11}{10}$, then $z = 10$. ○ True ○ False

D. If $\frac{7}{14} = \frac{b}{9}$, then $b = 4.5$. ○ True ○ False

E. If $\frac{3}{8} = \frac{6}{s}$, then $s = 16$. ○ True ○ False

11. Write each ratio in the correct box.

$$\boxed{\frac{16}{40}} \quad \boxed{\frac{36}{96}} \quad \boxed{\frac{8}{20}} \quad \boxed{\frac{42}{112}} \quad \boxed{\frac{38}{95}} \quad \boxed{\frac{27}{72}}$$

Equal to $\frac{12}{32}$	Equal to $\frac{32}{80}$

12. Circle the number that makes the statement true.

The value $f =$ $\boxed{\begin{array}{c} 0.45 \\ 0.55 \\ 0.65 \end{array}}$ makes the proportion $\frac{0.4}{f} = \frac{1.6}{1.8}$ true.

13. Which pair of ratios do **not** form a true proportion? Circle all that apply.

A. 20:5 and 4:2

B. 3 to 4 and 12 to 16

C. $\frac{18}{8}$ and $\frac{3}{2}$

D. 12 to 24 and 3 to 4

E. 6:9 and 3:2

F. $\frac{8}{6}$ and $\frac{4}{3}$

14. Draw a line from each proportion to the value that makes the proportion true.

A. $\dfrac{\frac{1}{8}}{\frac{3}{4}} = \dfrac{\frac{1}{2}}{x}$ •   • 6

B. $\dfrac{\frac{2}{5}}{\frac{3}{8}} = \dfrac{x}{\frac{15}{4}}$ •   • 3

C. $\dfrac{2}{x} = \dfrac{36}{90}$ •   • 5

D. $\dfrac{2.4}{4.2} = \dfrac{x}{10.5}$ •   • 4

15. Look at each proportion. Does $z = 6$? Select Yes or No.

A. $\dfrac{2}{6} = \dfrac{z}{36}$ ○ Yes   ○ No

B. $\dfrac{18}{14} = \dfrac{3}{z}$ ○ Yes   ○ No

C. $\dfrac{z}{24} = \dfrac{12}{45}$ ○ Yes   ○ No

D. $\dfrac{4}{z} = \dfrac{32}{48}$ ○ Yes   ○ No

E. $\dfrac{84}{24} = \dfrac{21}{z}$ ○ Yes   ○ No

16. Use numbers from the box to solve the proportion.

$$\frac{h}{42} = \frac{18}{63}$$

$$\underline{\hspace{1cm}} \times h = \underline{\hspace{1cm}} \times 18$$

$$\underline{\hspace{1cm}} \times h = \underline{\hspace{1cm}}$$

$$h = \underline{\hspace{1cm}}$$

9	63
12	126
18	216
42	756

Proportional Relationships

Getting the Idea

You can use proportions to solve problems. Proportional relationships, such as the number of miles driven at a constant speed and the amount of time spent driving, can be represented by equal ratios. Relationships that are not proportional, such as a person's age and height, cannot be represented by equal ratios.

Example 1

Derek counted 24 marshmallows in 3 servings of Marshy Morsels. At this rate, how many marshmallows are in 12 servings?

Strategy   **Write and solve a proportion.**

Step 1   Set up a proportion.

   Keep the units consistent.

   $\dfrac{24 \text{ marshmallows}}{3 \text{ servings}} = \dfrac{m \text{ marshmallows}}{12 \text{ servings}}$

Step 2   Find a common denominator.

   3 is a factor of 12.

Step 3   Rename $\dfrac{24}{3}$ as a fraction with 12 as the denominator.

   $\dfrac{24}{3} \times \dfrac{4}{4} = \dfrac{96}{12}$

   $m = 96$

Solution   **At this rate, there are 96 marshmallows in 12 servings.**

In a proportional relationship, when one quantity increases, the other quantity also increases. The ratio of the two quantities stays constant in a proportional relationship. The constant ratio is also called the unit rate, or the **constant of proportionality**.

Example 2

A train travels 120 miles in 1.5 hours. At this rate, how many miles can it travel in 5 hours?

Strategy   **Find and use the unit rate.**

Step 1   Write the rate as a fraction.

$$\frac{120 \text{ mi}}{1.5 \text{ hr}}$$

Step 2   Divide to find the unit rate, or the constant of proportionality.

$120 \div 1.5 = 80$

The unit rate is 80 mph.

Step 3   Write the distance equation.

rate × time = distance

Step 4   Substitute the known values into the equation and solve for the distance.

rate = 80 mph

time = 5 hr

rate × time = distance

$80 \times 5 = 400$ miles

Solution   **At this rate, the train can travel 400 miles in 5 hours.**

In Example 2, you could also have solved the problem by writing and solving a proportion.

$\frac{120}{1.5} = \frac{x}{5}$ Let x represent the distance traveled in 5 hours.

$120 \times 5 = 1.5 \times x$ Write the factors of the cross products.

$600 = 1.5x$ Find the cross products.

$\frac{600}{1.5} = \frac{1.5x}{1.5}$ Divide to solve for x.

$400 = x$

Some problems involving percents can be solved by writing and solving a proportion.

Example 3

18 is what percent of 60?

Strategy   **Write and solve a proportion.**

Step 1   Let x represent the percent, which is unknown.

Write a proportion that compares 18 and 60 to x%.

$$\frac{18}{60} = \frac{x}{100}$$

Step 2   Cross multiply.

$$\frac{18}{60} = \frac{x}{100}$$
$$60 \times x = 18 \times 100$$
$$60x = 1{,}800$$
$$\frac{60x}{60} = \frac{1{,}800}{60}$$
$$x = 30$$

Solution   **18 is 30% of 60.**

Coached Example

Mr. Collins is planning a party for his homeroom class. There are 30 students in his class. He wants each student to have a serving of 8 fluid ounces of juice. Each jug of juice contains 40 fluid ounces. At this rate, how many jugs of juice will he need for the party?

First find the unit rate, the number of servings of juice in each jug.

Write the number of fluid ounces for each student. _____

Write the number of fluid ounces in each jug. _____

To find the unit rate, write a _____ that compares the number of fluid ounces in each jug to the number of fluid ounces for each student. _____

Simplify the ratio to write the unit rate. _____ servings per jug

To find the number of jugs Mr. Collins needs, _____ the number of students in the class by the number of servings per jug.

_____ ÷ _____ = _____

Mr. Collins will need _____ jugs of juice for the party.

Duplicating any part of this book is prohibited by law.

Lesson Practice • Part 1

Choose the correct answer.

1. Mrs. Simpson drove 105 miles in $2\frac{1}{2}$ hours. What was Mrs. Simpson's speed in miles per hour?

   A. 35 miles per hour

   B. 42 miles per hour

   C. 45 miles per hour

   D. 52.5 miles per hour

2. A restaurant charges a single price for its buffet. The total bill for a table of 6 people having the buffet was $294. Each of the 8 people at a second table also had the buffet. What was the total bill at the second table?

   A. $392

   B. $441

   C. $490

   D. $588

3. On a standardized test, Raul answered the first 22 questions in 5 minutes. There are 77 questions on the test. If he continues to answer questions at the same rate, how long will it take him to complete the test from start to finish?

   A. 15 minutes

   B. 16 minutes

   C. 16.5 minutes

   D. 17.5 minutes

4. Kendall knows that a 45-fluid ounce pitcher can hold enough lemonade for 6 people. At this rate, how many fluid ounces of lemonade will Kendall need to serve 26 people?

   A. 45 fluid ounces

   B. 71 fluid ounces

   C. 180 fluid ounces

   D. 195 fluid ounces

5. One 50-pound bag of fertilizer will cover 75 square feet of lawn. How many pounds of fertilizer will Tawny need to cover 120 square feet of lawn?

   A. 80 pounds

   B. 70 pounds

   C. 60 pounds

   D. 50 pounds

6. A factory uses 15 pounds of steel for every 18 pounds of copper. How much copper will the factory use for 2,700 pounds of steel?

   A. 2,250 pounds

   B. 2,400 pounds

   C. 3,240 pounds

   D. 3,700 pounds

7. A computer downloads a 48-kilobyte file in 5 seconds. At this rate, how long will it take the computer to download a file that is 120 kilobytes?

    A. 2 seconds

    B. 11 seconds

    C. 12.5 seconds

    D. 14.4 seconds

8. Taylor buys 8 comic books for $18. Each comic book costs the same amount.

    A. What is the cost per comic book that Taylor pays? Show your work.

    _____

    _____

    B. At this rate, how many comic books can Taylor buy with $27? Show your work.

    _____

    _____

Lesson Practice • Part 2

Choose the correct answer.

Use this information for questions 1 and 2.

Mrs. Graham put 150 gallons of water into a swimming pool in 6 minutes.

1. At that rate, how many minutes would it take to fill a 20,000-gallon pool?

   A. $133\frac{1}{3}$ minutes

   B. 156 minutes

   C. 800 minutes

   D. 900 minutes

2. Which describes the constant of proportionality?

   A. 25 gallons per minute
   B. 25 gallons per hour
   C. 900 gallons per minute
   D. 900 gallons per hour

3. Two gallons of paint will cover 700 square feet. How many gallons of paint are needed to cover 1,960 square feet?

   A. $3\frac{4}{5}$ gallons

   B. $4\frac{3}{5}$ gallons

   C. $4\frac{4}{5}$ gallons

   D. $5\frac{3}{5}$ gallons

4. What value of b makes this proportion true?

   $$\frac{12}{16} = \frac{21}{b}$$

   A. $b = 25$ C. $b = 28$
   B. $b = 27$ D. $b = 30$

Use this information for questions 4 and 5.

A bullet train traveled 270 kilometers in 1.5 hours. The entire trip is scheduled to last 5 hours.

5. If the train continues at the same rate, which proportion can be used to find the length, in kilometers, k, of the trip?

   A. $\frac{1.5}{270} = \frac{5}{k}$

   B. $\frac{1.5}{k} = \frac{5}{270}$

   C. $\frac{270}{1.5} = \frac{5}{k}$

   D. $\frac{270}{k} = \frac{5}{1.5}$

6. What is the value of k?

   A. $k = 630$ C. $k = 900$
   B. $k = 810$ D. $k = 945$

7. Luna has scored 75 points in her first 6 games. If she keeps scoring at the same rate per game, how many points will she score in 20 games?

   A. 240   C. 260
   B. 250   D. 270

8. Major league baseball teams play a 162-game schedule. So far, Grace's favorite team has won 11 games and lost 7 games. If Grace's team wins at the same rate, how many games can she expect for them to win this season?

A. 63   C. 85

B. 77   D. 99

9. Alejandro has a 2,400-word paper to type on his computer. He has typed 450 words in 12 minutes. At that rate, how many more minutes will it take him to complete typing?

A. 48 minutes

B. 52 minutes

C. 64 minutes

D. 120 minutes

Use this information for questions 10 and 11.

Thomas received $79 for exchanging 50 British pounds for dollars.

10. How many dollars would Thomas receive for 160 British pounds?

A. $252.80

B. $173.80

C. $132.91

D. $101.27

11. What is the constant of proportionality?

A. $0.31 per British pound

B. $0.63 per British pound

C. $1.58 per British pound

D. $2.03 per British pound

12. A person who weighs 150 pounds weighs 25 pounds on the Moon.

A. What is the weight of a 1,800-pound car on the Moon? Show your work.

B. Suppose an object weighs 80 pounds on the Moon. What is that object's weight on Earth? Show your work.

13. Draw a line from each price ratio for cans to the cost of five cans.

A. cans of peas: $17.28 for 12 cans   •   • $7.00

B. cans of corn: $16.80 for 12 cans   •   • $7.25

C. cans of green beans: $8.52 for 6 cans   •   • $7.20

D. cans of lima beans: $13.05 for 9 cans   •   • $7.10

14. One 6.25 pound bag of grass seed covers 125 square feet. Circle the number that makes the statement true.

The unit rate is
| 15 |
| 18.5 |
| 20 |
| 20.8 |
square feet per pound.

15. A recipe for 80 fluid ounces of lemonade uses $1\frac{1}{2}$ cups of lemon juice. Which ratio is proportional to 80 fluid ounces per $1\frac{1}{2}$ cups? Circle all that apply.

   A. 160 fluid ounces to 3.5 cups

   B. 640 fluid ounces to 11.5 cups

   C. 240 fluid ounces to 4.5 cups

   D. 320 fluid ounces to 6 cups

   E. 560 fluid ounces to 10.5 cups

16. Write each ratio in the correct box.

| 220 mi per 4.5 hr | 660 mi per 11.5 hr | 825 mi per 14 hr | 385 mi per 7.5 hr | 715 mi per 12 hr | 990 mi per 17.5 hr |

Speed < 55 mph	Speed > 55 mph

17. Look at each statement. Does $k = 35$? Select Yes or No.

A. 28 is k% of 80.   ○ Yes ○ No

B. 36 is k% of 102.   ○ Yes ○ No

C. 84 is k% of 230.   ○ Yes ○ No

D. 77 is k% of 220.   ○ Yes ○ No

E. 49 is k% of 140.   ○ Yes ○ No

18. Chris had 72 hits in 200 at-bats. Use numbers from the box to make the statements true.

Find the unit rate. Divide _____ by _____.

The unit rate is _____ hits per at-bat.

At that rate, the number of hits in 275 at-bats is found by calculating unit rate × _____ = _____.

0.35	99
0.36	200
72	272
84	275

19. The length-to-width unit rate for picture frame size is $1\frac{1}{2}$ to 1. In each picture frame dimension below, are the length and width in proportion to this unit rate? Select Yes or No.

A. length = 21 inches, width = 14 inches   ○ Yes ○ No

B. length = 34 inches, width = 51 inches   ○ Yes ○ No

C. length = 63 inches, width = 42 inches   ○ Yes ○ No

D. length = 39 inches, width = 27 inches   ○ Yes ○ No

E. length = 42 inches, width = 28 inches   ○ Yes ○ No

Represent Proportional Relationships

Getting the Idea

A **directly proportional** relationship has an equation of the form $y = kx$. It is a relationship between two quantities in which one is a constant multiple of the other. When one quantity changes, the other quantity changes by a constant factor, k. The constant factor k is the constant of proportionality.

Example 1

The function table below shows the relationship between the side lengths of a regular octagon and its perimeter.

Side Lengths, s (inches)	Perimeter, P (inches)
1	8
2	16
3	24
4	32
9	?

If a regular octagon has side lengths of 9 inches, what is its perimeter?

Strategy   **Write and solve an equation.**

   Step 1   Write an equation to represent the situation.

The perimeter is always 8 times the side length of a regular octagon.

So, 8 is the constant of proportionality.

$P = 8s$

   Step 2   Substitute the side length of 9 for s and find the perimeter.

$P = 8 \times 9$ in.

$= 72$ in.

Solution   **A regular octagon with a side length of 9 inches has a perimeter of 72 inches.**

A directly proportional relationship is a **linear relationship** because it forms a straight line when graphed. The graph of a proportional relationship is a straight line that passes through the **origin** at (0, 0). It will also pass through the point (1, k), where k is the constant of proportionality, or the unit rate.

Example 2

An empty swimming pool is being filled at a rate of 10 gallons per minute. Make a graph to display the amount of water in the pool each minute for 6 minutes.

Strategy   **Write an equation and create a function table to represent the situation.**

Step 1   Write an equation to represent the situation.

Let x = the number of minutes and y = the number of gallons.

$y = 10x$

Step 2   Make a function table to show the number of gallons in the pool each minute.

At 0 minutes, when $x = 0$, there is no water going into the pool, so $y = 0$.

At 1 minute, when $x = 1$, the pool is filled with 10 gallons of water.

At 2 minutes, when $x = 2$, the pool is filled with 20 gallons of water.

Complete the rest of the table.

Number of Minutes (x)	0	1	2	3	4	5	6
Number of Gallons (y)	0	10	20	30	40	50	60

Step 3   Make a line graph, using the ordered pairs from the function table.

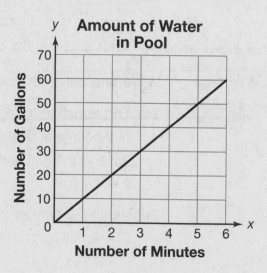

Solution   **The graph is shown in Step 3.**

Example 3

The graph below shows the amounts charged for purchasing different numbers of roses from a florist. Is there a proportional relationship between the number of roses bought and the cost? If so, what is the constant of proportionality and what does it mean in this context?

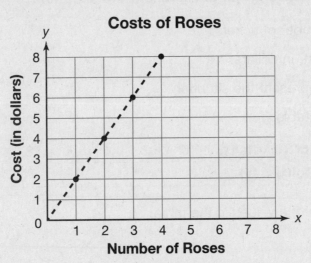

Costs of Roses

| **Strategy** | **Analyze the graph to determine if the relationship is proportional.** |

Step 1 Think about the graph of a proportional relationship.

The graph of a proportional relationship is a straight line that passes through the origin. Since this graph matches that description, it shows a proportional relationship.

Step 2 Determine the constant of proportionality.

The graph must pass through the point $(1, k)$, where k is the constant of proportionality.

The graph passes through the point $(1, 2)$. So, k is 2.

Step 3 Determine what the constant of proportionality means in this context.

In this situation, the fact that $k = 2$ means that each rose costs $2.

Solution **The relationship is proportional and the constant of proportionality, 2, means that each rose costs $2.**

Coached Example

A movie theater charges $16 for 2 tickets, and $32 for 4 tickets. How much would is cost for 12 tickets? Make a graph to represent the situation.

Let x represent the number of tickets.

Let y represent the cost, in dollars.

Write an equation to represent the situation. _____

Complete the function table.

Number of Tickets (x)	0	2	4	6	8	10	12
Cost in Dollars, (y)							

Create a graph to show the values in the table.

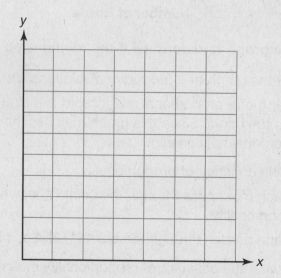

The graph passes through the point (1, _____). So, _____ is the constant of proportionality, or the unit rate.

It would cost _____ for 12 people.

Lesson Practice • Part 1

Choose the correct answer.

Use the function table for questions 1 and 2.

The table shows the relationship between the side lengths of a regular pentagon and its perimeter.

Side Length, s (inches)	Perimeter, P (inches)
1	5
2	10
3	15
4	20
5	25

1. Which equation shows the relationship between the side length and the perimeter of a regular pentagon?

   A. $P = s + 5$

   B. $P = 5s$

   C. $P = \frac{1}{5}s$

   D. $P = 5s + 5$

2. If a regular pentagon has side lengths of 8 inches, what is its perimeter?

   A. 13 inches

   B. 30 inches

   C. 40 inches

   D. 45 inches

Use the graph for questions 3–5.

The graph shows the relationship between the cost and the number of uniforms ordered by a sports team.

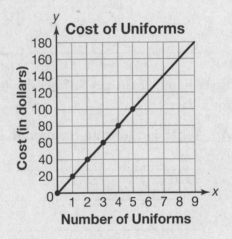

3. Which equation shows the relationship between the number of uniforms, x, and the cost, y?

   A. $y = 20x$ **C.** $y = 2x$

   B. $y = 10x$ **D.** $y = x$

4. What is the unit cost of a uniform?

   A. $2 per uniform

   B. $5 per uniform

   C. $10 per uniform

   D. $20 per uniform

5. How much will it cost the team to order 8 uniforms?

   A. $20   **C.** $160

   B. $140   **D.** $180

6. Amber rides 30 miles in 2 hours. Which equation shows the relationship between the distance, d, and the time, t, that she rides?

A. $d = 2t$

B. $d = 15t$

C. $d = 30t$

D. $d = 32t$

7. Pasha bought 3 pounds of onions for $2.67. Which ratio is proportional to 3 pounds at $2.67?

A. $\dfrac{\$3.48}{4 \text{ pounds}}$

B. $\dfrac{\$3.67}{4 \text{ pounds}}$

C. $\dfrac{\$4.45}{5 \text{ pounds}}$

D. $\dfrac{\$4.57}{5 \text{ pounds}}$

8. River Rambler charges $25 per day to rent a kayak. How much will it cost to rent a kayak for 5 days?

A. Write and solve an equation to solve the problem.

_____

_____

_____

B. Make a graph to display the relationship.

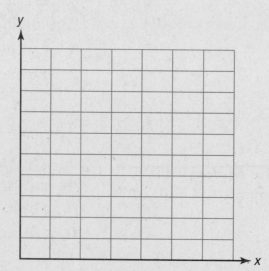

Lesson Practice • Part 2

Choose the correct answer.

Use the function table for questions 1 and 2.

The table shows the relationship between the number of touchdowns, *t* and the number of points, *p*.

Number of Touchdowns, *t*	Number of Points, *p*
1	6
2	12
3	18
4	24
5	30

1. Which equation shows the relationship between the number of touchdowns and the number of points?

A. $p = 6t$

B. $p = 6 + t$

C. $p = \frac{1}{6t}$

D. $p = \frac{t}{6}$

2. How many touchdowns are worth 72 points?

A. 11

B. 12

C. 13

D. 14

Use the graph for questions 3–5.

The graph shows the distance that a train traveled in 5 hours.

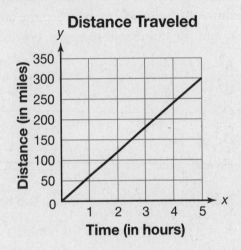

3. Which equation shows the relationship between the number of number of hours, *x*, and the number of miles, *y*?

A. $y = 50x$

B. $y = 60x$

C. $y = 100x$

D. $y = 120x$

4. At the rate it is traveling, how long will it take the train to travel 450 miles?

A. $7\frac{1}{2}$ hours

B. 8 hours

C. $8\frac{1}{2}$ hours

D. 9 hours

5. At the rate it is traveling, how many miles will the train travel in $6\frac{3}{4}$ hours?

   A. 360 miles   **C.** 405 miles

   B. 390 miles   **D.** 420 miles

6. To bowl two games costs $7 and to bowl four games costs $14. Which equation shows the relationship between the cost, c, and the number of games, g, bowled?

   A. $c = 14g$

   B. $c = 7g$

   C. $c = 3.5g$

   D. $c = 2g$

7. What does the ordered pair $(1, y)$ represent on a graph of a proportional relationship?

   A. the origin

   B. the ratio of x to the total

   C. the ratio of y to x

   D. the unit rate

8. At Bob's Second Chance Books, two books cost $6, four books cost $12, and six books cost $18.

   A. What is the cost for 10 books?

   B. Make a graph to display the relationship between the cost and the number of books bought.

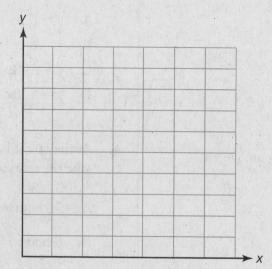

9. Look at each equation. Does the equation represent a directly proportional relationship? Select Yes or No.

   A. $y = 4x + 1$ ○ Yes ○ No

   B. $y = 3x - 1$ ○ Yes ○ No

   C. $\frac{y}{x} = 5$ ○ Yes ○ No

   D. $y = x$ ○ Yes ○ No

   E. $\frac{x}{y} = 7$ ○ Yes ○ No

   F. $xy = 8$ ○ Yes ○ No

10. Which table represents a directly proportional relationship? Circle all that apply.

    A.

x	1	2	3	4
y	4	8	12	16

    B.

x	1	2	3	4
y	9	8	6	5

    C.

x	1	2	3	4
y	5	10	15	20

    D.

x	1	2	3	4
y	2.5	6	7.5	12

    E.

x	1	2	3	4
y	0.5	1	1.5	2

11. Is each ratio of cost per pound proportional to $23.40 for 4 pounds of trail mix? Select Yes or No.

    A. 1 pound for $5.85 ○ Yes ○ No
    B. 2 pounds for $11.75 ○ Yes ○ No
    C. 5 pounds for $29.25 ○ Yes ○ No
    D. 7 pounds for $45.20 ○ Yes ○ No
    E. 12 pounds for $70.12 ○ Yes ○ No

12. The table shows distances that a train travels while going at a constant speed. Use numbers from the box to make the table represent a directly proportional relationship.

Time (h), x	0	3		6	9	
Distance (mi), y	0		360	432		

4	216
5	648
11	791
12	864

13. The graphs show Wayne's and Rama's pay for helping their parents do yard work. Write each point in the correct box.

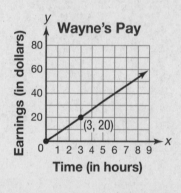

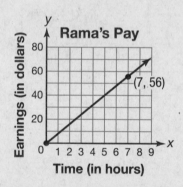

(8, 52)	(5, 32.5)	(8, 64)	(7, 45.5)	(4, 32)	(5, 40)

Points on Wayne's Graph	Points on Rama's Graph

Domain 2: Cumulative Assessment for Lessons 9–12

1. A delivery truck traveled 133 miles in 3.5 hours. What was the average speed of the delivery truck in miles per hour?

   A. 33 miles per hour

   B. 35 miles per hour

   C. 38 miles per hour

   D. 43 miles per hour

2. What value of x makes this proportion true?
   $$\frac{120}{165} = \frac{x}{11}$$

   A. 8

   B. 9

   C. 10

   D. 12

3. A recipe for whole grain rolls calls for $\frac{3}{4}$ cup rye flour. The recipe makes 6 rolls. How many cups of rye flour are needed to make 32 rolls?

   A. $3\frac{1}{4}$ cups

   B. 4 cups

   C. $4\frac{3}{4}$ cups

   D. 8 cups

4. It takes Joaquin $\frac{1}{5}$ hour to hike $\frac{1}{4}$ mile. What is Joaquin's unit rate, in miles per hour?

   A. $\frac{1}{20}$ mile per hour

   B. $1\frac{1}{4}$ miles per hour

   C. 2 miles per hour

   D. 20 miles per hour

5. What value of n makes this proportion true?
   $$\frac{4.5}{n} = \frac{27}{37.8}$$

   A. $n = 3.2$

   B. $n = 6.3$

   C. $n = 10.8$

   D. $n = 22.5$

6. A candle crafter packs 180 candles in 5 boxes. Each box holds the same number of candles. Which equation shows the relationship between the number of boxes, b, and the number of candles, n?

   A. $n = 5b$

   B. $n = 24b$

   C. $n = 36b$

   D. $n = 900b$

7. The function table shows the relationship between the height and the age in weeks of a plant.

Age, *w* (in weeks)	Height, *h* (in inches)
1	3
2	6
3	9
4	12
5	15

Which equation shows the relationship between the height and age of the plant?

A. $h = w + 3$

B. $h = \frac{1}{3}w$

C. $h = 3w$

D. $h = 5w$

8. Kiran bought 6 yards of ribbon for $3.90. Which ratio is proportional to 6 yards at $3.90?

A. $\frac{\$1.36}{2 \text{ yards}}$

B. $\frac{\$1.92}{3 \text{ yards}}$

C. $\frac{\$2.64}{4 \text{ yards}}$

D. $\frac{\$3.25}{5 \text{ yards}}$

9. A stage designer is making a rectangular drape that is 7 yards in length and 16 yards in width. The fabric for the drape costs $2.90 per square yard. How much will it cost to make the drape?

_____

10. Friendship bracelets sell for $7 each. How much will it cost to buy 5 friendship bracelets?

A. Write and solve an equation to solve the problem.

_____

_____

B. Make a graph to display the relationship.

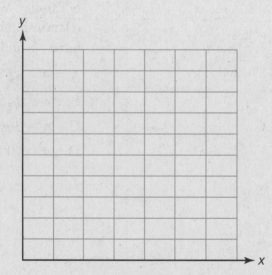

Domain 3

Expressions and Equations

Domain 3: Diagnostic Assessment for Lessons 13–19

Lesson 13 Write Algebraic Expressions

Lesson 14 Simplify and Evaluate Algebraic Expressions

Lesson 15 Add and Subtract Algebraic Expressions

Lesson 16 Write Algebraic Equations

Lesson 17 Solve Equations

Lesson 18 Use Algebra to Solve Word Problems

Lesson 19 Inequalities

Domain 3: Cumulative Assessment for Lessons 13–19

Domain 3: Diagnostic Assessment for Lessons 13–19

1. Brad sold 5 times as many raffle tickets as Doug. They sold 120 raffle tickets in all. Which equation can be used to find how many tickets, t, Doug sold?

   A. $5t + t = 120$

   B. $5t - t = 120$

   C. $5t = 120$

   D. $\frac{t}{5} = 120$

2. Which is equivalent to the expression below?

   $$8x + 4x + y + 3y$$

   A. $3(4x + y)$

   B. $4(3x + y)$

   C. $2(6x + y)$

   D. $2(6x + 2y)$

3. What is the value of the expression below when $n = 12$ and $p = 2$?

   $$\frac{n}{3} - 1 + p$$

   A. 5

   B. 6

   C. $12\frac{1}{3}$

   D. $12\frac{2}{3}$

4. At the school book fair, the number of books sold on Tuesday was 10 less than half the number sold on Monday. Let b represent the number of books sold on Monday. Which expression represents the total number of books sold on Tuesday?

   A. $\frac{b}{2} - 10$

   B. $2b - 10$

   C. $10 - \frac{b}{2}$

   D. $10 - 2b$

5. Troy is at most 5 years older than 3 times Levi's age. If Troy is 29 years old, which inequality best represents x, Levi's age?

   A. $3x + 5 < 29$

   B. $3x + 5 \leq 29$

   C. $3x + 5 > 29$

   D. $3x + 5 \geq 29$

6. Julia walked 8% more miles this week than Andy walked. If Andy walked m miles, which expression represents how far Julia walked?

   A. $0.08m$

   B. $0.8m$

   C. $1.08m$

   D. $1.8m$

7. Mr. Weston has 4 boxes of pencils and 7 single pencils. In all, he has 79 pencils. How many pencils are in a box?

   A. 9

   B. 13

   C. 16

   D. 18

8. Solve for x.

   $$2x - 7 = 9$$

   A. $x = 1$

   B. $x = 3\frac{1}{2}$

   C. $x = 4\frac{1}{2}$

   D. $x = 8$

9. Tanner has budgeted no more than \$20 a month for entertainment and an additional \$15 for possible one-time fees. If Tanner has \$155 to use for entertainment, what is the greatest number of months, m, he budgeted for? Write and solve an inequality to represent the situation.

   _____

10. Marisa bought 3 sweaters on sale for the same price. After using a coupon for \$25, the total cost was \$80.

    A. Write an algebraic equation to represent the situation.

       _____

       _____

    B. How much did each sweater cost? Show your work.

       _____

       _____

       _____

Write Algebraic Expressions

Getting the Idea

An **expression** is a statement that combines numbers, operation signs, and sometimes variables. An algebraic expression includes at least one variable. To write an algebraic expression from words, look for the relationship between the words and the numbers in the situation. This list can help you to translate many, but not all, math word problems.

Operation	Problem	Numerical Expression
addition	3 more than x the sum of x and 3 3 increased by x the total of x and 3 3 combined with x	$3 + x$
subtraction	3 minus x x fewer than 3 x less than 3 x subtracted from 3 3 decreased by x the difference of x from 3	$3 - x$
multiplication	3 times x 3 multiplied by x the product of 3 and x x groups of 3	$3x$
division	x partitioned into 3 equal groups x shared by 3 equally	$\frac{x}{3}$

Example 1

Write an expression to represent the phrase below.

2 less than the product of 7 and a number n

Strategy   **Decompose the word expression into parts.**

Step 1   Look at the first part of the word expression.

"2 less" means to subtract 2.

2 will be subtracted from the second part of the word expression.

Step 2   Look at the second part of the word expression.

"The product of 7 and a number n" means to multiply 7 and n or $7n$.

Step 3   Put the parts together to form one expression.

2 less than $7n$ means $7n - 2$.

Solution   **The expression $7n - 2$ represents the phrase "2 less than the product of 7 and a number n."**

Example 2

The number of stamps in Ethan's collection is 4 more than half the number of stamps in Helen's collection.

Write an expression to show the number of stamps in Ethan's collection.

Strategy   **Decompose the word expression into parts.**

Step 1   Look at the first part of the word expression.

"4 more" means to add 4.

Step 2   Look at the second part of the word expression.

Let h represent the number of stamps in Helen's collection.

"Half the number" can mean to multiply $\frac{1}{2}$ or to divide by 2.

This can be represented by $\frac{h}{2}$ or $\frac{1}{2}h$.

Step 3   Put the two parts together to form one expression.

"4 more" than "half the number" can be represented by $4 + \frac{h}{2}$ or $4 + \frac{1}{2}h$.

Solution   **There are different expressions that represent the stamps in Ethan's collection. Two of them are $4 + \frac{h}{2}$ or $4 + \frac{1}{2}h$.**

Example 3

Lucy babysat for 2 hours on Friday, 3 hours on Saturday, and 2.5 hours on Sunday. She earns d dollars per hour for babysitting.

Write an expression to represent her total earnings for the three babysitting jobs.

Strategy   **Decompose the word expression into parts.**

Step 1   Write what you know.

Lucy babysat three times for the same amount of money each time.

To find how much Lucy earned, add the hours and multiply the number of hours by her rate per hour.

Step 2   Add the hours Lucy worked.

$2 + 3 + 2.5 = 7.5$

Step 3   Write the expression.

Lucy worked 7.5 hours at a rate of d dollars per hour.

That can be shown as $7.5d$.

Solution   The expression $7.5d$ represents Lucy's total earnings for the three jobs.

Coached Example

Kerrigan is k years old. Mia is twice as old as Kerrigan. William is 3 years younger than Mia.

Write an expression to represent William's age.

Mia is twice as old as Kerrigan.

The word "twice" indicates you could _____ by 2.

William is 3 years younger than Mia.

The words "younger than" mean that William's age is _____ than Mia's age.

What operation should you use to show "younger than"? _____

Translate the words into an algebraic expression.

3 years younger than ⟍ ⟋ Mia is twice as old as Kerrigan

_____   −   _____

The expression _____ represents William's age.

Lesson Practice • Part 1

Choose the correct answer.

1. Which expression represents the phrase below?

   83 less than a number n

   A. $83 - n$

   B. $n - 83$

   C. $83 \div n$

   D. $n \div 83$

2. If n stands for the unknown number, which expression represents the phrase below?

   the sum of a number and three, divided by seven

   A. $n + \dfrac{7}{3}$

   B. $\dfrac{7}{n} + 3$

   C. $\dfrac{7}{n + 3}$

   D. $\dfrac{n + 3}{7}$

3. Johanna has s yards of string. For an art project, she can cut an equal number of pieces of string if each piece is $\dfrac{11}{12}$ foot long. Which expression shows the number of pieces she can cut?

   A. $s + \dfrac{11}{12}$

   B. $s \cdot \dfrac{11}{12}$

   C. $s \div \dfrac{11}{12}$

   D. $s - \dfrac{11}{12}$

4. The Hamied family stayed at a hotel for n nights. The cost was $80 per night plus a one-time fee of $20 because they brought their dog. Which expression represents the total cost of their hotel stay?

   A. $80n + 20n$

   B. $80n + 20$

   C. $80 + 20n$

   D. $80 + 20 + n$

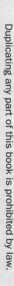

5. The number of pledges that Melissa collected for this year's charity walk is 8 less than half the number of pledges she collected last year. She collected p pledges last year. Which expression represents the number of pledges she collected this year?

A. $2p - 8$

B. $p - \dfrac{8p}{2}$

C. $\dfrac{p}{2} - 8$

D. $8 - \dfrac{p}{2}$

6. Aiden is shopping for school supplies. He has \$35 to spend on a calculator and notebooks. He will buy one calculator for \$18. Let n represent the cost of one notebook. Which expression represents the number of notebooks Aiden can buy with the \$35?

A. $(35 - 18) \div n$

B. $(18 - 35) \times n$

C. $(18 - 35) \div n$

D. $(35 + 18) \div n$

7. A landscaper charges \$30 for each job plus an additional \$20 for each hour worked.

A. Write an expression to represent the total cost of a landscape job. Explain what the variable used in the expression represents.

_____

_____

_____

B. Explain how you identified the operations used in the expression.

_____

_____

_____

Lesson Practice • Part 2

Choose the correct answer.

1. Which expression means the same as an increase of 20%?

   A. $x + 0.2$

   B. $x + 0.2x$

   C. $x + 20x$

   D. $x + 20$

2. Which expression can represent the difference of a number from four times three?

   A. $3(n - 4)$

   B. $(4 \times 3) - n$

   C. $3n - 4$

   D. $n - (4 \times 3)$

3. Levi scored 3 more than 5 times as many points as Emilio. Emilio scored e points. How many points did Levi score?

   A. $3e + 5$

   B. $3e - 5$

   C. $5e - 3$

   D. $5e + 3$

4. It costs $4 to skate each hour and there is a one-time fee of $5 for the skate rental. Which expression represents the cost to skate for someone who has to rent skates?

   A. $4s - 5$

   B. $4s + 5$

   C. $5s - 4$

   D. $5s + 4$

5. A pair of pants normally costs p dollars. The pants are on sale for 15% off. Which expression represents the sale price of the pants?

   A. $p - 0.15$

   B. $p + 0.15$

   C. $p - 0.15p$

   D. $p + 0.15p$

6. There were z babies named Zayden born in New Mexico in 2014. There were 8 fewer than double the number of babies named Jace born in New Mexico that same year. Which expression represents the number of babies named Jace born in New Mexico in 2014?

   A. $2z - 8$

   B. $2z + 8$

   C. $8z - 2$

   D. $8z + 2$

7. Enrollments for the running club are 4 fewer than one third of the enrollments for the swimming club. The swimming club has s enrollments. Which expression represents the enrollments for the running club?

A. $\frac{s}{3} + 4$

B. $\frac{s}{3} - 4$

C. $3s + 4$

D. $3s - 4$

8. Piper's Plumbing charges $120 per hour. They offer a $10 discount for first-time customers. Which expression represents the charge for h hours for a first-time customer?

A. $10h - 120$

B. $10h + 120$

C. $120h - 10$

D. $120h + 10$

9. During college, Jade earned $3 less than half the money per hour than her starting pay at her first job after graduating. Let d represent the amount of money that Jade earned per hour at her first job after college.

A. Write an expression to represent the amount of money that Jade earned per hour in her college job.

_____

B. Jade worked 20 hours per week during her college job. Write an expression to represent the amount of money Jade earned per week at her college job.

_____

10. Antonia had s stickers. She kept 8 and divided the rest equally among 3 friends. Use values from the box to write an expression to represent the situation.

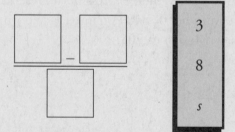

11. Circle the part that completes each expression.

8 more than 2 times a number n

$8 + \begin{array}{|c|} \hline 2 + n \\ \\ n \\ \\ 2n \\ \hline \end{array}$

45 minus the sum of 10 and a number n

$45 - \begin{array}{|c|} \hline (10 + n) \\ \\ 10 + n \\ \\ 10n \\ \hline \end{array}$

4 times 15 less than a number n

$4 \times \begin{array}{|c|} \hline (15 - n) \\ \\ (15 + n) \\ \\ (n - 15) \\ \hline \end{array}$

12. Maelin raised $50 plus $3 for each mile, m, that she walked in a fund-raiser walk. Which expression represents the situation? Circle all that apply.

A. $50 + 3m$

B. $50m + 3$

C. $3 + 50m$

D. $50 \times 3m$

E. $3m + 50$

F. $(50 + 3)m$

G. $50 - 3m$

13. Select True or False for each statement.

    A. 5 less than a number n is written as $5 - n$.   ○ True ○ False

    B. 11 times half of a number n is written as $11\frac{n}{2}$.   ○ True ○ False

    C. 25 more than a number n is written as $25 + n$.   ○ True ○ False

    D. 40 divided by the sum of a number n and 12 is written as $\frac{12 + n}{40}$.   ○ True ○ False

14. Draw a line from each phrase to the numerical expression that it represents.

    A. 5 less than g •   • $5 - \frac{g}{2}$

    B. 5 less than one-half g •   • $g - 5$

    C. g less than 5   •   • $5 - g$

    D. one-half g less than 5   •   • $\frac{g}{2} - 5$

15. Lonnie earned 10 tickets for each game, g, he played at a carnival. He also received 25 tickets for coming to the carnival. Which expression represents the situation? Circle all that apply.

    A. $10 + 25g$

    B. $(25 + 10)g$

    C. $25 + 10g$

    D. $25 \times 10g$

    E. $25 - 10g$

    F. $25g + 10$

    G. $10g + 25$

16. Brogan earns $5 per week. He can earn extra money by helping with chores. He earns $2 per chore, c. Look at each expression. Does the expression represent how much money Brogan earns in a week? Select Yes or No.

    A. $5 + 2c$ ○ Yes ○ No

    B. $2 + 5c$ ○ Yes ○ No

    C. $(5 + 2)c$ ○ Yes ○ No

    D. $2c + 5$ ○ Yes ○ No

Simplify and Evaluate Algebraic Expressions

Getting the Idea

To simplify a numerical expression, follow the **order of operations**.

> **Order of Operations**
> 1. Perform operations inside parentheses or other grouping symbols.
> 2. Evaluate exponents.
> 3. Multiply or divide in order from left to right.
> 4. Add or subtract in order from left to right.

An **exponent** tells how many times the **base** is used as a factor. For example, in 3^2, 3 is the base and 2 is the exponent.

Example 1

Simplify this expression.

$$\frac{1}{2}(2^3 + 2)$$

Strategy   **Follow the order of operations.**

Step 1   Perform operations within parentheses.

The expression within parentheses is $(2^3 + 2)$.

Evaluate the exponent first, then add.

$$2^3 + 2 =$$
$$8 + 2 = 10$$

So, $\frac{1}{2}(2^3 + 2) = \frac{1}{2}(10)$.

Step 2   Multiply.

$$\frac{1}{2}(10) = \frac{1}{2} \times 10 = 5$$

Solution $\frac{1}{2}(2^3 + 2) = 5$

You can use number properties and like terms to help you simplify algebraic expressions.

Like terms are terms that contain the same variable(s) raised to the same power(s).

Commutative Properties	
commutative property of addition	**commutative property of multiplication**
$a + b = b + a$	$ab = ba$

Associative Properties	
associative property of addition	**associative property of multiplication**
$(a + b) + c = a + (b + c)$	$(a \times b) \times c = a \times (b \times c)$

Example 2

Simplify this expression.

$(11k + 5) + 2k$

Strategy	**Use number properties and like terms.**
Step 1	Use the commutative property to reorder the first two terms.
	$(11k + 5) + 2k =$
	$(5 + 11k) + 2k$
	$11k$ and $2k$ are like terms. The like terms are next to each other.
Step 2	Use the associative property to group like terms.
	$(5 + 11k) + 2k =$
	$5 + (11k + 2k)$
Step 3	Combine the like terms.
	$5 + (11k + 2k) =$
	$5 + 13k$
Solution	**The expression can be simplified as $5 + 13k$.**

Example 3

Simplify this expression.

$4s + 5t + (-3s) + 4t$

Strategy	**Use the properties of addition.**
Step 1	Use the commutative property to reorder the terms.
	$4s + 5t + (-3s) + 4t =$
	$4s + (-3s) + 5t + 4t$

Step 2   Use the associative property to group like terms and combine them.

$$4s + (-3s) + 5t + 4t =$$
$$[4s + (-3s)] + (5t + 4t) =$$
$$s + 9t$$

Solution   **The expression can be simplified to $s + 9t$.**

To expand an expression is to remove parentheses or brackets.

You can use the distributive property to expand an expression.

Distributive Properties	
distributive property over addition	**distributive property over subtraction**
$a(b + c) = ab + ac$	$a(b - c) = ab - ac$

Example 4

Simplify this expression.

$$2(4m + n) - 2n$$

Strategy   **Use number properties and combine like terms.**

Step 1   Expand the first part of the expression using the distributive property.

$$2(4m + n) = (2 \times 4m) + (2 \times n)$$
$$= 8m + 2n$$

Step 2   Rewrite the expression.

$$2(4m + n) - 2n = 8m + 2n - 2n$$

Step 3   Use the associative property to group and combine like terms.

$$8m + (2n - 2n) =$$
$$8m + 0n = 8m$$

Solution   **The expression can be simplified to $8m$.**

The opposite of expanding is factoring. You can also use the distributive property to help you factor an expression. An expression is completely factored when there are no more common factors among terms.

Example 5

Simplify and factor this expression.

$$6x + 3x + 15y + 12y$$

Strategy   **Combine like terms. Then use the distributive property to find the GCF.**

Step 1   Combine like terms.
$$6x + 3x + 15y + 12y =$$
$$9x + 27y$$

Step 2   Find the GCF of the terms $9x$ and $27y$.
        The GCF of $9x$ and $27y$ is 9.

Step 3   Factor 9 from each term in $9x + 27y$.
$$9x + 27y =$$
$$9 \times x + 9 \times 3y = 9(x + 3y)$$

Solution   **The simplified and factored expression is $9(x + 3y)$.**

To evaluate an algebraic expression, substitute the given values for the variables. Remember to follow the order of operations.

Example 6

Evaluate this expression when $a = 8$ and $b = -7$.

$$12 + 3a - b$$

Strategy   **Substitute the value of each variable into the expression. Then evaluate.**

Step 1   Substitute 8 for a and -7 for b.
$$12 + 3a - b = 12 + 3(8) - (-7)$$

Step 2   Use the order of operations to simplify.
        First, multiply and divide from left to right.
$$12 + 3(8) - (-7) = 12 + 24 - (-7)$$
        Next, add and subtract from left to right.
        Add: $12 + 24 - (-7) = 36 - (-7) = 36 + 7 = 43$

Solution   **The value of the expression is 43.**

Example 7

Evaluate this algebraic expression when $m = -3$ and $n = -4$.

$m^2 + n$

Strategy Substitute the value of each variable into the expression. Then evaluate.

Step 1 Substitute -3 for m and -4 for n.
$m^2 + n = (-3)^2 + (-4)$

Step 2 Use the order of operations to simplify.

First, evaluate the exponent.

$(-3)^2 + (-4) =$

$(-3 \times -3) + (-4) =$

$9 + (-4)$

Add.

$9 + (-4) = 5$

Solution The value of the expression is 5.

Coached Example

What is the value of this expression when $p = 8$ and $q = 5$?

$\frac{16}{p} - 3q$

Substitute _____ for p and _____ for q in the expression.

$\frac{16}{p} - 3q = $ _____

Use the order of operations to simplify.

First, multiply and divide from left to right.

_____

_____

_____

Now, add and subtract in order from left to right.

_____

The value of the expression is _____.

Lesson Practice • Part 1

Choose the correct answer.

1. Simplify the expression.

   $$(8 - 5)^2 \cdot 3 - 8 \div 2$$

   A. -3
   B. 9.5
   C. 14
   D. 23

2. Simplify the expression.

   $$\frac{28 + 4^2}{2}$$

   A. 9
   B. 11
   C. 16
   D. 22

3. Which is equivalent to the expression below?

   $$4a + 5 - a + 2$$

   A. $10a$
   B. $11a$
   C. $3a + 7$
   D. $4a + 7$

4. Expand the expression.

   $$6(2k - 3)$$

   A. $8k - 3$
   B. $9k$
   C. $12k - 3$
   D. $12k - 18$

5. What is the value of this expression when $c = 4$?

   $$4c + 3c - 2c$$

   A. 20
   B. 28
   C. 36
   D. 40

6. What is the value of this expression when $a = -3$ and $b = 5$?

   $$a + b^2$$

   A. -28
   B. -13
   C. 22
   D. 28

7. Which is equivalent to the expression below?

$$3p + 4 + p + 12 + 3q$$

A. $4p + 3q + 16$

B. $4p + 19q$

C. $6p + q + 16$

D. $20p + 3q$

8. Which shows the simplified and completely factored form of the following expression?

$$12x + 4x + 25y + 15y$$

A. $2(8x + 10y)$

B. $4(4x + 10y)$

C. $5(3x + 5y)$

D. $8(2x + 5y)$

9. Winnie wrote out the following expression.

$$8a - 2b + 12a - 2a - 4b$$

A. Show how to simplify the expression. Write the answer in factored form.

_____

_____

_____

_____

B. Evaluate the expression when $a = 4$ and $b = -2$. Show your work.

_____

_____

_____

Lesson Practice • Part 2

Choose the correct answer.

1. Which is equivalent to the expression below?

   $$6a - 7 + 2a - 4$$

   A. $4a - 11$

   B. $4a - 3$

   C. $8a - 11$

   D. $8a - 3$

2. Simplify the expression.

   $$\frac{1}{2}(3^2 - 4)$$

   A. $-1\frac{3}{4}$

   B. $-\frac{1}{2}$

   C. $\frac{1}{2}$

   D. $2\frac{1}{2}$

3. Expand the expression.

   $$-5(3b - 7)$$

   A. $-15b - 7$

   B. $-15b + 35$

   C. $15b - 7$

   D. $15b + 35$

4. What is the value of this expression when $c = 6$ and $d = 4$?

   $$\frac{5}{2}c - 3d$$

   A. 3

   B. 8

   C. 9

   D. $11\frac{1}{2}$

5. Which is equivalent to the expression below?

   $$4e + 6 - 2e + 5f + 2 - 2f$$

   A. $6e + 3f + 4$

   B. $6e + 7f + 8$

   C. $2e + 7f + 4$

   D. $2e + 3f + 8$

6. Which shows the simplified and completely factored form of this expression?

   $$8g + 12g + 10h + 18h$$

   A. $2(10g + 14h)$

   B. $4(5g + 7h)$

   C. $5(4g + 6h)$

   D. $10(2g + 3h)$

7. Simplify the expression.

$$(3 + 5)^2 - 4 \cdot 6 - 8 \div 2$$

- **A.** 16
- **B.** 36
- **C.** 120
- **D.** 176

8. Simplify the expression.

$$\frac{42 - 6^2}{3}$$

- **A.** 2
- **B.** 10
- **C.** 30
- **D.** 432

9. Which shows the simplified and completely factored form of this expression?

$$4j + 6k + 8j + 10k$$

- **A.** $2(6j + 8k)$
- **B.** $3(4j + 5k)$
- **C.** $4(3j + 4k)$
- **D.** $6(2j + 3k)$

10. What is the value of this expression when $m = -6$ and $n = 4$?

$$m^3 - 2n^2$$

- **A.** -248
- **B.** -152
- **C.** 152
- **D.** 184

11. Luis wrote this expression on the board.

$$16p + 8q + 12p + 6q$$

A. Write the simplified and completely factored form of the expression.

_____

B. Evaluate the expression when $p = 6$ and $q = -3$. Show your work.

_____

_____

12. Draw a line from each expression to its value.

- **A.** $6^2 - 30 + 5$ •   • 1
- **B.** $(20 + 4 \times 9) \div 8$ •   • 7
- **C.** $10(7 - 2) + 20$ •   • 11
- **D.** $28 \div 7 - 3$ •   • 70

13. Which expression is equivalent to the one given below? Circle all that apply.

$$18r + (7 - 2) \times 3m$$

A. $18r + 5 + 3m$

B. $18r + 15m$

C. $18r + m$

D. $3(6r + 5m)$

E. $15m + 18r$

F. $23r + 3m$

G. $m + 18r$

14. Evaluate the expression for each given value of x. Circle each correct value.

$$7x - 5(2x + 9)$$

$x = -3$ value of expression =

-6
-36
-54

$x = 10$ value of expression =

-21
-39
-75

$x = 7$ value of expression =

$1,012$
-30
-66

15. Look at each equation. Is the expression on the left simplified correctly on the right? Select Yes or No.

A. $8p + 10q - 4p = 12p + 10q$ ◯ Yes   ◯ No

B. $15p - 2(3q + p) = 13p - 6q$ ◯ Yes   ◯ No

C. $\dfrac{10p}{2q} = \dfrac{5p}{q}$ ◯ Yes   ◯ No

D. $-5p \times -3q = -15pq$ ◯ Yes   ◯ No

16. Select True or False for each equation.

A. $-10 \times 3(6 - 4) = -60$ ◯ True   ◯ False

B. $\dfrac{9}{6^2} = \dfrac{1}{4}$ ◯ True   ◯ False

C. $15 - 6 \times -4 = -36$ ◯ True   ◯ False

D. $7^2 + (10 - 5) = 54$ ◯ True   ◯ False

Add and Subtract Algebraic Expressions

Getting the Idea

The same rules you learned for adding and subtracting rational numbers also apply to adding and subtracting algebraic expressions.

Number properties and the order of operations can also help you solve problems involving addition or subtraction of expressions.

Example 1

What is the perimeter of the triangle below?

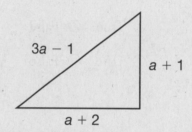

Strategy	Add the expressions for the 3 sides. Simplify the sum.
Step 1	Write an expression to represent the perimeter.

The perimeter of a figure is the sum of its side lengths.

$(a + 1) + (a + 2) + (3a - 1)$

Step 2	Use the commutative and associative properties to reorder and group like terms.

$(a + 1) + (a + 2) + (3a - 1) =$

$a + 1 + a + 2 + 3a - 1 =$

$a + a + 3a + 1 + 2 - 1$

Step 3	Add.

$a + a + 3a + 1 + 2 - 1 =$

$(a + a + 3a) + (1 + 2 - 1) =$

$5a + 2$

Solution	The expression $5a + 2$ represents the perimeter of the triangle.

Remember that subtracting an integer is the same as adding its opposite. You can use the same strategy to subtract an algebraic expression.

Example 2

Subtract.

$4x + 8 - (3 + 4y)$

Strategy   **Find the opposite of the expression being subtracted. Then add the opposite to the original expression.**

Step 1   Find the opposite of the quantity being subtracted.

The opposite of $3 + 4y$ is $-(3 + 4y)$.

$-(3 + 4y)$ is the same as $-1(3 + 4y)$, so distribute -1 over the two terms.

$-(3 + 4y) = (-3) - 4y$

Step 2   Rewrite the problem as an addition problem by adding the opposite.

$4x + 8 - (3 + 4y) =$

$4x + 8 + (-3) - 4y$

Step 3   Use the commutative and associative properties to reorder and group like terms.

$4x + 8 + (-3) - 4y = 4x - 4y + 8 + (-3)$

Then add.

$4x - 4y + 8 + (-3) = 4x - 4y + 5$

Solution   **The difference is $4x - 4y + 5$.**

Example 3

Drew baked c corn muffins. He brought $\frac{3}{4}$ of the corn muffins to the bake sale and gave $\frac{1}{8}$ of the muffins to his grandmother. How many muffins did Drew have left?

Strategy   **Translate the problem into an expression. Then simplify.**

Step 1   Write an expression for the number of muffins Drew had left.

Drew baked c muffins. He brought $\frac{3}{4}$ of the muffins to the bake sale.

He also gave $\frac{1}{8}$ of the muffins to his grandmother.

This can be represented as $c - \frac{3}{4}c - \frac{1}{8}c$.

| Step 2 | Simplify the expression using a common denominator. |

$$c - \frac{3}{4}c - \frac{1}{8}c =$$

$$1c - \frac{3}{4}c - \frac{1}{8}c =$$

$$\frac{8}{8}c - \frac{6}{8}c - \frac{1}{8}c =$$

$$\frac{(8 - 6 - 1)}{8}c = \frac{1}{8}c$$

Solution   Drew had $\frac{1}{8}c$ muffins left.

Coached Example

Carter bought a ruler for $2 and a compass for x dollars. He paid for the items with a $5 bill and y-dollar bills. How much did Carter receive in change? Write your answer in simplest form.

Translate the problem into an expression.

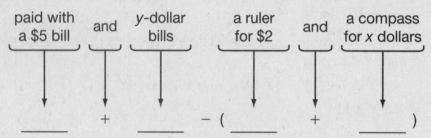

| paid with a $5 bill | and | y-dollar bills | a ruler for $2 | and | a compass for x dollars |

_____   +   _____   − (_____   +   _____)

Simplify the expression you wrote.

Find the opposite of the expression being subtracted.

The opposite of $2 + x$ is _____.

Distribute the −1 over the two terms. _____.

Rewrite the problem as an addition problem by adding the opposite.

_____   +   _____

Use number properties to reorder and group like terms. Then add.

_____

In simplest form, Carter received _____ in change.

Lesson Practice • Part 1

Choose the correct answer.

1. Add.

   $$7y + 5 + (3 - y)$$

   A. $8y + 8$

   B. $6y + 8$

   C. $-6y + 8$

   D. $-8y + 8$

2. Subtract.

   $$5 + 5q - (3q - 9)$$

   A. $2q - 9$

   B. $2q - 4$

   C. $-2q + 4$

   D. $2q + 14$

3. Add.

   $$5k + 4 + (6 - 2m)$$

   A. $5k - 2m + 10$

   B. $3k + m + 10$

   C. $5k + 2m + 10$

   D. $10k + 3m$

4. Subtract.

   $$5r + 3 - (1 + 6r)$$

   A. $-11r + 2$

   B. $-2r + 2$

   C. $-r + 2$

   D. $11r + 2$

5. Which expression represents the perimeter, in units, of this trapezoid?

   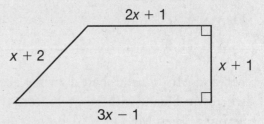

   A. $7x + 3$

   B. $7x - 1$

   C. $2x + 1$

   D. $2x - 1$

6. Angelo and Jimmy went shopping. Angelo had a dollars in his wallet. He spent $\frac{1}{3}$ of that money on new jeans. Jimmy had j dollars in his wallet. He spent $\frac{1}{2}$ of that money on a new jacket. Jimmy had more money left than Angelo. Which expression shows the difference between the amounts of money, in dollars, that each boy had left?

   A. $\frac{1}{3}a - \frac{1}{2}j$

   B. $\frac{2}{3}a - \frac{1}{2}j$

   C. $\frac{1}{2}j - \frac{2}{3}a$

   D. $\frac{1}{2}j - \frac{1}{3}a$

7. Which expression is equivalent to the expression below?

$$4r + 9 + r + 2s - 3$$

A. $14r - s$

B. $7r + 6$

C. $5r + 2s - 12$

D. $5r + 2s + 6$

8. Which of the following shows a simplified version of this expression?

$$2k + (-3m) - 6k + 2m$$

A. $-4k - 2m$

B. $-4k - m$

C. $4k - 5m$

D. $4k - m$

9. Mr. and Mrs. Duane share a savings account. There were d dollars in the savings account when Mr. Duane withdrew \$45 from the account. Mrs. Duane deposited m dollars into the account. Then Mr. Duane deposited an additional \$65 into the account.

A. Write an expression to show how much money, in dollars, is in the account after the transactions.

_____

_____

_____

B. Simplify the expression. Explain your thinking.

_____

_____

_____

Lesson Practice • Part 2

Choose the correct answer.

1. Add.

   $8a + 6 + (4 - a)$

   A. $7a + 2$
   B. $7a + 10$
   C. $9a + 2$
   D. $9a + 10$

2. Subtract.

   $7b + 4 - (2b - 2)$

   A. $5b + 2$
   B. $5b + 6$
   C. $9b + 2$
   D. $9b + 6$

3. Add.

   $6c + 8 + (3 - 2d)$

   A. $6c - 2d + 11$
   B. $6c + 2d + 11$
   C. $6c - 2d + 5$
   D. $6c + 2d + 5$

4. Subtract.

   $8e + 4 - (3 + 9e)$

   A. $17e + 1$
   B. $17e + 7$
   C. $-e + 1$
   D. $-e + 7$

5. Which expression is equivalent to the expression below?

   $-4p - 3q - (2p - 4q)$

   A. $-6p - 7q$
   B. $-6p + q$
   C. $-2p - 7q$
   D. $-2p + q$

6. Dawn bought a magazine for $6 and a book for b dollars. She paid for the items with a $20 bill and d dollars bills. Which represents the amount of change that Dawn received?

   A. $14 + d - b$
   B. $14 - d + b$
   C. $26 + d - b$
   D. $26 - d + b$

7. Which expression is equivalent to the expression below?

   $5f - 8 + 2f - 4g + 2$

   A. $3f - 4g - 10$
   B. $3f - 4g - 6$
   C. $7f - 4g - 10$
   D. $7f - 4g - 6$

8. Which expression is equivalent to the expression below?

$$4j + (-5k) - 2j + 3k$$

A. $2j - 8k$ **C.** $6j - 8k$

B. $2j - 2k$ **D.** $6j - 2k$

9. Which expression is equivalent to the expression below?

$$-6m + 2n + 4m - 3n$$

A. $-10m - 5n$

B. $-10m - n$

C. $-2m - 5n$

D. $-2m - n$

10. What is the perimeter of the triangle?

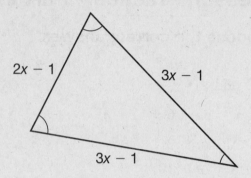

A. $5x - 2$

B. $5x - 3$

C. $8x - 2$

D. $8x - 3$

11. Camila was given this expression.

$$4r - 3 + 6s - 8r - (4s - 6)$$

A. Simplify the expression.

_____

B. Explain how you used the properties of operations to simplify the expression.

_____

_____

_____

_____

12. The expression below shows the perimeter of a rectangle with sides $(2 + s)$ and $(5 - m)$. Which is an equivalent expression? Circle all that apply.

$$(2 + s) + (5 - m) + (2 + s) + (5 - m)$$

A. $(4 + 2s) + (10 - 2m)$

B. $(2 + s) + (5 - m)$

C. $2(2 + s) + 2(5 - m)$

D. $14 + 2s - 2m$

E. $14 + 2s + 2m$

F. $14 + 4sm$

G. $14sm$

13. Draw a line from each expression to the equivalent simplified expression.

A. $3a + 11 - (2 + 4a)$ •	• $7a - 9$
B. $3a + 11 + (2 + 4a)$ •	• $-a + 9$
C. $3a - 11 + (2 + 4a)$ •	• $7a + 9$
D. $3a + 11 - (2 - 4a)$ •	• $7a + 13$

14. Landon biked 4 miles on Monday, $2m$ miles on Wednesday, and $(10 - m)$ miles on Friday. How many miles did he bike during the week? Use values from the box to complete a simplified expression that represents the situation.

$$-6$$

$$14$$

$$3m$$

$$m$$

_____ + _____

15. Look at each equation. Is the expression on the left simplified correctly on the right? Select Yes or No.

   A. $6x - 7y + 3x = 3x - 7y$ ○ Yes   ○ No

   B. $10 - 3x - 4x = 3x$ ○ Yes   ○ No

   C. $(22x + 5) - (3x + 9) = 19x - 4$ ○ Yes   ○ No

   D. $12x - y - 5x = 7x - y$ ○ Yes   ○ No

16. Tania bought three shirts for $(12 + d)$, $(7d + 5)$, and $(20 - 2d)$ dollars. Which expression represents the total cost? Circle all that apply.

   A. $37 + 6d$

   B. $12 + d + 7d + 5 - 20 - 2d$

   C. $(12 + 5 - 20) + (d + 7d - 2d)$

   D. $(12 + 5 + 20) + (d + 7d - 2d)$

   E. $12 + d + 7d + 5 + 20 - 2d$

   F. $37 + 10d$

   G. $(d + 12) + (5 + 7d) + (-2d + 20)$

17. Select True or False for each equation.

   A. $2p + 3d - (p + d) = p + 2d$ ○ True   ○ False

   B. $4p + 22d - (21p + 54d) = -17p + 76d$ ○ True   ○ False

   C. $-p + 100d + 79p - 6d = 78p + 94d$ ○ True   ○ False

   D. $56p - 32d - (25p + d) = 31p - 31d$ ○ True   ○ False

Write Algebraic Equations

Getting the Idea

An **equation** is a mathematical sentence that contains an equal sign (=).

An algebraic equation contains at least one variable.

You may need to write equations to solve word problems.

Example 1

Nicholas has 28 coins. That is 5 more than his brother Sam has. Write an equation that represents s, the number of coins Sam has.

Strategy   Decompose the situation into two expressions.

Step 1   Write what you know.

Nicholas has 28 coins.

Nicholas has 5 more coins than Sam.

Step 2   Translate the words into a number sentence.

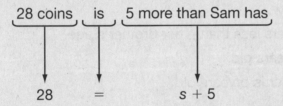

$$28 \qquad = \qquad s + 5$$

Solution   The equation $28 = s + 5$ represents the number of coins Sam has.

Example 2

Mr. Edwards purchased 3 bags of potatoes. He bought 36 potatoes in all. Each bag contains the same number of potatoes. Write an equation that represents this situation.

Strategy   **Decompose the situation into two expressions.**

Step 1   Write what you know.

Mr. Edwards bought 36 potatoes.

The potatoes came in 3 bags, each with an equal number of potatoes.

Step 2   Translate the words into an equation.

Let p = the number of potatoes in each bag.

$3p = 36$

Solution   **The equation $3p = 36$ represents this situation.**

Example 3

Phoebe is 3 years less than half her brother's age. Phoebe is 13 years old. Her brother is b years old. Write an equation that could be used to find her brother's age.

Strategy   **Decompose the situation into two expressions.**

Step 1   Write what you know.

Phoebe is 3 years less than $\frac{1}{2}$ her brother's age.

Phoebe is 13 years old.

Phoebe's brother is b years old.

Step 2   Decompose the situation.

Phoebe is 13 years old, so 13 goes on one side of the equation.

If Phoebe's brother is b years old, then Phoebe is $\frac{b}{2} - 3$ years old.

Step 3   Translate the words into an equation.

$\frac{b}{2} - 3 = 13$

Solution   **The equation $\frac{b}{2} - 3 = 13$ could be used to find her brother's age.**

Example 4

Rafael's tennis racket cost 5% more than Carl's tennis racket. Rafael's racket cost $126. Write an equation that could be used to find the cost of Carl's tennis racket.

Strategy   **Use mathematical sense to translate the words into an equation.**

Step 1   Understand how the quantities are related.

Rafael's racket cost 5% more than 100% of the cost of Carl's racket.

Step 2   Write an expression for the cost of Rafael's racket.

Let c = the cost of Carl's tennis racket.

$5\%c + 100\%c = 0.05c + 1c = 1.05c$ or $105\%c$

The cost of Rafael's racket is 105% of the cost of Carl's racket.

Step 3   Write the equation for the cost of Rafael's racket.

$1.05c = 126$

Solution   **The equation $1.05c = 126$ could be used to find the cost of Carl's tennis racket.**

Coached Example

Nigel went to an ice rink and paid $5 for admission plus an additional $2.50 per hour to rent skates. The total cost was $15. Write an equation that represents h, the number of hours for which Nigel rented skates.

Translate the words into a mathematical sentence.

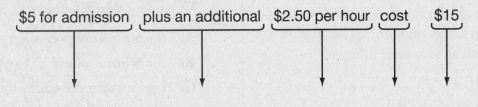

$5 for admission   plus an additional $2.50 per hour   cost $15

_____   _____   _____   _____   _____

The equation _____ represents the situation.

Lesson Practice • Part 1

Choose the correct answer.

1. Lou had r rocks in his collection. He separated his rocks into 3 equal piles. He now has 12 rocks in each pile. Which equation represents this situation?

   A. $r - 3 = 12$

   B. $r \div 3 = 12$

   C. $r + 3 = 12$

   D. $r \times 3 = 12$

2. Magdalena bought a sweater that cost d dollars. She paid the clerk $40.00. She received $5.19 in change. Which equation represents this situation?

   A. $40.00 - d = 5.19$

   B. $40.00 + d = 5.19$

   C. $d - 40.00 = 5.19$

   D. $d - 5.19 = 40.00$

3. Kevin sold 5 times as many raffle tickets as Alice. If Kevin sold 45 raffle tickets in all, which equation can be used to find a, the number of tickets Alice sold?

   A. $5 + a = 45$

   B. $45 + a = 5$

   C. $5a = 45$

   D. $45a = 5$

4. Clarissa had a strip of leather that was n yards long. She cut the strip into pieces that were each $\frac{1}{4}$ yard long, with no leather left over. She used all of the pieces and made 9 bracelets. Which equation represents this situation?

   A. $n + \frac{1}{4} = 9$

   B. $n - \frac{1}{4} = 9$

   C. $n \times \frac{1}{4} = 9$

   D. $n \div \frac{1}{4} = 9$

5. This season, the number of points Reggie scored was 36 less than 4 times the number of points Larry scored. Reggie scored 64 points this season. The equation below represents this situation.

   $$4n - 36 = 64$$

   What does n represent in this equation?

   A. the number of points Reggie scored

   B. the number of points Larry scored

   C. how many more points Reggie scored than Larry

   D. how many points Reggie and Larry scored in all

6. Jonas bought 3 books. Each book was the same price. After using a $10-off coupon, the total charge was $20. Which equation can be used to find b, the cost of each book?

   A. $3b + 10 = 20$

   B. $3b - 10 = 20$

   C. $10b + 3 = 20$

   D. $10b - 3 = 20$

7. A rectangle has a length of x centimeters and a width that is equal to half of its length. The perimeter of the rectangle is 22.5 centimeters. Which equation represents this situation?

   A. $(x)\left(\frac{x}{2}\right) = 22.5$

   B. $\frac{1}{2}\left(x + \frac{x}{2}\right) = 22.5$

   C. $x + \frac{x}{2} = 22.5$

   D. $x + 2x = 22.5$

8. Irina bought 2 songbooks and a new guitar. Each songbook cost the same price. The guitar cost $250.10. Before tax, she spent a total of $301.80. Which equation can be used to find c, the cost in dollars, of each songbook?

   A. $\frac{c}{2} + 250.10 = 301.80$

   B. $2c - 250.10 = 301.80$

   C. $2c + 250.10 = 301.80$

   D. $2 + c + 250.10 = 301.80$

9. Madison's skateboard cost 10% more than Tony's skateboard. Madison's skateboard cost $83.

   A. Choose a variable to represent the unknown value in the situation. Explain what the variable represents.

   _____

   _____

   _____

   B. Write an equation that could be used to find the cost of Tony's skateboard. Explain your thinking.

   _____

   _____

   _____

Lesson Practice • Part 2

Choose the correct answer.

1. There are 8 fewer than double the number of students in the chorus than in the band. There are 54 members in the chorus. Which equation represents how to find the number of students in the band?

   A. $2x - 8 = 54$

   B. $2x + 8 = 54$

   C. $8x - 2 = 54$

   D. $8x + 2 = 54$

2. Everly's age is 2 years more than 3 times Gage's age. If Everly is 23 years old, which equation represents how to find Gage's age?

   A. $2e + 3 = 23$

   B. $2e - 3 = 23$

   C. $3e + 2 = 23$

   D. $3e - 2 = 23$

3. Katrina's ski boots cost 8% more than her skis. Her ski boots cost $162. Which equation can be used to find the cost, c, of Katrina's skis?

   A. $c + 0.08c = 162$

   B. $c + 0.8c = 162$

   C. $c - 0.08c = 162$

   D. $c - 0.8c = 162$

4. Tucker read 10 pages more than 3 times the number of pages that Ivy read. Ivy read 72 pages yesterday. Which equation can be used to find the number of pages that Tucker read?

   A. $3n + 10 = 72$

   B. $3n - 10 = 72$

   C. $\frac{n}{3} + 10 = 72$

   D. $\frac{n}{3} - 10 = 72$

5. The perimeter of a rectangle is 60 inches. The width of the rectangle is 8 inches. Which equation can be used to find the length of the rectangle?

   A. $2l + 8 = 60$

   B. $2l - 8 = 60$

   C. $2l + 16 = 60$

   D. $2l - 16 = 60$

6. Lexi scored 27 points fewer than 3 times as many points as Madelyn this season. If Lexi scored 120 points, which equation shows how many points Madelyn scored?

   A. $3p + 27 = 120$

   B. $3p - 27 = 120$

   C. $27p - 3 = 120$

   D. $27p + 3 = 120$

7. Cal spent 4 times as much time working on the science fair project as Emmett. Together they spent 720 minutes working on the project. Which equation can be used to find how many minutes each spent on the science fair project?

    A. $\frac{m}{4} = 720$

    B. $4m = 720$

    C. $4m - m = 720$

    D. $4m + m = 720$

8. Ryan bought 4 shirts that cost $60 after he applied a $10-off coupon. The shirts all cost the same amount. Which equation can be used to find the cost of each shirt?

    A. $4s - 10 = 60$
    B. $4s + 10 = 60$
    C. $10s - 4 = 60$
    D. $10s + 4 = 60$

9. Toni's grandmother is 3 years more than 6 times Toni's age. The sum of their ages in years is 87. Which equation can be used to find each of their ages?

    A. $6y + 3 = 87$
    B. $6y - 3 = 87$
    C. $6y + y - 3 = 87$
    D. $6y + y + 3 = 87$

10. Jose has a board that is f feet long. He cut the board into pieces that were each $\frac{3}{4}$ foot long. He used all of the pieces and built 6 shelves for a bookshelf. Which equation can be used to find the length, in feet, of each piece?

    A. $f + \frac{3}{4} = 6$

    B. $\frac{f}{\frac{3}{4}} = 6$

    C. $f - \frac{3}{4} = 6$

    D. $\frac{3}{4f} = 6$

11. Adrian's computer cost 20% less than Jocelyn's computer. Adrian's computer cost $640. Adrian's computer cost 15% more than Corbin's computer.

    A. Write an equation that could be used to find the cost of Jocelyn's computer.

    _____

    B. Write an equation that could be used to find the cost of Corbin's computer.

    _____

12. David practiced his saxophone for m minutes on Monday. On Tuesday, he practiced for 30 minutes more than twice as long as Monday. He practiced for 80 minutes on Tuesday. Use values from the box to write an equation to represent how long David practiced on Tuesday.

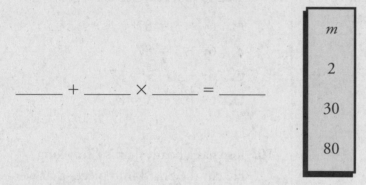

_____ + _____ × _____ = _____

| m |
| 2 |
| 30 |
| 80 |

13. Which situation could be represented by the equation below? Circle all that apply.

$$8x - 17 = 30$$

A. Steve had 8 times as many dollars as Juan, x, and spent $17. Steve has $30 left.

B. Jennifer had 30 dollars. She spent 8 times as many dollars as Tia, x, and has $17 left.

C. Bella is 17 years younger than 8 times Jonah's age, x. Jonah is 30.

D. KeShawn is 17 years younger than 8 times Billy's age, x. KeShawn is 30.

E. Heath scored 30 points, which is 17 less than 8 times the number of points that Tyrese scored, x.

F. Lena scored 17 less than 8 times the number of points Kevin scored, x. Lena scored 30 points.

G. Nadia has two trees. The shorter tree is 17 inches less than 8 times the height of the other. The taller tree is 30 inches tall.

14. Pedro had 6 packs of gum with p pieces in each pack. He had a total of 72 pieces of gum. Decide whether each equation represents the situation. Select True or False for each equation.

A. $p + 6 = 72$ ○ True   ○ False

B. $6p = 72$ ○ True   ○ False

C. $72 \div p = 6$ ○ True   ○ False

D. $p \times 6 = 72$ ○ True   ○ False

15. Kyra read 45 pages of her book on Saturday. On Sunday, she read 100 more pages than she read on Saturday. Use values from the box to write an equation to represent how many pages Kyra read on Sunday, s.

$$\rule{1.5cm}{0.4pt} + \rule{1.5cm}{0.4pt} = \rule{1.5cm}{0.4pt}$$

s

45

100

16. Patty has $75. Latisha has L dollars. Patty has $20 more than 3 times the amount of money that Latisha has. Which equation represents the situation? Circle all that apply.

A. $75 = 20 + 3L$

B. $3L + 20 = 75$

C. $3 \times 75 + 20 = L$

D. $L = 3 \times 20 + 75$

E. $20L + 3 = 75$

F. $3L - 20 = 75$

G. $75 - 20 = 3L$

17. Nina is 5 years older than half of Robin's age, r. Nina is 8 years old. Does each equation show how to find Robin's age? Select Yes or No.

A. $2r + 5 = 8$ ○ Yes ○ No

B. $5 + \frac{r}{2} = 8$ ○ Yes ○ No

C. $5 - \frac{r}{2} = 8$ ○ Yes ○ No

D. $\frac{r}{2} + 5 = 8$ ○ Yes ○ No

Solve Equations

Getting the Idea

To solve an equation, you must isolate the variable by using **inverse operations**. Inverse operations undo each other.

The first step to solving a two-step equation is to add or subtract to remove the **constant** to leave one side of the equation with a **coefficient** and variable. If the coefficient is an integer, the second step will be to divide to isolate the variable.

Example 1

What is the value of n in the equation $6n + 9 = 36$?

Strategy   **Use inverse operations to isolate the variable.**

> **Step 1**   Subtract 9 from both sides of the equation to remove the constant.
>
> $$6n + 9 - 9 = 36 - 9$$
> $$6n = 27$$

> **Step 2**   Divide both sides of the equation by the coefficient to isolate the variable and write the solution in simplest form.
>
> $$\frac{6n}{6} = \frac{27}{6}$$
> $$n = 4\frac{3}{6} = 4\frac{1}{2}$$

Solution $n = 4\frac{1}{2}$

When the coefficient is a fraction, multiply both sides by the reciprocal of the coefficient.

Example 2

What is the value of z in the equation $\frac{2}{3}z - 6 = 15$?

Strategy   **Use inverse operations to isolate the variable.**

> **Step 1**   Add 6 to both sides of the equation to remove the constant.
>
> $$\frac{2}{3}z - 6 + 6 = 15 + 6$$
> $$\frac{2}{3}z = 21$$

> **Step 2**   Multiply both sides of the equation by the reciprocal of the coefficient to isolate the variable.

The reciprocal of $\frac{2}{3}$ is $\frac{3}{2}$.

$$\frac{2}{3}z \times \frac{3}{2} = 21 \times \frac{3}{2}$$

$$z = \frac{63}{2} = 31\frac{1}{2}$$

Solution $z = 31\frac{1}{2}$

When a coefficient comes before a term in parentheses, use the distributive property to rename the equation.

Example 3

What is the value of b in the equation $4(b - 3) = 24$?

Strategy	**Use the distributive property to rename the equation.**

Step 1 Use the distributive property to simplify the left side of the equation.

Multiply 4 by each term inside the parentheses.

$$4(b - 3) = 4 \cdot b + 4 \cdot -3$$
$$= 4b - 12$$

The equation is now $4b - 12 = 24$.

Step 2 Add 12 to both sides of the equation to remove the constant.

$$4b - 12 + 12 = 24 + 12$$
$$4b = 36$$

Step 3 Divide both sides of the equation by the coefficient to isolate the variable.

$$4b \div 4 = 36 \div 4$$
$$b = 9$$

Solution $b = 9$

Example 4

What is the value of g in the equation $\frac{3}{4}\left(g - \frac{1}{2}\right) = 1\frac{7}{8}$?

Strategy **Use the distributive property to rename the equation.**

Step 1 Use the distributive property to simplify the left side of the equation.

Multiply $\frac{3}{4}$ by each term inside the parentheses.

$$\frac{3}{4}\left(g - \frac{1}{2}\right) = \frac{3}{4}g - \frac{3}{8}$$

The equation is now $\frac{3}{4}g - \frac{3}{8} = 1\frac{7}{8}$.

Step 2   Add $\frac{3}{8}$ to both sides of the equation to remove the constant.

$$\frac{3}{4}g - \frac{3}{8} + \frac{3}{8} = 1\frac{7}{8} + \frac{3}{8}$$

$$\frac{3}{4}g = 1\frac{10}{8} = 2\frac{1}{4}$$

Step 3   Multiply both sides of the equation by the reciprocal of the coefficient to isolate the variable.

Rename the mixed number as an improper fraction.

$$\frac{3}{4}g \cdot \frac{4}{3} = \frac{\overset{3}{\cancel{9}}}{\cancel{4}} \times \frac{\overset{1}{\cancel{4}}}{\underset{1}{\cancel{3}}}$$

$$g = 3$$

Solution $g = 3$

Use the rules for computing with rational numbers to solve equations involving negative numbers.

Example 5

What is the value of p in the equation $-4p - 8 = 24$?

Strategy   **Use inverse operations to isolate the variable.**

Step 1   Add 8 to both sides of the equation to remove the constant.

$$-4p - 8 + 8 = 24 + 8$$

$$-4p = 32$$

Step 2   Divide both sides of the equation by the coefficient to isolate the variable.

The signs are different, so the solution will be negative.

$$\frac{-4p}{-4} = \frac{32}{-4}$$

$$p = -8$$

Solution $p = -8$

Use the distributive property for a negative coefficient as you would a positive coefficient.

Example 6

What is the value of q in the equation $-0.8(q - 0.5) = -2.6$?

Strategy   **Use the distributive property to rename the equation.**

Step 1   Use the distributive property to simplify the left side of the equation.

Multiply -0.8 by each term inside the parentheses.

$$-0.8(q - 0.5) = -0.8q + 0.4$$

The equation is now $-0.8q + 0.4 = -2.6$.

Step 2 Subtract 0.4 from both sides of the equation to remove the constant.

$$-0.8q + 0.4 - 0.4 = -2.6 - 0.4$$
$$-0.8q = -3$$

Step 3 Divide both sides of the equation by the coefficient to isolate the variable.

$$\frac{-0.8q}{-0.8} = \frac{-3}{-0.8}$$

The signs are the same, so the solution will be positive.

$$q = 3.75$$

Solution $q = 3.75$

Coached Example

What is the solution for *r* in this equation?

$$-\frac{1}{2}\left(r - \frac{3}{4}\right) = \frac{-4}{5}$$

The first step is to use the _____ to simplify the left side of the equation.

Multiply both terms inside the parentheses by _____.

The left side of the equation is now _____.

The equation can be rewritten as _____.

Now you have a two-step equation to solve.

Subtract _____ from both sides of the equation. _____.

What is the difference of the right side of the equation? _____.

The equation is now _____.

Multiply both sides of the equation by the _____ of the coefficient.

Solve. _____.

Write the solution is simplest form. ***r*** = _____

Lesson Practice • Part 1

Choose the correct answer.

1. Solve for d.

$$2d + 8 = 24$$

A. $d = 4$

B. $d = 8$

C. $d = 12$

D. $d = 16$

2. What is the value of g?

$$\frac{1}{3}g - 6 = 4$$

A. $g = 2$

B. $g = 6$

C. $g = 10$

D. $g = 30$

3. Solve for k.

$$3(k - 2) = 15$$

A. $k = 3$

B. $k = 4\frac{1}{3}$

C. $k = 5\frac{2}{3}$

D. $k = 7$

4. Solve for b.

$$-3b + 5 = 13$$

A. $b = -6$

B. $b = -2\frac{2}{3}$

C. $b = 2\frac{2}{3}$

D. $b = 6$

5. What is the value of n?

$$\frac{3}{8}n - \frac{1}{3} = \frac{5}{6}$$

A. $n = 3\frac{1}{9}$

B. $n = 2\frac{1}{12}$

C. $n = 1\frac{7}{9}$

D. $n = 1\frac{1}{3}$

6. Solve for q.

$$-\frac{2}{3}\left(q + \frac{1}{6}\right) = -\frac{11}{12}$$

A. $q = 1\frac{5}{24}$

B. $q = 1\frac{13}{24}$

C. $q = 1\frac{5}{8}$

D. $q = 3$

7. What is the value of m?

$$2.5m - 5 = 9$$

A. $m = 1.6$

B. $m = 3.6$

C. $m = 5.6$

D. $m = 9.2$

8. Solve for j.

$$-\frac{3}{4}j + \frac{1}{5} = \frac{3}{5}$$

A. $j = -1\frac{1}{15}$

B. $j = -\frac{8}{15}$

C. $j = \frac{8}{15}$

D. $j = 1\frac{1}{15}$

9. What is the value of v?

$$0.6(v - 2) = 1.5$$

A. $v = 0.5$

B. $v = 2.5$

C. $v = 4.5$

D. $v = 5.8\overline{3}$

10. Solve for x.

$$-5(x + 2) = -20$$

A. $x = -6$

B. $x = -2$

C. $x = 2$

D. $x = 6$

---

11. Ms. Ruiz is 9 years older than 6 times as many years old as Carlos. Ms. Ruiz is 57 years old.

A. Write an equation that can be used to find Carlos's age in years. Use c as your variable.

_____

B. What is Carlos's age in years? Show your work.

Lesson Practice • Part 2

Choose the correct answer.

1. Solve for a.

$$-4a - 6 = -12$$

A. $a = -4\frac{1}{2}$

B. $a = -1\frac{1}{2}$

C. $a = 1\frac{1}{2}$

D. $a = 4\frac{1}{2}$

2. What is the value of z?

$$\frac{3}{5}z - \frac{1}{4} = \frac{17}{20}$$

A. $z = \frac{33}{50}$

B. $z = 1$

C. $z = 1\frac{5}{12}$

D. $z = 1\frac{5}{6}$

3. Solve for e.

$$2\frac{1}{2}\left(e - 1\frac{3}{4}\right) = 5\frac{1}{2}$$

A. $e = \frac{9}{20}$

B. $e = 1\frac{1}{2}$

C. $e = 2\frac{9}{10}$

D. $e = 3\frac{19}{20}$

4. Solve for w.

$$3w + 7 = 20$$

A. $w = 4\frac{1}{3}$

B. $w = 6\frac{2}{3}$

C. $w = 7\frac{1}{3}$

D. $w = 9$

5. What is the value of p?

$$-0.2p + 0.4 = -1.2$$

A. $p = 8$

B. $p = 4$

C. $p = -4$

D. $p = -8$

6. Solve for y.

$$\frac{y}{4} - \frac{3}{5} = \frac{13}{20}$$

A. $y = \frac{1}{5}$

B. $y = 1\frac{1}{4}$

C. $y = 2\frac{14}{25}$

D. $y = 5$

7. What is the value of u?

    $$-6(u - 2.4) = 9$$

    A. $u = 3.9$
    B. $u = 0.9$
    C. $u = -1.1$
    D. $u = -1.9$

8. Solve for x.

    $$-\frac{2}{3}x - \frac{3}{5} = \frac{1}{2}$$

    A. $x = -1\frac{13}{20}$
    B. $x = -\frac{11}{15}$
    C. $x = \frac{11}{15}$
    D. $x = 1\frac{13}{20}$

9. What is the value of b?

    $$2b + 0.8 = 5.4$$

    A. $b = 0.4$
    B. $b = 2.3$
    C. $b = 2.7$
    D. $b = 3.1$

10. Solve for m.

    $$-6m + 3 = 2$$

    A. $m = -\frac{5}{6}$
    B. $m = -\frac{1}{2}$
    C. $m = \frac{1}{6}$
    D. $m = \frac{1}{3}$

11. Curtis bought 4 DVDs that each cost the same amount. He had a $10-off coupon and spent $46 in all.

    A. Write an equation that can be used to find the cost of each DVD before the coupon was applied. Use d as your variable.

    _____

    B. What was the cost of each DVD before the coupon was applied? Show your work.

12. Draw a line from each equation to its solution.

    A. $2x - 3 = 9$　●　　　　●　$x = 2$

    B. $3x + 2 = 11$　●　　　　●　$x = 3$

    C. $4x - 2 = 6$　●　　　　●　$x = 4$

    D. $\frac{1}{2}x + 3 = 5$　●　　　　●　$x = 6$

13. Select True or False for each equation.

A. $3(x + 2) = 15$, $x = 3$ ○ True   ○ False

B. $2(x - 4) = 6$, $x = -1$ ○ True   ○ False

C. $\frac{1}{2}x + 3 = 9$, $x = 3$ ○ True   ○ False

D. $4x - 2 = 8$, $x = 2\frac{1}{2}$ ○ True   ○ False

E. $\frac{2}{5}x - \frac{1}{2} = \frac{3}{10}$, $x = 2$ ○ True   ○ False

F. $\frac{1}{3}(x + 9) = 6$, $x = 9$ ○ True   ○ False

14. Use numbers from the box to complete each equation. The same number may be used more than once.

$\frac{2}{3}x + 6 = 9$

$\frac{2}{3}x + 6 - \underline{\hspace{1cm}} = 9 - \underline{\hspace{1cm}}$

$\frac{2}{3}x = \underline{\hspace{1cm}}$

$\frac{2}{3}x \cdot \underline{\hspace{1cm}} = \underline{\hspace{1cm}} \cdot \underline{\hspace{1cm}}$

$x = \underline{\hspace{1cm}}$

$$\frac{3}{2}$$

$$3$$

$$4\frac{1}{2}$$

$$6$$

15. Which equations have solutions of $x = 4$? Select all that apply.

A. $5x - 4 = 14$

B. $\frac{1}{2}x + 2 = 4$

C. $2.4x - 3.2 = 6.4$

D. $-3x - 2 = -14$

E. $2(x + 4) = 20$

16. Circle the number that makes each equation true.

$-\dfrac{3}{5}x + \dfrac{1}{2} = -\dfrac{7}{10}$	$x = -2$
	$x = -\dfrac{1}{3}$
	$x = \dfrac{1}{3}$
	$x = 2$

$0.4(x - 0.8) = -1.6$	$x = -4.8$
	$x = -3.2$
	$x = 3.2$
	$x = 4.8$

17. Solve each equation. Write each equation in the correct box.

$2x - 6 = 14$

$3x + 5 = 11$

$\dfrac{1}{2}x - 4 = 1$

$2(x - 2) = 6$

$0.8x + 2.4 = 6.4$

$x = 2$	$x = 5$	$x = 10$

Use Algebra to Solve Word Problems

Getting the Idea

One way to solve a word problem is arithmetically. Problem solving strategies can help you recognize the sequence of steps needed to solve a problem arithmetically.

Example 1

The art teacher has 6 packages of brushes and 8 single brushes. Each package has the same number of brushes. In all, he has 80 brushes for his students to use. How many brushes are in a package?

Strategy   **Work backward to undo the sequence of operations in the problem.**

Step 1   Understand the problem.

There are 6 packages of brushes, each with the same number of brushes.

There are also 8 single brushes.

There are 80 brushes in all.

Step 2   Identify the first operation to undo.

The 8 single brushes are in addition to the packages of brushes.

Subtract 8 from the total of 80 to find how many brushes are in the packages in all.

$80 - 8 = 72$

There are 72 brushes in the packages in all.

Step 3   Identify the next operation to undo.

There are 72 brushes in the 6 packages. Since each package has the same number of brushes, divide to find the number in each package.

$72 \div 6 = 12$

Solution   **There are 12 brushes in each package.**

Another way to solve a word problem is algebraically. First, define the variable in the problem situation. Next, write an equation to represent the situation. Then solve the equation using inverse operations and the properties of equality.

The properties of equality tell you that if you perform an operation to one side of an equation, you must perform the same operation to the other side of the equation to keep both sides equal.

When you solve an equation, you must isolate the variable on one side of the equation.

Example 2

Solve the problem in Example 1 algebraically.

Strategy   **Write and solve an equation.**

Step 1   Write the problem as an equation.

Let x represent the number of brushes in each package.

There are 6 packages of brushes and 8 single brushes: $6x + 8$.

There are 80 brushes in all: 80.

$6x + 8 = 80$

Step 2   Solve the equation.

$$6x + 8 = 80$$
$$6x + 8 - 8 = 80 - 8 \qquad \text{Subtract 8 from both sides.}$$
$$6x = 72 \qquad \text{Simplify.}$$
$$\frac{6x}{6} = \frac{72}{6} \qquad \text{Divide both sides by 6.}$$
$$x = 12$$

The solution is the same whether you solve the equation arithmetically or algebraically.

Example 3

Troy is 3 times as old as Mia's and Dan's ages combined. If Troy is 36 and Mia is 5, how old is Dan?

Strategy   **Translate the problem into an algebraic equation. Then solve.**

Step 1   Translate the problem into an algebraic equation.

Let d represent Dan's age.

The total of Mia's and Dan's ages combined is $5 + d$.

Troy is 3 times the total. Troy is 36 years old.

$3(5 + d) = 36$

Step 2   Solve for d.

$$\frac{3(5 + d)}{3} = \frac{36}{3} \qquad \text{Divide both sides of the equation by 3.}$$
$$5 + d = 12 \qquad \text{Simplify.}$$
$$5 - 5 + d = 12 - 5 \qquad \text{Subtract 5 from both sides to isolate } d.$$
$$d = 7$$

Solution   **Dan is 7 years old.**

You can rename an expression to better relate how to solve a word problem. You may rename a percent to a fraction or a decimal or visa versa. Use whichever method is best for you.

Example 4

Ali was earning $15 per hour before receiving a 10% raise. What is Ali's new hourly rate?

Strategy   **Write and solve an equation.**

Step 1   Write an expression to represent Ali's hourly rate after her raise.

$15 was 100% of her hourly rate.

Her rate increased by 10%, so add 100% + 10% = 110%.

Step 2   Find Ali's new hourly rate.

Rename 110% to 1.1 and multiply 1.1 times the original rate.

Let n represent Ali's new hourly rate.

$n = 15 \times 1.1$

$n = 16.5$

Solution   **Ali's new hourly rate is $16.50.**

Example 5

Aaron bought a stock at $42.80 per share. The value of the stock dropped 20% in its first week. What is the value of the stock after one week?

Strategy   **Write and solve an equation.**

Step 1   Write an expression to represent the value of Aaron's stock.

$42.80 was 100% of the value of the stock when Aaron bought it.

The value decreased by 20%, so subtract 100% − 20% = 80%.

Step 2   Find the value of the stock.

Rename 80% to 0.8 and multiply 0.8 times the original value.

Let s represent the value of the stock after one week.

$s = 42.8 \cdot 0.8$

$s = \$34.24$

Solution   **The value of the stock after one week is $34.24.**

Example 6

Ron wants to place a painting that is $32\frac{1}{2}$ inches wide in the horizontal center of a wall that is $89\frac{1}{2}$ inches wide. How far from each corner of the wall should he place the painting for it to be centered?

Strategy   **Solve the problem algebraically.**

Step 1   Translate the problem into an algebraic equation.

Let n represent the distance from each corner.

If the painting is centered, the distance from each corner plus the width of the painting is equal to the width of the wall.

$$32\frac{1}{2} + 2n = 89\frac{1}{2}$$

Step 2   Solve the equation for n.

$$32\frac{1}{2} - 32\frac{1}{2} + 2n = 89\frac{1}{2} - 32\frac{1}{2}$$ Subtract $32\frac{1}{2}$ from both sides.

$$2n = 57$$ Simplify.

$$\frac{2n}{2} = \frac{57}{2}$$ Divide both sides by 2.

$$n = 28\frac{1}{2}$$

Solution   **Ron should place the painting $28\frac{1}{2}$ inches from each corner.**

Coached Example

The cost of the sneakers that Janeel wants to buy is $84.20. This week those sneakers are 30% off. What is the sale price of the sneakers, s?

What percent of the cost does $84.20 represent? _____

Will Janeel pay for less than or more than 100% of the total cost? _____

What percent of the cost will Janeel pay? _____

Write an equation to represent how to find the sale price of the sneakers.

_____

Solve your equation.

_____

Janeel will spend _____ for the sneakers.

Lesson Practice • Part 1

Choose the correct answer.

1. Claire wants to place a mirror that is $18\frac{1}{2}$ inches wide in the center of a wall that is 31 inches wide. How far from each corner should she place the mirror for it to be centered?

   A. $6\frac{1}{4}$ in.

   B. $9\frac{1}{4}$ in.

   C. $10\frac{1}{3}$ in.

   D. $12\frac{1}{2}$ in.

2. Justin is 10 years less than half his father's age. If Justin is 12 years old, how old is his father?

   A. 22

   B. 24

   C. 32

   D. 44

3. The school media specialist has catalogued $\frac{2}{3}$ of the new books in a shipment. If she has catalogued 52 books, what is the total number of books in the shipment?

   A. 35

   B. 78

   C. 104

   D. 156

4. A video game is on sale for 30% off the regular price of $50. What is the sale price of the video game?

   A. $20

   B. $30

   C. $33

   D. $35

5. One school bus can seat 42 passengers. How many school buses will be needed to transport a total of 180 passengers on a trip to the state legislature?

   A. 138

   B. 10

   C. 5

   D. 4

6. Nate bought shares of a stock at $36.85. The value of the shares increased by $2 more than 40% when Nate sold them. At what price did Nate sell the stock?

   A. $37.65

   B. $40.32

   C. $53.59

   D. $54.39

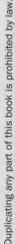

7. In his bank account, Hal has $70 more than one-fifth the amount of money that Bob has in his account. Hal has $170 in his bank account. How much money does Bob have in his account?

   A. $240

   B. $350

   C. $420

   D. $500

8. Rudy wants to teach a hip-hop dance workshop. The cost of renting a dance studio is $109.50 plus $15 per person attending the workshop. Rudy can spend $318 at most to rent the space. What is the greatest number of people Rudy can allow to attend the workshop?

   A. 13 people

   B. 14 people

   C. 28 people

   D. 29 people

9. Sylvie bought 13 bagels and a container of cream cheese. Each bagel cost the same price. The cream cheese cost $2.95. Sylvie spent a total of $7.50.

   A. Write an algebraic equation to represent the situation. Identify the variable.

   _____

   _____

   B. What was the cost of each bagel? Explain your thinking.

   _____

   _____

   _____

Lesson Practice • Part 2

Choose the correct answer.

1. Preston is 8 years less than twice as many years old as Tyler. If Tyler is 12 years old, how old is Preston?

   A. 14 years old

   B. 16 years old

   C. 20 years old

   D. 32 years old

2. Mr. Campbell earns $24 per hour for the first 40 hours that he works in a week. He earns 1.5 times that hourly rate for any hours greater than 40 in a week. Last week Mr. Campbell earned $1,248. How many hours did he work?

   A. $34\frac{2}{3}$ hours

   B. 48 hours

   C. 52 hours

   D. $74\frac{2}{3}$ hours

3. Kinley bought 3 notebooks that cost the same and a poster that cost $6. She spent $20.40 in all. What was the cost of each notebook?

   A. $8.80

   B. $6.80

   C. $4.80

   D. $0.80

4. The perimeter of a rectangle is 84 inches. The width of the rectangle is 12 inches. What is the length of the rectangle?

   A. 30 inches

   B. 36 inches

   C. 42 inches

   D. 72 inches

5. Sharice bought 8 songs that cost $0.79 each. She also bought an album. The total price for these items before tax was $15.21. What was the price of the album?

   A. $6.32

   B. $8.89

   C. $14.42

   D. $21.53

6. Eight friends went on a hiking trip. They took 40 bottles of water and iced tea. Each friend carried the same number of bottles. They each carried 2 bottles of iced tea. How many water bottles did each friend carry?

   A. 3

   B. 5

   C. 7

   D. 24

7. A golfer played four rounds and finished with a composite score of -12. The golfer shot three rounds of -5 each. What was the score in the other round?

    A. -7

    B. -3

    C. -2

    D. 3

8. Slaggers Restaurant decided to add an 18% tip to all of its bills. If the food bill was $64.50, what was the total including the tip?

    A. $46.50

    B. $52.89

    C. $76.11

    D. $82.50

9. Brielle wants to center a print that is $25\frac{3}{4}$ inches wide in the horizontal center of a wall that is 150 inches wide.

    A. How far from each corner of the wall should she place the print for it to be centered?

    B. Did you solve the problem arithmetically or algebraically? Explain your reasoning.

10. In miniature golf, Janelle scored 5 strokes less than 150% of what Adam scored. Which situation could be true? Circle all that apply.

    A. Adam scored 76 and Janelle scored 54.

    B. Adam scored 71 and Janelle scored 54.

    C. Adam scored 60 and Janelle scored 85.

    D. Adam scored 52 and Janelle scored 73.

    E. Adam scored 60 and Janelle scored 87.

    F. Adam scored 50 and Janelle scored 70.

    G. Adam scored 72 and Janelle scored 103.

11. Remy made cupcakes in batches of 12. There are 28 students in the class. Select True or False for each statement.

  A. Remy made 2 batches and had 4 cupcakes left over. ○ True ○ False

  B. Remy made 3 batches and had 4 cupcakes left over. ○ True ○ False

  C. Remy made 3 batches and had 8 cupcakes left over. ○ True ○ False

  D. Remy made 4 batches and had 20 cupcakes left over. ○ True ○ False

12. Grant is 5% taller than he was last year. How tall is Grant if his height last year was as given below? Circle each correct height.

56 inches:	56.8 in. 58.8 in. 61.6 in.	60 inches:	63 in. 66 in. 69 in.	68 inches:	68.8 in. 71.4 in. 74.8 in.

13. Marnel ran 3 miles less than twice as far as James. Marnel ran 7 miles. How far did James run, j? Use values from the box to complete the equations and solve the problem.

$$\underline{\hspace{1cm}}\, j - \underline{\hspace{1cm}} = 7$$

$$2 \times \underline{\hspace{1cm}} = 7 + \underline{\hspace{1cm}}$$

$$\underline{\hspace{1cm}} = 10 \div \underline{\hspace{1cm}}$$

$$j = \underline{\hspace{1cm}}$$

j
2
3
5

14. To get to the amusement park, 14 people need to have a seat in a car. Each car holds 4 people. Is each given number of cars enough to hold all the people? Select Yes or No.

A. 3   ○ Yes   ○ No

B. 4   ○ Yes   ○ No

C. 2   ○ Yes   ○ No

D. 6   ○ Yes   ○ No

15. Elise paid $\frac{2}{3}$ as much for a sweater as she did for a pair of shoes. How much did Elise pay for the sweater if the shoes cost each given amount? Circle each correct amount.

Shoes cost $60: Sweater cost

$20

$40

$90

Shoes cost $75: Sweater cost

$25

$50

$112.50

Shoes cost $42: Sweater cost

$14

$28

$63

Inequalities

Getting the Idea

An **inequality** is a mathematical statement that two quantities are not equal. Inequalities are represented by using the symbols > **(is greater than)**, < **(is less than)**, ≥ **(is greater than or equal to)**, and ≤ **(is less than or equal to)**.

To solve an inequality, follow the same rules as when solving an equation. The solution of an inequality is a set of numbers called the **solution set**.

You can graph the solution set of an inequality on a number line. Draw a circle and an arrow to show all of the numbers that are part of the solution. If the circled number is part of the solution set, fill in the circle. If the circled number is not part of the solution set, leave the circle open. Here are some examples.

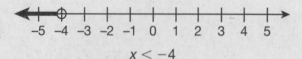

$x < -4$

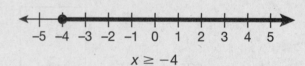

$x > -4$

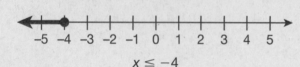

$x \leq -4$

$x \geq -4$

Example 1

Graph the solution set for this inequality.

$2x - 7 < 11$

Strategy   **Use inverse operations to isolate the variable.**

Step 1   Add 7 to both sides of the inequality.

$2x - 7 + 7 < 11 + 7$

$2x < 18$

Step 2   Divide both sides of the inequality by 2.

$\frac{2x}{2} < \frac{18}{2}$

$x < 9$

Step 3	Graph the solution set.

9 is not part of the solution set, so use an open dot.

Since x is less than 9, the arrow points left.

Solution

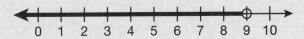

Example 2

Graph the solution set for this inequality.

$$\frac{3}{4}x + \frac{1}{4} \geq 2\frac{1}{2}$$

Strategy Use inverse operations to isolate the variable.

Step 1	Subtract $\frac{1}{4}$ from both sides of the inequality.

$$\frac{3}{4}x + \frac{1}{4} - \frac{1}{4} \geq 2\frac{1}{2} - \frac{1}{4}$$

$$\frac{3}{4}x \geq 2\frac{1}{4}$$

Step 2	Multiply both sides by the reciprocal of $\frac{3}{4}$.

$$\frac{3}{4}x \cdot \frac{4}{3} \geq \frac{\overset{3}{\cancel{9}}}{\cancel{4}} \times \frac{\overset{1}{\cancel{4}}}{\cancel{3}}$$

$$x \geq 3$$

Step 3	Graph the solution set.

3 is part of the solution set, so use a closed dot.

Since x is greater than or equal to 3, the arrow points right.

Solution

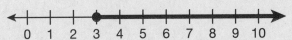

When you multiply or divide by a negative number in an inequality, it reverses the sign. For example, to find the solution set for x in $-2x > 4$, divide both sides by -2. This reverses the sign from $>$ to $<$. So the solution set would be $x < -2$.

Example 3

Find the solution set for $-4p + 6 > -10$.

Strategy Use inverse operations to isolate the variable.

Step 1	Subtract 6 from both sides of the inequality.

$$-4p + 6 - 6 > -10 - 6$$

$$-4p > -16$$

Step 2   Divide both sides of the inequality by -4.

$$\frac{-4p}{-4} > \frac{-16}{-4}$$

The sign reverses.

$$p < 4$$

Solution   **The solution set is $p = 4$.**

You can solve problems by writing and solving an inequality.

Example 4

On Saturday, Maya read at least 5 fewer than 3 times as many pages in her book as she did on Friday. On Saturday, she read 58 pages. How many pages did Maya read on Friday?

Strategy   **Translate the problem into an algebraic inequality. Then solve.**

Step 1   Translate the problem into an algebraic inequality.

Let n represent the number of pages Maya read on Friday.

"5 fewer than 3 times as many pages" translates to $3n - 5$.

Use the inequality sign $\geq$ for "at least."

$$3n - 5 \geq 58$$

Step 2   Solve the inequality using inverse operations.

$$3n - 5 + 5 \geq 58 + 5 \qquad \text{Add 5 to both sides.}$$

$$3n \geq 63$$

$$\frac{3n}{3} \geq \frac{63}{3} \qquad \text{Divide both sides by 3.}$$

$$n \geq 21$$

Step 3   Interpret the solution.

The solution set $n \geq 21$ means Maya read 21 pages or more on Friday.

Solution   **Maya read at least 21 pages on Friday.**

Example 5

A taxi driver charges a flat fee of $4 plus $6 per mile. The tip is included in the mileage rate. Orlando only has $22 to pay for a taxi ride. How many miles at most can Orlando ride in the taxi? Graph the solution set.

Strategy   **Translate the problem into an algebraic inequality. Then solve.**

Step 1   Translate the problem into an algebraic inequality.

Let m represent the number of miles.

"Flat fee of $4 plus $6 per mile" translates to $4 + 6m$.

Use the inequality sign $\leq$ for "at most."

$4 + 6m \leq 22$

Step 2   Solve the inequality using inverse operations.

$4 - 4 + 6m \leq 22 - 4$ Subtract 4 from both sides.

$6m \leq 18$

$\dfrac{6m}{6} \leq \dfrac{18}{6}$ Divide both sides by 6.

$m \leq 3$

Step 3   Interpret the solution.

The solution set $m \leq 3$ means Orlando can ride 3 miles or less.

Step 4   Graph the solution set.

The graph must start at 0 since he cannot ride less than 0 miles.

Orlando can ride between 0 and 3 miles. So, draw closed circles on 0 and 3.

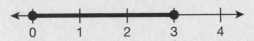

Solution   **Orlando can ride between 0 and 3 miles in the taxi.**

Coached Example

A middle school is sponsoring a 5K Fun Run to raise money for the library. Each runner will receive a T-shirt. The T-shirts for the race cost $345. Timers and other race equipment cost $85. Local businesses donated $50. If each runner pays $15, how many people must enter the race for it to make a profit?

The expenses for the race are the _____, the timers, and other race equipment.

The total expenses are _____ + _____ = _____.

Let *n* represent the number of people _____.

Write an expression for the total amount raised by entry fees. _____

How much money was donated to help with expenses? _____

Write an expression for the total amount of money raised. _____

To make a profit, the amount raised by the entry fees plus the money donated must be _____ the total expenses for the race.

Write an inequality to show how many people must enter the race to make a profit.

_____

Solve the inequality.

The solution of the inequality is a mixed number. Since you cannot have a fraction of a person, round the number up to the next whole number.

What is the least number of people who can enter for the race to make a profit? _____

At least _____ people must enter the race for it to make a profit.

Lesson Practice • Part 1

Choose the correct answer.

1. A waitress earned $7 per hour at her job plus an additional $50 in tips on Friday. She earned more than $99 total. Which inequality best represents the situation, where h represents the number of hours she worked on Friday?

   A. $7 + 50h > 99$

   B. $7 + 50h \geq 99$

   C. $7h + 50 > 99$

   D. $7h + 50 \geq 99$

2. Which is the solution set of this inequality?

   $$-2n - 7 > -25$$

   A. $n > 16$

   B. $n < 16$

   C. $n > 9$

   D. $n < 9$

3. Which graph represents the solution set of this inequality?

   $$5y + 9 < 24$$

   A.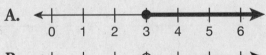

   B.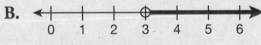

   C.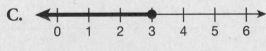

   D.

4. Josef has at least 296 photos. He bought an album that holds 6 photos on each page. Which best describes the number of photo album pages he will use?

   A. at least 50 pages

   B. more than 50 pages

   C. less than 50 pages

   D. at most 50 pages

5. Margo has $80 to spend. She wants to buy as many DVDs as possible after buying a CD that costs $8. The DVDs cost $18 each at most. What is the greatest number of DVDs she can buy?

   A. 3

   B. 4

   C. 5

   D. 6

6. Cory earns $20 per day plus $6 for every sale he makes. On Friday, he wants to earn at least $50. Which best describes the number of sales he needs to make to reach his goal?

   A. at least 5 sales

   B. at most 5 sales

   C. at least 6 sales

   D. at most 6 sales

7. Sharona's age is at most 3 more than twice Kayla's age. If Sharona is 35 years old, which inequality best represents the situation, where a represents Kayla's age?

A. $2a + 3 < 35$

B. $2a + 3 \leq 35$

C. $2a + 3 > 35$

D. $2a + 3 \geq 35$

8. Which graph represents the solution set to this inequality?

$3x + 9 \geq 21$

A.

B.

C.

D.

9. The soccer team is selling key chains to raise money for the team. They ordered 100 key chains that cost $0.25 each. There is a flat shipping rate of $8. The team sells the key chains for $2 each.

A. Write an algebraic inequality to find the fewest number of key chains, k, the team must sell to make a profit.

_____

B. What is the fewest number of key chains the team must sell to make a profit?

Show your work and explain your thinking.

_____

_____

_____

_____

_____

Lesson Practice • Part 2

Choose the correct answer.

1. Which is the solution set of this inequality?

$$-\frac{1}{4}r - \frac{3}{5} < \frac{5}{8}$$

A. $r > -4\frac{9}{10}$

B. $r < -4\frac{9}{10}$

C. $r > 4\frac{9}{10}$

D. $r < 4\frac{9}{10}$

Use this information for questions 2 and 3.

Josh wants to spend less than $80 to buy 4 shirts and a pair of pants. The pants cost $24. The shirts he wants all cost the same.

2. Which inequality can be used to find how much Josh will spend on each shirt?

A. $4s + 24 > 80$

B. $4s + 24 < 80$

C. $4s + 24 \geq 80$

D. $4s + 24 \leq 80$

3. What is the greatest amount that Josh is willing to pay for each shirt?

A. $13.99

B. $14.00

C. $25.99

D. $26.00

4. Which shows the solution set to the inequality below?

$$2x + 3 \leq -5$$

A.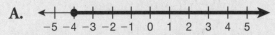

B.

C.

D.

Use this information for questions 5 and 6.

Rylee read 36 pages of a book before putting it down for a month. She wants to resume reading the book that is more than 480 pages long. She plans on finishing the book in 12 days, reading the same amount each day.

5. Which inequality can be used to determine, p, the number of pages that Rylee must read each day to attain her goal?

A. $12p - 36 < 480$

B. $12p + 36 < 480$

C. $12p - 36 > 480$

D. $12p + 36 > 480$

6. Which best describes the number of pages that Rylee has to read to achieve her goal?

A. less than 37 pages per day

B. more than 37 pages per day

C. less than 43 pages per day

D. more than 43 pages per day

Use this information for questions 7 and 8.

Aspen scored no fewer than 18 points in her last basketball game. She scored 6 points on free throws that are worth 1 point each. The rest of the points she scored on 3-point field goals.

7. Which inequality can be used to determine, p, the number of 3-point field goals that Aspen made?

    A. $3p + 6 > 18$

    B. $3p + 6 < 18$

    C. $3p + 6 \geq 18$

    D. $3p + 6 \leq 18$

8. Which graph shows the number of 3-point field goals Aspen could have made in the game?

A.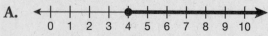

B.

C.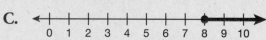

D.

9. For a party, Mrs. Williams spent $140 on food and bought 8 containers of fruit drink that each cost d dollars. She spent less than $172 in all.

    A. Write an inequality that can be used to find the cost of each bottle of fruit drink.

    B. What is the greatest amount that Mrs. Williams could have spent on each bottle of fruit drink?

    C. Graph the inequality from Part A.

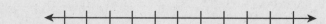

10. Which symbol does each of the given words indicate to use in an inequality? Circle each correct symbol.

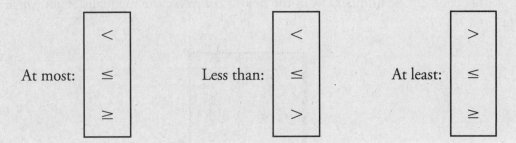

At most:

```
<
≤
≥
```

Less than:

```
<
≤
>
```

At least:

```
>
≤
≥
```

11. Landon's baseball practice lasts more than twice as long as math class. Select True or False for each statement.

A. If math class lasts 52 minutes, then baseball practice could last 95 minutes.　　　○ True　○ False

B. If math class lasts 45 minutes, then baseball practice could last 90 minutes.　　　○ True　○ False

C. If math class lasts 65 minutes, then baseball practice could last 45 minutes.　　　○ True　○ False

D. If math class lasts 57 minutes, then baseball practice could last 120 minutes.　　　○ True　○ False

12. Corey graphed a solution set to a problem. Which value is part of the solution set? Circle all that apply.

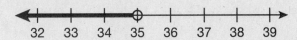

A. 17

B. 37

C. 34.5

D. 0

E. 35

F. 35.5

G. 40

13. Caitlin has $80 and earns $7.25 an hour babysitting. To take a creative writing course during the summer, she needs to have at least $250. How many hours must she babysit to cover the cost of the writing course? Use numbers from the box to complete the inequalities and solve the problem.

_____ + _____ $h \geq 250$

_____ $h \geq$ _____

$h \geq$ _____

Caitlin has to babysit _____ hours.

7.25	46
23.4	80
24	170
45.5	330

14. Payson filled a 10-gallon jug by using a smaller container. She needed to fill the container at most 18 times. Could each measure be the size of the container? Select Yes or No.

A. 1 gal ○ Yes ○ No

B. 2 gal ○ Yes ○ No

C. $\frac{1}{2}$ gal ○ Yes ○ No

D. $\frac{3}{4}$ gal ○ Yes ○ No

15. Sean has at most $50 to spend while shopping. He wants to buy some books that cost $4 each and a DVD that cost $17. What is the greatest number of books he can buy? Use numbers from the box to complete the inequalities and solve the problem.

_____ $x +$ _____ ≤ 50

_____ $x \leq$ _____

$x \leq$ _____

Sean can buy _____ books.

4	16.25
8	17
8.25	33
16	67

Domain 3: Cumulative Assessment for Lessons 13–19

1. Sarvenanda saved $\frac{3}{5}$ of the money he earned doing yard work. He saved $120 in all. Which equation can be used to find how much money, m, he earned doing yard work?

   A. $m - \frac{3}{5} = 120$

   B. $\frac{3}{5} + m = 120$

   C. $m \div \frac{3}{5} = 120$

   D. $\frac{3}{5}m = 120$

2. Which is equivalent to the expression below?

   $$4x + 2x - 2y - y$$

   A. $-6(x + y)$ C. $6(x - y)$

   B. $-3(2x + y)$ D. $3(2x - y)$

3. What is the value of the expression below when $a = 3$ and $b = 7$?

   $$a^2 b - 2b$$

   A. 28   C. 49

   B. 33   D. 54

4. Dora found 6 less than 3 times the number of shells that Tess found at the beach. Let s represent the number of shells that Tess found. Which expression represents the number of shells that Dora found?

   A. $3s - 6$ C. $6 - 3s$

   B. $3s + 6$ D. $3 + 6s$

5. Cicely has $30 to spend on art supplies. She wants to buy as many pastels as possible after buying a sketchbook that costs $6. The pastels cost at most $4 each. What is the greatest number of pastels she can buy?

   A. 4

   B. 5

   C. 6

   D. 7

6. Dennis sold his skateboard for 15% more than he paid for it. If Dennis paid d dollars for the skateboard, which expression represents how much he sold it for?

   A. $0.15d$

   B. $1.15d$

   C. $1.5d$

   D. $1.55d$

7. The cafeteria has 4 cases of tuna and 9 single cans of tuna. In all, there are 65 cans of tuna. How many cans of tuna are in a case?

   A. 5

   B. 13

   C. 14

   D. 16

8. Solve for x.

$$\frac{3}{5}\left(x - \frac{1}{4}\right) = 1\frac{1}{2}$$

A. $x = 2\frac{1}{12}$

B. $x = 2\frac{1}{4}$

C. $x = 2\frac{3}{4}$

D. $x = 2\frac{11}{12}$

9. Monica earns $140 per week plus $15 for every painting she sells at the gallery. She wants to earn at least $200 this week. How many paintings, p, does she need to sell to reach her goal? Write and solve an inequality to represent the situation.

_____

10. The cost of renting a private room at a restaurant is $400. There is also a charge of $25 for each person who attends. The total cost for Christian's party at the restaurant was $775.

A. Write an algebraic equation to represent the situation.

_____

_____

B. How many people attended Christian's party? Explain your thinking.

_____

_____

_____

Domain 4

Geometry

Domain 4: Diagnostic Assessment for Lessons 20–27

Domain 4: Cumulative Assessment for Lessons 20–27

Domain 4: Diagnostic Assessment for Lessons 20–27

1. A warehouse 25 feet tall casts a shadow that is 15 feet long. At the same time of day, how long is the shadow cast by an apartment building that is 90 feet tall?

   A. 54 ft
   B. 57 ft
   C. 60 ft
   D. 66 ft

2. A cube has edges of 7 inches. What is the surface area of the cube?

   A. 49 in.^{2}
   B. 168 in.^{2}
   C. 294 in.^{2}
   D. 343 in.^{2}

3. Cynthia wants to construct a triangle with angles measuring 34°, 21°, and 125°. Which best describes a triangle with these angle measures?

   A. ambiguously defined
   B. nonexistent
   C. a unique, acute triangle
   D. a unique, obtuse triangle

4. The prism below is sliced by a plane parallel to its base.

   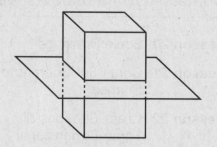

   What is the shape of the cross section?

   A. cube
   B. rectangle
   C. trapezoid
   D. triangle

5. A circular pond has a diameter of 4.5 feet. Which is closest to the circumference of the pond?

   A. 7.07 ft
   B. 14.13 ft
   C. 28.26 ft
   D. 63.59 ft

6. A computer monitor makes a 65° angle with the desk it rests on. What is the measure of its complementary angle?

   A. 20°
   B. 25°
   C. 115°
   D. 125°

7. The blacktop at the park is 30 feet wide. The blacktop is 6 feet longer than it is wide. What is the area of the blacktop?

   A. 1,080 ft²

   B. 3,240 ft²

   C. 6,480 ft²

   D. 9,720 ft²

8. What is the volume of this rectangular prism?

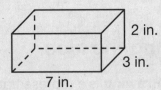

   A. 21 in.³

   B. 41 in.³

   C. 42 in.³

   D. 82 in.³

9. An artist is making a circular stained glass window. The window has a radius of 20 inches. What is the area of the window? Use 3.14 for π.

_____

10. Kerry drew the rectangular prism below.

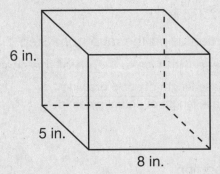

   A. What is the surface area of the rectangular prism? Show your work.

_____

_____

   B. What is the volume of the rectangular prism? Show your work.

_____

_____

Scale Drawings

Getting the Idea

A **scale drawing** is a representation of an actual object. The **scale** tells how to reduce or enlarge the dimensions of a scale drawing. Scale drawings are similar to and, therefore, proportional to the actual object.

Example 1

Ray went to visit the Great Pyramids. He learned that the base length of each triangular face is about 750 ft. He wants to make a scale drawing of the pyramids using the scale 1 in. = 150 ft. What will be the base length of his scale drawing?

Strategy   Use the scale to write a proportion.

Step 1   Write the scale as a ratio.

The scale is 1 in. = 150 ft.

This means that, for each inch of the scale drawing, the actual length is 150 feet.

The ratio is $\frac{1 \text{ in.}}{150 \text{ ft}}$.

Step 2   Write a proportion using the ratio from Step 1.

Let x represent the base length of the scale drawing.

$$\frac{1 \text{ in.}}{150 \text{ ft}} = \frac{\text{base length of scale drawing}}{\text{base length of actual pyramid}}$$

$$\frac{1}{150} = \frac{x}{750}$$

Step 3   Solve the proportion.

$$\frac{1}{150} = \frac{x}{750}$$
$$150 \times x = 750 \times 1$$
$$150x = 750$$
$$\frac{150x}{150} = \frac{750}{150}$$
$$x = 5$$

Solution   The base length of Ray's scale drawing will be 5 inches.

Example 2

Loretta made a scale drawing of an elephant. What is the actual length of the elephant?

|← —— 1.5 in. —— →|

Scale
$\frac{1}{4}$ in. = 2 ft

Strategy   **Use the scale to write a proportion.**

Step 1   Write the scale as a ratio.

The scale is $\frac{1}{4}$ inch = 2 feet.

So the ratio is $\frac{\frac{1}{4} \text{ in.}}{2 \text{ ft}}$.

Step 2   Write a proportion.

Let x represent the actual length of the elephant.

$$\frac{\frac{1}{4} \text{ in.}}{2 \text{ ft}} = \frac{\text{scale drawing length}}{\text{actual length}}$$

$$\frac{\frac{1}{4}}{2} = \frac{1.5}{x}$$

Step 3   Solve the proportion.

$$\frac{\frac{1}{4}}{2} = \frac{1.5}{x}$$

$$\frac{1}{4} \times x = 2 \times 1.5$$

$$\frac{1}{4}x = 3$$

$$4 \times \frac{1}{4}x = 3 \times 4$$

$$x = 12$$

Solution   **The actual length of the elephant is 12 feet.**

A map is a type of scale drawing. You can use the scale on a map to find real-world distances, or use the scale to make an accurate map.

Example 3

The poster of Happy Campground shows the distance between the lake and the cabins.

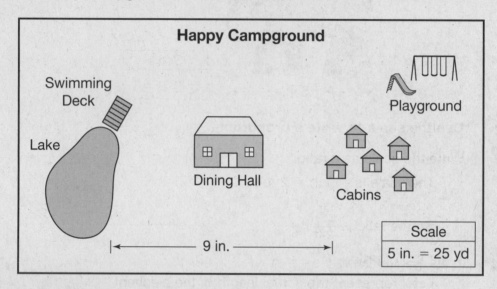

What is the actual distance between the lake and the cabins?

Strategy   **Use the scale to write a proportion.**

Step 1   Write the scale as a ratio.

The scale is 5 inches = 25 yards.

So, the ratio is $\frac{5 \text{ in.}}{25 \text{ yd}}$.

Step 2   Write a proportion.

Let x represent the actual distance.

$$\frac{5 \text{ in.}}{25 \text{ yd}} = \frac{\text{scale drawing distance}}{\text{actual distance}}$$

$$\frac{5}{25} = \frac{9}{x}$$

Step 3   Solve the proportion.

$$\frac{5}{25} = \frac{9}{x}$$

$$5 \times x = 25 \times 9$$

$$5x = 225$$

$$\frac{5x}{5} = \frac{225}{5}$$

$$x = 45$$

Solution   **The actual distance between the cabins and the lake is 45 yards.**

Example 4

Drake made the scale drawing below of the lounge at a recreation center.

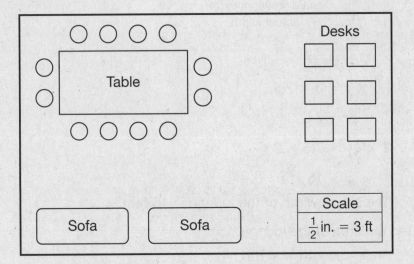

What is the actual area of the lounge?

Strategy   **Find the actual length and width of the lounge.**

Step 1   Measure the length and width of the scale drawing.

The drawing is 4 inches long and 2.5 inches wide.

Step 2   Write a ratio of the scale.

The scale is $\frac{1}{2}$ inch = 3 feet.

So, the ratio is $\frac{\frac{1}{2}\text{ in.}}{3\text{ ft}}$.

Step 3   Write and solve a proportion to find the actual length.

Let x represent the actual length of the lounge.

$$\frac{\frac{1}{2}\text{ in.}}{3\text{ ft}} = \frac{\text{scale drawing length}}{\text{actual length}}$$

$$\frac{\frac{1}{2}}{3} = \frac{4}{x}$$

$$\frac{1}{2} \times x = 3 \times 4$$

$$\frac{1}{2}x = 12$$

$$2 \times \frac{1}{2}x = 12 \times 2$$

$$x = 24$$

The actual length of the lounge is 24 feet.

Step 4 Write and solve a proportion to find the actual width.

Let y represent the actual width of the lounge.

$$\frac{\frac{1}{2} \text{ in.}}{3 \text{ ft}} = \frac{\text{scale drawing width}}{\text{actual width}}$$

$$\frac{\frac{1}{2}}{3} = \frac{2.5}{y}$$

$$\frac{1}{2} \times y = 3 \times 2.5$$

$$\frac{1}{2}y = 7.5$$

$$2 \times \frac{1}{2}y = 7.5 \times 2$$

$$y = 15$$

The actual width of the lounge is 15 feet.

Step 5 Find the area of the lounge.

Area = length × width

$\qquad$ = 24 ft × 15 ft

$\qquad$ = 360 ft^2

Solution **The actual area of the lounge is 360 ft^2.**

Coached Example

Two cities are 420 miles apart. Kerri wants to draw a map that has a scale of $\frac{1}{2}$ inch = 50 miles. How far apart should Kerri draw the two cities on the map?

The scale is _____ inch = _____ miles.

Write a ratio of the scale as a fraction. _____

Let x represent the scale drawing distance.

Write a proportion to find the scale drawing distance. _____

Solve the proportion.

The scale drawing distance is _____ inches.

Kerri should draw the two cities _____ apart on the map.

Lesson Practice • Part 1

Choose the correct answer.

1. Travis made a scale drawing of a horsefly. What is the actual wingspan of the horsefly?

←— 22 mm —→

Scale
4 mm = 1 cm

   A. 4.4 cm
   B. 5.0 cm
   C. 5.5 cm
   D. 6.4 cm

2. The scale of a map is $1\frac{1}{4}$ inches = 100 miles. On that map, two cities are $4\frac{1}{8}$ inches apart. What is the actual distance between the cities?

   A. 275 mi
   B. 330 mi
   C. 375 mi
   D. 412.5 mi

3. The scale on a map is 3 centimeters = 25 kilometers. Two rivers on the map are located 8.1 centimeters apart. What is the actual distance between the two rivers?

   A. 62.5 km
   B. 67.5 km
   C. 68.75 km
   D. 75 km

4. Asia made a scale drawing of her bedroom using a scale of 0.5 centimeter = 1 meter. The actual length of her bedroom is 4.5 meters. What is the length of Asia's bedroom on the scale drawing?

   A. 2.25 cm
   B. 2.5 cm
   C. 4.5 cm
   D. 5.0 cm

5. The length between consecutive bases on a major league baseball diamond is 90 feet. Alvin wants to make a scale drawing of a baseball field. If the bases are $2\frac{1}{2}$ inches apart on his scale drawing, what is Alvin's scale?

   A. 1 in. = 2.5 ft
   B. 1 in. = 3 ft
   C. 1 in. = 30 ft
   D. 1 in. = 36 ft

6. The length of the kitchen floor on the scale drawing is $1\frac{1}{2}$ inches.

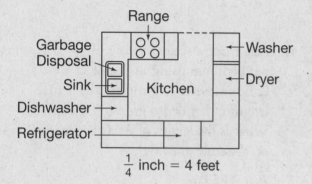

Range
Garbage Disposal
Washer
Sink
Dryer
Kitchen
Dishwasher
Refrigerator

$\frac{1}{4}$ inch = 4 feet

What is the actual length of the kitchen floor?

A. 16 ft   **C.** 24 ft

B. 22 ft   **D.** 28 ft

7. Two fields of a state park are 1,200 meters from each other. On a map, the two fields are 8 centimeters apart. What scale is the map using?

A. 1 cm = 120 m

B. 1 cm = 130 m

C. 1 cm = 150 m

D. 1 cm = 160 m

8. Bella made a drawing of her rectangular bedroom with the scale of 1 inch = 3 feet.

The drawing was 6 inches long by 4 inches wide.

A. What are the dimensions of Bella's room? Show your work.

_____

_____

_____

B. What is the actual area of Bella's room? Show your work.

_____

_____

_____

Lesson Practice • Part 2

Choose the correct answer.

1. A map has a scale of $\frac{1}{2}$ inch $=$ 16 miles. The distance between two parks on the map is $2\frac{3}{4}$ inches. How far apart are the parks?

    A. 40 miles

    B. 44 miles

    C. 76 miles

    D. 88 miles

Use this information for questions 2 and 3.

From end zone to end zone, a football field is 360 feet long and 160 feet wide. Ethan wants to make a scale drawing of a football field. From end-to-end, Ethan's end zones are 6 inches apart.

2. What is Ethan's scale?

    A. 1 in. $= 26\frac{2}{3}$ ft

    B. 1 in. $=$ 60 ft

    C. 1 in. $=$ 80 ft

    D. 1 in. $=$ 180 ft

3. What is the width of Ethan's scale drawing?

    A. $1\frac{3}{5}$ in.   **C.** 9 in.

    B. $2\frac{2}{3}$ in.   **D.** $13\frac{1}{2}$ in.

4. The floor of a building is 120 feet long and 80 feet wide. A scale model of the building has a length of 24 inches. What is the width of the model?

    A. 16 in.

    B. 18 in.

    C. $26\frac{2}{3}$ in.

    D. 36 in.

5. This map shows the state of Utah.

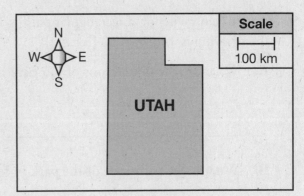

    Based on the map, what is the approximate length of the western border of Utah?

    A. 140 km   **C.** 240 km

    B. 180 km   **D.** 360 km

6. The scale of a map is 1.5 centimeters $=$ 120 kilometers. If two cities are 4.75 centimeters apart on the map, what is their actual distance?

    A. 420 km   **C.** 380 km

    B. 390 km   **D.** 360 km

7. The map shows the distance between the swings and an obstacle course.

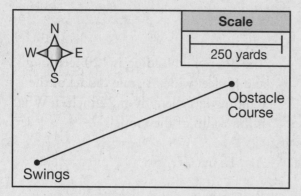

What is the actual distance from the swings to the obstacle course?

A. 500 yd   **C.** 625 yd

B. 562.5 yd   **D.** 750 yd

8. A scale drawing of a rectangular blacktop is 21 inches by 12 inches. If the actual blacktop is 126 feet by 72 feet, which is the scale used for the drawing?

A. 1 in. = 6 ft

B. 1 in. = 6 in.

C. 1 in. = $10\frac{1}{2}$ in.

D. 1 in. = $10\frac{1}{2}$ ft

9. The scale drawing of a rectangular park is 18 inches long and 15 inches wide. The scale on the drawing is 1 inch = 40 feet.

A. What are the dimensions of the park in yards? Show your work.

_____

_____

B. What is the perimeter of the park in feet? Show your work.

_____

_____

C. What is the area of the park in square yards? Show your work.

_____

_____

10. A map of several bicycle trails uses a scale of 2 cm = 5 km. The actual lengths of three trails are given. How long is each trail on the map? Circle each correct number of centimeters.

12.5 km:

2.5
5
31.25

cm

25 km:

5
10
62.5

cm

67.5 km:

13.5
27
168.75

cm

11. A scale drawing uses a scale of $\frac{1}{4}$ inch = 4 feet. Draw a line from each actual size to the corresponding scale size.

A. 6 ft •   • $1\frac{3}{4}$ in.

B. 28 ft •   • $1\frac{1}{2}$ in.

C. 24 ft •   • $\frac{3}{8}$ in.

D. 14 ft •   • $\frac{7}{8}$ in.

12. A golf course uses markers in the tee box of each golf hole to show a scale map of the hole. The markers have a scale of 1 in. = 14 yd. Which is an accurate marker-distance combination? Circle all that apply.

A. 215 in. = 3,010 yd

B. 15 in. = 210 yd

C. $39\frac{1}{4}$ in. = 550 yd

D. $23\frac{1}{2}$ in. = 329 yd

E. 10 in. = 160 yd

F. 154 in. = 11 yd

G. $30\frac{1}{2}$ in. = 427 yd

13. A state map uses a scale of 1 inch = 25 miles. Select True or False for each statement.

    A. 465 miles is equivalent to 18.6 inches on the map.   ○ True ○ False

    B. 1,000 miles is equivalent to 4 inches on the map.   ○ True ○ False

    C. 15 miles is equivalent to 375 inches on the map.   ○ True ○ False

    D. 225 miles is equivalent to 9 inches on the map.   ○ True ○ False

14. Two students each made a map of the school library using a different scale. An actual size and scale size is given for each map. Circle each correct scale.

15-ft long bookshelf = 3 cm   9-ft long sofa = 1.5 cm

Scale:
| 5 ft = 1 cm |
| 3 ft = 1 cm |
| 1 ft = 5 cm |

Scale:
| 3 ft = 1 cm |
| 6 ft = 1 cm |
| 8 ft = 1 cm |

15. The map shows a scale drawing of Wilson's backyard. Circle every item whose actual size is shown.

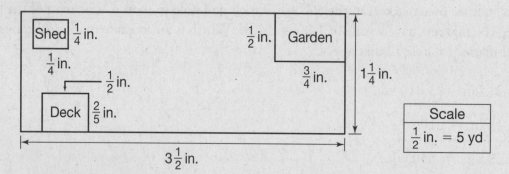

    A. Shed: $2\frac{1}{2}$ yd by $2\frac{1}{2}$ yd

    B. Garden: 5 yd by $2\frac{1}{2}$ yd

    C. Deck: 4 yd by 5 yd

    D. Backyard: $12\frac{1}{2}$ yd by $17\frac{1}{2}$ yd

    E. Area of shed: $6\frac{1}{4}$ yd^2

    F. Area of garden: $37\frac{1}{2}$ yd^2

Domain 4 • Lesson 21

Construct Geometric Shapes

Getting the Idea

Triangles can be constructed using simple tools such as a ruler and protractor, or using more complex tools such as computer drawing technology. When drawing triangles with a ruler and/or a protractor by hand, you may sometimes need to erase your work and start over again. It can involve some trial and error.

Acute triangles have 3 **acute angles**, a **right triangle** has 1 **right angle**, and an **obtuse triangle** has 1 **obtuse angle**. The sum of the angle measures of any triangle is 180°.

Example 1

Using a ruler, construct a triangle with side lengths of 3 centimeters, 4 centimeters, and 5 centimeters. What kind of triangle is it? Is it possible to draw another kind of triangle?

Strategy   Use a ruler.

Step 1   Try drawing a triangle with one obtuse angle—an obtuse triangle.

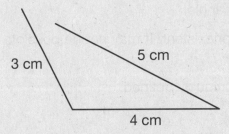

The figure is not closed. An obtuse triangle is not possible.

Step 2   Try drawing a triangle with only acute angles—an acute triangle.

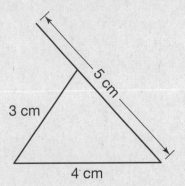

The endpoints do not meet. An acute triangle is not possible.

Step 3   Try drawing a triangle with one right angle—a right triangle.

3 cm 5 cm 4 cm

You can draw one unique triangle with those side lengths, and it is a right triangle.

Solution   **It is only possible to draw a right triangle with side lengths of 3 centimeters, 4 centimeters, and 5 centimeters.**

When trying to construct a triangle with given side lengths or angle measures, there are several possibilities:

- The triangle may be uniquely defined. In other words, you may only be able to draw one triangle.

- The triangle may be ambiguously defined. That just means you may be able to draw more than one triangle.

- The triangle may be nonexistent. It may not be possible to draw a triangle with those measures.

The triangle in Example 1 is uniquely defined.

Example 2

Is it possible to construct a triangle with angles measuring 61°, 33°, and 86°? If so, can you draw only a unique triangle or can you draw many different triangles?

Strategy   **Find the sum of the angle measures.**

Step 1   Determine if the angle measures add to 180°.

$$61° + 33° + 86° \stackrel{?}{=} 180°$$

$$180° = 180° \checkmark$$

So, a triangle with these angle measures is possible.

Step 2   Use a protractor to draw one or more triangles with those angle measures.

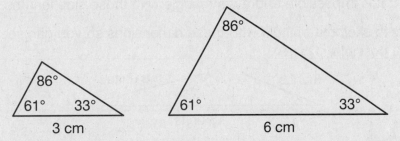

The two triangles are **similar** to each other because they have the same angle measures.

It is possible to draw many different triangles with those angle measures.

Solution   **A triangle with angles measuring 61°, 33°, and 86° is ambiguously defined because no side lengths are mentioned. It is possible to draw many different similar triangles with those angle measures.**

The sum of the lengths of any two sides of a triangle is greater than the length of the third side.

Example 3

Can you construct a triangle with sides measuring 5 inches, 8 inches, and 15 inches?

Strategy **Determine if one length is greater than the sum of the other two lengths.**

Step 1 Determine if one length is greater than the sum of the other two lengths.

$$5 + 8 \overset{?}{>} 15$$

$13 < 15$, so the inequality $5 + 8 > 15$ is not true.

It is impossible to draw a triangle with those side lengths.

Step 2 Try to sketch a triangle with those dimensions so you can see why it is not possible.

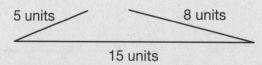

5 units   8 units

15 units

There is no way to connect all three sides. It is impossible to draw a triangle with those side lengths.

Solution **A triangle with sides measuring 5 inches, 8 inches, and 15 inches does not exist.**

Coached Example

Is it possible to construct a triangle with sides measuring 8 feet, 9 feet, and 12 feet?

The sum of the lengths of any two sides of a triangle must be _____ than the length of the third side.

Determine if this triangle is possible or not.

Is $8 + 9 > 12$? _____

Is $8 + 12 > 9$? _____

Is $9 + 12 > 8$? _____

The inequalities above are all true, so it _____ possible to draw a triangle with side lengths of 8 feet, 9 feet, and 12 feet.

Lesson Practice • Part 1

Choose the correct answer. Use a ruler.

1. Which best describes a triangle with side lengths of 6 inches, 8 inches, and 9 inches?

   A. ambiguously defined
   B. nonexistent
   C. a unique, acute triangle
   D. a unique, right triangle

2. Which best describes a triangle with angles measuring 60°, 40°, and 100°?

   A. ambiguously defined
   B. nonexistent
   C. a unique, acute triangle
   D. a unique, right triangle

3. Which best describes a triangle with side lengths of 3 inches, 4 inches, and 8 inches?

   A. ambiguously defined
   B. nonexistent
   C. a unique, obtuse triangle
   D. a unique, right triangle

4. Which best describes a triangle with side lengths of 5 centimeters, 12 centimeters, and 13 centimeters?

   A. ambiguously defined
   B. nonexistent
   C. a unique, acute triangle
   D. a unique, right triangle

5. Lincoln constructs a triangle with one side 5 inches long and another side 7 inches long. Which is **not** a possible length for the third side?

   A. 3 inches
   B. 6 inches
   C. 11 inches
   D. 12 inches

6. Maggie constructs a triangle with one side 7 centimeters long and another side 10 centimeters long. Which is **not** a possible length for the third side?

   A. 2 centimeters
   B. 4 centimeters
   C. 7 centimeters
   D. 16 centimeters

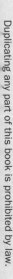

7. Chantelle constructs a triangle with angles measuring 65° and 38°. What must be true of the measure of the third angle in her construction?

A. It must measure exactly 77°.

B. It must measure exactly 87°.

C. It can have any measure less than 103°.

D. It can have any measure greater than 27°.

8. Josh constructs a triangle with angles measuring 54°, 23°, and 103°. He wants to construct a different triangle with those angle measures. What will he find if he does?

A. It is not possible to construct a different triangle with those angle measures.

B. Any other triangle he constructs with those angle measures will be congruent to his original triangle.

C. Any other triangle he constructs with those angle measures will be similar to his original triangle.

D. He can construct many other triangles with those angle measures, and none of them will be similar to the first triangle he constructed.

9. Use a ruler for this problem.

A. In the space below, construct a triangle with side lengths of 1 centimeter, 2 centimeters, and 2 centimeters.

B. Is the triangle you constructed above unique or ambiguously defined? Use words and a sketch to support your answer.

_____

_____

_____

Lesson Practice • Part 2

Choose the correct answer. Use a ruler.

1. Which quadrilateral can be drawn with exactly 2 right angles?

   A. parallelogram

   B. rectangle

   C. rhombus

   D. trapezoid

2. Which best describes a triangle with side lengths of 4 inches, 5 inches, and 6 inches?

   A. ambiguously defined

   B. nonexistent

   C. a unique, acute triangle

   D. a unique, right triangle

3. Which best describes a triangle with angle measures of 58°, 47°, and 85°?

   A. ambiguously defined

   B. nonexistent

   C. a unique, acute triangle

   D. a unique, right triangle

4. Two of the sides of a triangle are 7 inches and 8 inches. If the third side is a whole number of inches, what is its greatest possible measure?

   A. 14 inches

   B. 15 inches

   C. 16 inches

   D. There is no limit to its measure.

5. Which best describes a triangle with side lengths of 6 inches, 8 inches, and 10 inches?

   A. ambiguously defined

   B. nonexistent

   C. a unique, acute triangle

   D. a unique, right triangle

6. How many angle combinations are there for an isosceles, right triangle?

   A. 1

   B. 2

   C. 3

   D. infinite

7. At least one of the measures of an isosceles triangle is 42°. Which can **not** be one of the other angle measures?

A. 42°

B. 48°

C. 69°

D. 106°

8. Two of the sides of a triangle are 3 centimeters and 8 centimeters. If the third side is a whole number of centimeters, what is its least possible measure?

A. 5 centimeters

B. 6 centimeters

C. 10 centimeters

D. 11 centimeters

9. At least one of the measures of an isosceles triangle is 74°.

A. What are the two possible angle measure combinations of this triangle?

_____

_____

B. Describe your triangles as acute or obtuse.

_____

_____

C. Are each of the triangles you created unique or ambiguously defined? Explain your answer.

_____

_____

_____

10. Select True or False for each statement.

 A. An ambiguously defined triangle can have angle measures of 43°, 79°, and 58°.   ○ True   ○ False

 B. A triangle **cannot** have angle measures of 32°, 78°, and 80°.   ○ True   ○ False

 C. A unique, acute triangle can have angle measures of 60°, 70°, and 90°.   ○ True   ○ False

 D. A unique, right triangle can have angle measures of 30°, 60°, and 90°.   ○ True   ○ False

11. Write each set of triangle side lengths in the correct box.

2 cm, 3 cm, 6 cm	4 mi, 9 mi, 13 mi
5 ft, 12 ft, 13 ft	6 in., 8 in., 10 in.
15 mm, 36 mm, 39 mm	14 yd, 16 yd, 30 yd

Unique Triangle	Nonexistent Triangle

12. Brandon drew a triangle with one side 6 centimeters long and another side 10 centimeters long. Look at each length below. Is the length a possible side length of Brandon's triangle? Select Yes or No.

A. 2 centimeters   ○ Yes ○ No

B. 4 centimeters   ○ Yes ○ No

C. 6 centimeters   ○ Yes ○ No

D. 10 centimeters   ○ Yes ○ No

E. 14 centimeters   ○ Yes ○ No

F. 18 centimeters   ○ Yes ○ No

13. Draw a line from each triangle description to a possible set of side lengths.

A. nonexistent triangle   •   • 5 m, 18 m, 27 m

B. unique, right triangle   •   • 10 ft, 10 ft, 10, ft

C. unique, acute triangle   •   • 12 in., 16 in., 20 in.

14. Use angle measures from the box to complete each set of three angle measures of a triangle.

59°, 63°, _____

64°, 48°, _____

72°, 56°, _____

60°, 58°, _____

| 52° |
| 58° |
| 62° |
| 68° |

Cross Sections of Three-Dimensional Figures

> ## Getting the Idea
>
> A **three-dimensional figure** (also called a **solid figure**) has length, width, and height. It is not flat. Some examples of three-dimensional figures are below.

A **prism** has a pair of **bases** that are **parallel**, congruent polygons. Its other **faces** are rectangles.	A **rectangular prism** has 6 faces that are rectangles. 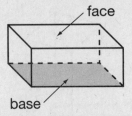 face base	A **cube** is a rectangular prism with 6 square faces.
A **pyramid** has one base that is a polygon. Its other faces are triangles. The height of a pyramid is called its **altitude**, and the height of its lateral face is called its **slant height**.	A **rectangular pyramid** has a base that is a rectangle. 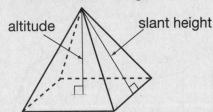 altitude slant height	A **square pyramid** has a base that is a square. 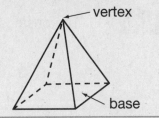 vertex base

A three-dimensional figure can be sliced by a plane to show a two-dimensional view. This view is called a **cross section**.

Example 1

A square pyramid is sliced by a plane that is parallel to its base, as shown.

What is the shape of the cross section?

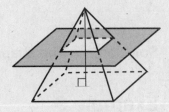

Strategy   **Visualize a plane, parallel to the base, slicing through the pyramid.**

The cross section will have the same shape as the base.

It will be a square.

Solution   **The shape of the cross section is a square.**

Example 2

A rectangular prism is cut by the slanted plane shown.

What is the shape of the cross section?

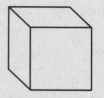

Strategy   **Visualize the prism being sliced by a thin piece of wire.**

Step 1   Determine the angle at which the plane intersects the prism.

The plane is neither horizontal nor vertical to the faces of the prism.

Step 2   Imagine slicing the rectangular prism with a piece of wire.

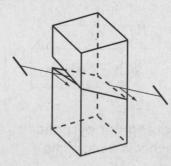

Step 3   The prism is now in two parts.

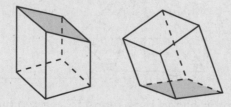

Step 4   Visualize the shape of the cross section.

Solution   **The shape of the cross section is a parallelogram.**

Example 3

Look at this cube.

How can a plane slice the cube so that the cross section is a triangle?

Strategy   **Visualize using a plane to slice the cube to get a triangular cross section.**

Slice through a corner of the cube with a plane.

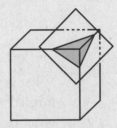

Solution   **The cross section of the cube is shown above.**

Coached Example

Nari will slice this pyramid with a plane that is perpendicular to the base and passes through the top vertex.

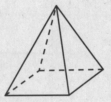

What is the shape of the cross section?

What does "perpendicular" mean?

Something at an angle of 90° to a given line, plane, or surface.

Visualize slicing the prism with a plane that is perpendicular to the base and passes through the top vertex.

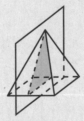

Make a sketch of the cross section in the space below.

The shape of the cross section is A triangle .

Lesson Practice • Part 1

Choose the correct answer.

1. The rectangular prism is being sliced by a plane parallel to its base.

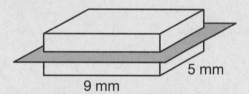

9 mm

5 mm

What will be the shape of the cross section formed?

- A. parallelogram that is not a rectangle
- **B.** rectangle that is not a square
- C. square
- D. triangle

2. What is the shape of the cross section formed when the square pyramid is sliced by a plane perpendicular to its base that does **not** pass through its top vertex?

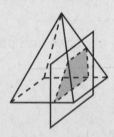

- A. parallelogram (not a square)
- B. square
- **C.** trapezoid
- D. triangle

3. What is the shape of the cross section formed when the rectangular pyramid is cut by the plane parallel to its base?

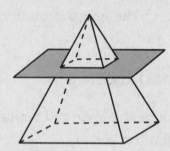

- A.
- B.
- C.
- **D.**

4. Matt molded a cube from clay. He then took piano wire and sliced through the clay, as shown by the dotted lines below.

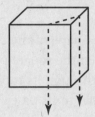

What is the shape of the cross section formed when he does this?

A. rectangle (not a square)

B. square

C. trapezoid

D. triangle

5. Which is the shape of the cross section formed when the triangular pyramid is cut by the plane, as shown?

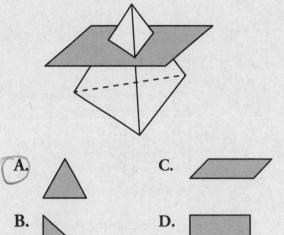

A.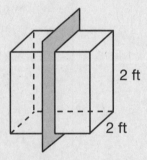

B.

C.

D.

6. The diagram shows a cube with each edge 2 feet long. The cube has been cut by a plane perpendicular to its base.

2 ft

2 ft

A. Identify and draw the shape of the cross section formed when the cube was cut by the plane shown. Label its dimensions.

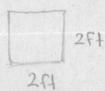

2ft

2ft

B. Suppose the plane were parallel to the base of the cube. What would be the shape of the cross section now? Explain your answer.

The shape of the cross section will remain a 2ft x 2ft square, since insted of being the base and top of the cube, the image will now show the sides of the cube, and since in a cube, all of the sides are congruent squares, the image will remain the same.

239

Lesson Practice • Part 2

Choose the correct answer.

1. The rectangular prism is sliced by a plane perpendicular to its base.

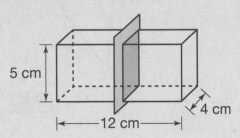

5 cm

12 cm

4 cm

Which best describes the shape of the cross section formed?

A. trapezoid

B. square

C. rectangle that is not a square

D. equilateral triangle

2. Which cross section of the cube will produce a square?

A.

B.

C.

D.

3. What is the shape of the cross section formed when the square pyramid is sliced by a plane through its top apex but is not perpendicular to its base?

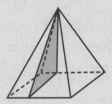

A. pentagon

B. rhombus

C. trapezoid

D. triangle

4. Which cross section does **not** produce a triangle?

A.

B.

C.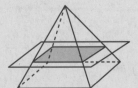

D.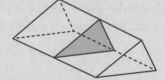

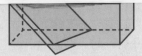

Which best describes the shape of the cross section?

A. parallelogram

B. pentagon

C. square

D. triangle

Which best describes the shape of the cross section formed?

A. triangle

B. trapezoid

C. square

D. rectangle that is not a square

---

7. The right rectangular prism is sliced by a plane that passes through six faces as shown.

A. Identify the shape of the cross section formed when the prism was cut by the plane.

_____

B. Suppose the plane sliced from one full edge of the prism through to its opposite edge. What would be the shape of the cross section? Explain your answer.

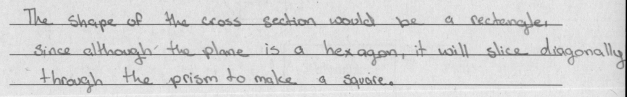

The shape of the cross section would be a rectangle, since although the plane is a hexagon, it will slice diagonally through the prism to make a square.

8. Draw a line from each cube to its cross section.

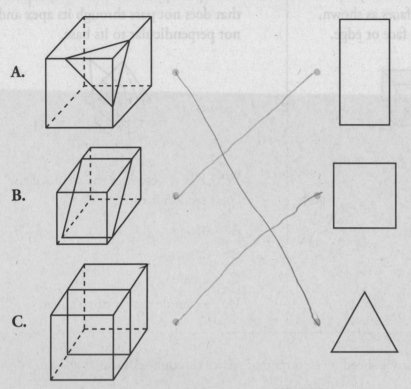

A.

B.

C.

9. A square prism is sliced by a plane that is perpendicular to its base. Circle the cross section.

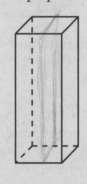

The cross section is a

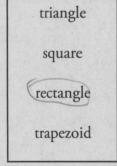

triangle

square

rectangle

trapezoid

10. A rectangular pyramid is sliced by a plane. Select True or False for each statement.

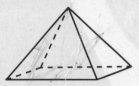

A. If the slice is parallel to the pyramid's base, the cross section is a triangle.

○ True ● False

B. If the slice is perpendicular to the pyramid's base but not through the vertex, the cross section is a triangle.

○ True ● False

C. If the slice is perpendicular to the pyramid's base through the vertex, the cross section is a triangle.

● True ○ False

D. If the slice is neither parallel nor perpendicular to the pyramid's base, the cross section is a trapezoid.

○ True ● False

11. Look at each figure. Is the cross section a triangle? Select Yes or No.

A. ● Yes ○ No

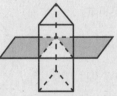

B. ● Yes ○ No

C. ○ Yes ● No

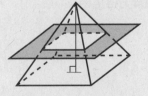

D. ○ Yes ● No

A **circle** is the set of all ~~~~~~ plane that are the same distance from a given point called the **center**. A circle is named by its center.

A **radius** is the distance from the center of a circle to any point on the circle. $\overline{OK}$, $\overline{OL}$, and $\overline{OM}$ are radii of circle O.

A **diameter** is the distance across a circle through its center.

The length of a diameter is always 2 times the length of a radius.

$\overline{LM}$ is a diameter of circle O.

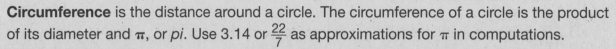

Circumference is the distance around a circle. The circumference of a circle is the product of its diameter and π, or *pi*. Use 3.14 or $\frac{22}{7}$ as approximations for π in computations.

The table below shows the formulas for finding the circumference and **area** of a circle.

Formulas	
circumference	$C = \pi d$ or $C = 2\pi r$
area	$A = \pi r^2$

Example 1

What is the approximate circumference of this circle? Use 3.14 for π.

Strategy Use the formula for the circumference of a circle.

Step 1 Write the formula for circumference when you know the radius.
$C = 2\pi r$

Step 2 Substitute 3 for r and 3.14 for π. Then multiply.
$C = 2\pi r$
$C \approx 2 \times 3.14 \times 3$ 　　Note: Use $\approx$ because 3.14 is an estimate.
$C \approx 18.84$

Solution **The circumference of the circle is about 18.84 meters.**

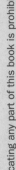

Example 2

The circumference of a circle is 9π inches. What is the diameter of the circle?

Strategy   **Use the formula for the circumference of a circle.**

Step 1   Write the formula for the circumference when you know the diameter.

$$C = \pi d$$

Step 2   Substitute 9π for C.

$$9\pi = \pi d$$

Step 3   Divide both sides of the equation by π.

$$9\pi = \pi d$$

$$\frac{9\pi}{\pi} = \frac{\pi d}{\pi}$$

$$9 = d$$

Solution   **The diameter of the circle is 9 inches.**

The formulas for the circumference of a circle and the area of a **parallelogram** can help you find a formula for the area of a circle.

Imagine cutting a circle into an equal number of pieces, such as 8 pieces. Arrange the pieces to form as close to a parallelogram as possible.

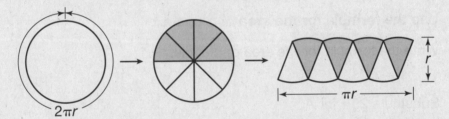

As you can see, the sides are not straight, so it is not a parallelogram. However, as the pieces of the circle get smaller, when arranged to make a parallelogram, the sides will be straight.

Since the circumference of a circle is $2\pi r$, the length of the parallelogram is $\frac{1}{2}$ the circumference. So, the length is $\frac{1}{2}C = \frac{1}{2} \times 2\pi r$, or πr.

The height of the parallelogram is about the same as the radius, r, of the circle. The area of a parallelogram is bh, so the area of the circle is $\pi r \times r$, or $A = \pi r^2$.

Example 3

A circle has a diameter of 8 inches. What is the approximate area of the circle? Use 3.14 for π.

Strategy   **Use the formula for the area of a circle.**

Step 1   Use the diameter to find the radius.

The length of the radius is $\frac{1}{2}$ the length of the diameter.

The diameter is 8.

$8 \div 2 = 4$, so the radius is 4 inches.

Step 2   Write the formula for the area of a circle.

$A = \pi r^2$

Step 3   Substitute 4 for r and 3.14 for π. Solve.

$A = \pi r^2$

$A \approx 3.14 \times 4 \text{ in.} \times 4 \text{ in.}$ Again, use $\approx$ because 3.14 is an estimate.

$A \approx 50.24 \text{ in.}^2$

Solution   **The area of the circle is about 50.24 in.^{2}**

Example 4

The area of a circle is 25π square centimeters. What is the radius of the circle?

Strategy   **Use the formula for the area of a circle.**

Step 1   Write the formula for the area of a circle.

$A = \pi r^2$

Step 2   Substitute 25π for A.

$25\pi = \pi r^2$

Step 3   Divide both sides of the equation by π.

$25\pi = \pi r^2$

$\frac{25\pi}{\pi} = \frac{\pi r^2}{\pi}$

$25 = r^2$

Step 4   Take the square root of both sides of the equation to find the value of r.

$25 = r^2$

$\sqrt{25} = \sqrt{r^2}$

$5 = r$

Solution   **When the area of a circle is 25π square centimeters, the radius is 5 centimeters.**

Coached Example

Philip is building a go-cart. The wheels he uses on the go-cart have a radius of 6 inches. What are the approximate circumference and the area of each wheel?

What is the formula for the circumference of a circle when the radius is given?

_____

Use 3.14 for π and substitute the length of the _____ into the formula.

$C \approx$ _____

Multiply.

$C \approx$ _____

What is the formula for the area of a circle? _____

Use 3.14 for π and substitute the length of the _____ into the formula.

$A \approx$ _____

Multiply.

$A \approx$ _____

The circumference of each wheel is about _____,

and the area is about _____.

Lesson Practice • Part 1

Choose the correct answer.

1. A rose garden is circular. The diameter of the garden is 18 feet. Which is closest to the total area of the garden? Use 3.14 for π.

 A. 56.52 ft^2

 B. 63.59 ft^2

 C. 113.04 ft^2

 D. 254.34 ft^2

2. A circular swimming pool has a radius of 15 feet. The family that owns the pool wants to put up a circular fence that is 5 feet away from the pool at all points. Which is closest to the circumference of the fence they will need? Use 3.14 for π.

 A. 94.2 ft

 B. 125.6 ft

 C. 157 ft

 D. 188.4 ft

3. Lana is putting lace trim around the border of a circular tablecloth. The tablecloth has a diameter of 1.2 meters. To the nearest meter, what is the least amount of lace she needs? Use 3.14 for π.

 A. 3 m

 B. 4 m

 C. 7 m

 D. 8 m

4. Randy's bicycle tires have a diameter of 42 centimeters. Which is closest to the circumference of one of the tires? Use 3.14 for π.

 A. 65.94 cm

 B. 87.14 cm

 C. 131.88 cm

 D. 441 cm

5. Pete needs to install a circular window with a radius of 7.25 inches. Which is closest to the amount of glass he will need? Use 3.14 for π.

 A. 22.77 in.^{2}

 B. 41.26 in.^{2}

 C. 45.53 in.^{2}

 D. 165.05 in.^{2}

6. At Palermo Pizzeria pizzas are sold by their diameter. Rihanna orders a 14-inch pizza. Which is closest to the area of the pizza? Use 3.14 for π.

 A. 21.98 in.^{2}

 B. 43.96 in.^{2}

 C. 153.86 in.^{2}

 D. 307.72 in.^{2}

7. A circular pin has a diameter of 6.2 centimeters. Which is closest to the area of the pin? Use 3.14 for π.

   A. 30.18 cm^2

   B. 19.47 cm^2

   C. 15.54 cm^2

   D. 9.74 cm^2

8. What is the radius of a circle when the circumference is 16π cm?

   A. 16 cm

   B. 12 cm

   C. 8 cm

   D. 4 cm

9. The circle below is divided into 6 equal pieces.

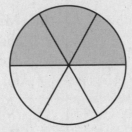

   A. Explain how to use the formulas for the circumference of a circle and the area of a rectangle to find the formula for the area of a circle.

   _____

   _____

   _____

   _____

   B. Use your explanation from Part A to find the area of the circle if the length of the radius is 3 centimeters. Check that the area is the same when you use the formula for the area of a circle. Show your work.

   _____

   _____

   _____

Lesson Practice • Part 2

Choose the correct answer.

Use this information for questions 1 and 2.

A CD is circular and has a diameter of 6 centimeters.

1. Which is closest to the circumference of the CD? Use 3.14 for π.

   A. 18.84 cm

   B. 28.26 cm

   C. 37.68 cm

   D. 113.04 cm

2. Which is closest to the area of the CD? Use 3.14 for π.

   A. 18.84 cm^2

   B. 28.26 cm^2

   C. 37.68 cm^2

   D. 113.04 cm^2

3. Mrs. Armstrong bought a circular, inflatable, above-ground pool for her family. The pool has a radius of 4.5 feet. Which is closest to the area of the pool? Use 3.14 for π.

   A. 14.13 ft^2

   B. 28.26 ft^2

   C. 63.59 ft^2

   D. 254.34 ft^2

4. A bicycle wheel has a circumference of 24π inches. What is the diameter of the wheel?

   A. 6 in.   C. 24 in.

   B. 12 in.   D. 48 in.

5. Mr. Higgins bought a circular area rug that has a diameter of 72 inches. Which is closest to the area of the rug? Use 3.14 for π.

   A. 113.04 in.^{2}

   B. 226.08 in.^{2}

   C. 452.16 in.^{2}

   D. 4,069.44 in.^{2}

6. Andy said that a circle with a radius of 2 centimeters has the same circumference and area. Which sentence is true? Use 3.14 for π.

   A. Andy is correct because the circumference and area are both approximately 12.56.

   B. Andy is incorrect because the circumference and area are measured in different units.

   C. Andy is incorrect because the circumference is approximately 6.28 and the area is approximately 12.56.

   D. Andy is incorrect because the circumference is approximately 12.56 and the area is approximately 6.28.

7. Circular pies at Perfect Pies come in 10-inch and 12-inch diameters. Which is closest to the difference in the areas of the pies? Use 3.14 for π.

   A.   3.14 in.^{2}

   B.   6.28 in.^{2}

   C.   34.54 in.^{2}

   D.   138.16 in.^{2}

8. A circular lid has an area of 50.24 square centimeters. What is the radius of the lid? Use 3.14 for π.

   A.   4 cm

   B.   8 cm

   C.   12 cm

   D.   16 cm

9. A shaded circle is inside a square.

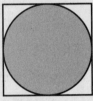

18 in.

   A.   What is the approximate difference between the perimeter of the square and the circumference of the circle? Use 3.14 for π. Show your work.

   B.   What is the approximate area of the part of the square that is **not** shaded? Use 3.14 for π. Show your work.

10. Tires come in several sizes. The radii of three tires are given. Circle the approximate circumference of each tire. Use 3.14 for π.

13 in.:
16.14
40.82
81.64
in.

14 in.:
43.96
87.92
615.44
in.

16 in.:
50.24
100.48
803.84
in.

11. Draw a line from each area of a circle in the left column to the corresponding circumference of the circle in the right column.

A. 25π units^2 •

B. 16π units^2 •

C. 100π units^2 •

D. 4π units^2 •

• 4π units

• 20π units

• 10π units

• 8π units

12. Look at the circle. Which is a true statement? Circle all that apply.

5 m

A. The diameter is 5 m.

B. The circumference is 5π m.

C. The diameter is 10 m.

D. The area is 25π m^2.

E. The circumference is 25π m.

F. The radius is 5 m.

G. The area is 10π m^2.

13. A circular flower garden has an area of 81π square inches. Select True or False for each statement.

    A. The circumference is 9π in.   ○ True   ○ False

    B. The radius is 9 in.   ○ True   ○ False

    C. The diameter is 9 in.   ○ True   ○ False

    D. The circumference is 18π in.   ○ True   ○ False

14. Dartboards come in different sizes. Circle the approximate area of a dartboard given each diameter. Use 3.14 for π.

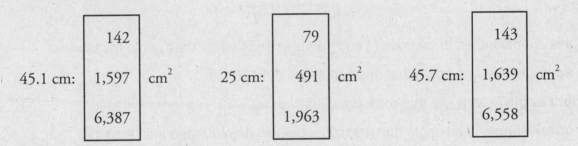

	142			79			143	
45.1 cm:	1,597	cm^2	25 cm:	491	cm^2	45.7 cm:	1,639	cm^2
	6,387			1,963			6,558	

15. The bottom of a cup is a circle with a diameter of $4\frac{1}{4}$ in. Which is a true statement? Circle all that apply. Use 3.14 for π.

    A. The radius is $8\frac{1}{2}$ in.

    B. The circumference is about 13.3 in.

    C. The area is about 14.2 in^2.

    D. The area is about 56.7 in^2.

    E. The circumference is about 26.7 in.

    F. The radius is $2\frac{1}{8}$ in.

16. A small swimming pool has a circumference of 3π feet. Is each statement about the pool true? Select Yes or No.

    A. The radius is 3 ft.   ○ Yes   ○ No

    B. The diameter is 3 ft.   ○ Yes   ○ No

    C. The diameter is 1.5 ft.   ○ Yes   ○ No

    D. The radius is 6 ft.   ○ Yes   ○ No

Angles

Getting the Idea

An **angle** is a geometric figure formed by two rays that have a common endpoint called the **vertex**. The angle below can be named ∠1, ∠JKL, ∠LKJ, or ∠K.

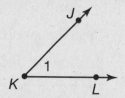

Angles are measured in degrees (°) and can be classified by their angle measures.

An **acute angle** is an angle that measures less than 90°.

A **right angle** is an angle that measures 90°.

An **obtuse angle** is an angle that measures greater than 90° and less than 180°.

Intersecting lines can form some special angle pairs.

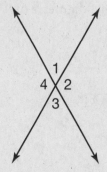

Adjacent angles are two angles with a side in common.
∠1 and ∠2 are one set of adjacent angles.

Vertical angles are two non-adjacent angles, formed by intersecting lines, and are congruent.
∠1 and ∠3 are one set of vertical angles.

Supplementary angles are two angles whose measures have a sum of 180°.
Supplementary angles that are adjacent angles have rays that form a line.
∠4 and ∠3 are one set of supplementary angles.

Complementary angles are two angles whose measures have a sum of 90°.

To write the measure of an angle, you can use the abbreviation, m.

For example, "the measure of angle x" can be written as "m∠x."

Example 1

Look at the diagram on the right.

Find the following:

- a pair of complementary angles
- a pair of supplementary angles
- a pair of adjacent angles
- a pair of vertical angles

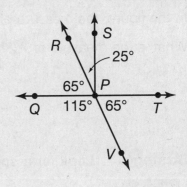

Strategy   **Use the definitions to identify the angle pairs.**

Step 1   Find a pair of complementary angles.

Find two angles that have a sum of 90°.

m∠QPR = 65° and m∠RPS = 25°.

65° + 25° = 90°

Step 2   Find a pair of supplementary angles.

Find two angles that have a sum of 180°.

m∠QPV = 115° and m∠TPV = 65°.

115° + 65° = 180°

Another pair of supplementary angles is ∠QPR and ∠QPV.

Step 3   Find a pair of adjacent angles.

Find two angles with a side in common.

∠QPR and ∠RPS have $\overrightarrow{PR}$ in common.

Other pairs of adjacent angles are ∠RPS and ∠SPT, ∠SPT and ∠TPV, ∠TPV and ∠QPV, and ∠QPV and ∠QPR.

Step 4   Find a pair of vertical angles.

Find two non-adjacent angles formed by intersecting lines.

$\overleftrightarrow{RV}$ and $\overleftrightarrow{QT}$ intersect at point P to form ∠QPR and ∠TPV.

These angles are vertical angles, and they are congruent.

Solution   **∠QPR and ∠RPS are a pair of complementary angles.**

∠QPV and ∠TPV are a pair of supplementary angles.

∠QPR and ∠RPS are a pair of adjacent angles.

∠QPR and ∠TPV are a pair of vertical angles.

Example 2

In the figure, the measure of ∠1 is 35°.

What is the measure of ∠2?

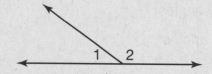

Strategy	**Look for a special angle pair.**
Step 1	Decide what type of angles are ∠1 and ∠2.
	The angles are adjacent angles that form a straight line.
	So, ∠1 and ∠2 are supplementary angles.
Step 2	What angle measures do you know?
	The measure of ∠1 is 35°.
	Supplementary angles have a sum of 180°.
Step 3	Subtract 35° from 180° to find the measure of ∠2.
	180° − 35° = 145°
Solution	**The measure of ∠2 is 145°.**

Example 3

What are the measures of $\angle x$ and $\angle z$?

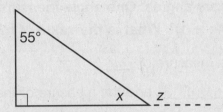

Strategy   **Look for special relationships between angles.**

Step 1   Find the measure of $\angle x$.

The measures of the angles in a triangle have a sum of 180°.

The measures given are 55° and a right angle, which measures 90°.

Write an equation and solve for the measure of $\angle x$.

$$55° + 90° + m\angle x = 180°$$
$$145° + m\angle x = 180°$$
$$145° - 145° + m\angle x = 180° - 145°$$
$$m\angle x = 35°$$

Step 2   Identify the angle relationship of $\angle x$ and $\angle z$.

$\angle x$ is adjacent to $\angle z$. The two angles form a straight line.

Supplementary angles that are adjacent angles form a straight line.

So, $\angle x$ and $\angle z$ are supplementary angles.

Step 3   Recall the definition of supplementary angles.

Supplementary angles have a sum of 180°.

Step 4   Write an equation to find the measure of $\angle z$.

$$m\angle x + m\angle z = 180°$$
$$35° + m\angle z = 180°$$
$$35° - 35° + m\angle z = 180° - 35°$$
$$m\angle z = 145°$$

Solution   **The measure of $\angle x$ is 35°. The measure of $\angle z$ is 145°.**

Coached Example

Two angles are complementary angles. One angle measures 59°.
The other angle measures $(4n - 1)°$. What is the value of n?

Complementary angles have a measure of _____.

The measure of one angle is _____, and the measure of the other angle is _____.

Write an equation for the total of the two angles.

_____ + _____ = 90

Solve the equation for n.

To find the measure of the unknown angle, substitute the value of n into $4n - 1$ and evaluate. _____

Check that the sum of the angle measures is 90°.

_____

The value of n is _____.

Lesson Practice • Part 1

Choose the correct answer.

Use the diagram for questions 1–4.

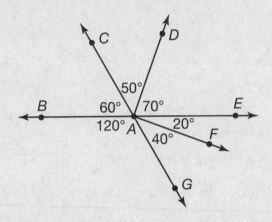

1. Which angle is complementary to ∠*FAE*?

    A. ∠*GAF*

    B. ∠*BAC*

    C. ∠*DAE*

    D. ∠*DAC*

2. Which angle is supplementary to ∠*GAB*?

    A. ∠*BAC*

    B. ∠*DAC*

    C. ∠*DAE*

    D. ∠*EAF*

3. Which pair of angles are adjacent angles?

    A. ∠*BAC* and ∠*GAF*

    B. ∠*DAC* and ∠*GAF*

    C. ∠*DAE* and ∠*BAC*

    D. ∠*CAD* and ∠*DAE*

4. Which pair of angles are vertical angles?

    A. ∠*EAG* and ∠*BAC*

    B. ∠*GAB* and ∠*DAF*

    C. ∠*DAC* and ∠*DAF*

    D. ∠*BAC* and ∠*CAE*

5. ∠*A* and ∠*B* are complementary angles. If m∠*A* is 35°, what is the measure of ∠*B*?

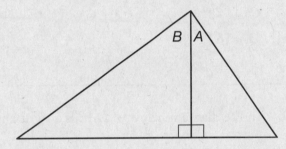

    A. 55°

    B. 65°

    C. 90°

    D. 145°

6. ∠*J* and ∠*K* are supplementary angles. If m∠*K* is 84°, what is the measure of ∠*J*?

    A. 16°

    B. 86°

    C. 96°

    D. 106°

Use the diagram for questions 7 and 8.

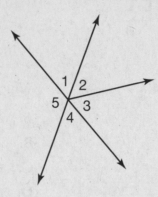

7. If m∠1 is 48°, what is the measure of ∠4?

   A. 42°

   B. 48°

   C. 58°

   D. 132°

8. If $m\angle 4 = 2x°$ and $m\angle 5 = 4x°$, what is the value of x?

   A. 20

   B. 30

   C. 60

   D. 120

9. In the diagram below, ∠DAE is a right angle and m∠BAF = 155°.

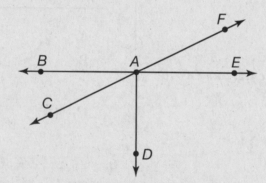

   A. What is the measure of ∠BAC? Explain your answer.

   _____

   _____

   B. What are the measures of ∠FAE and ∠CAD? Explain your answers.

   _____

   _____

Lesson Practice • Part 2

Choose the correct answer.

Use the diagram for questions 1–4.

Angle 3 measures 54°.

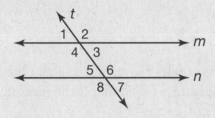

1. What is the measure of ∠1?

   A. 36°
   B. 54°
   C. 108°
   D. 126°

2. Which names a pair of vertical angles?

   A. ∠1 and ∠2
   B. ∠1 and ∠4
   C. ∠2 and ∠3
   D. ∠2 and ∠4

3. What is the measure of ∠4?

   A. 36°
   B. 54°
   C. 108°
   D. 126°

4. Which pair of angles are **not** supplementary angles?

   A. ∠3 and ∠4
   B. ∠5 and ∠8
   C. ∠5 and ∠7
   D. ∠6 and ∠7

Use the diagram for questions 5 and 6.

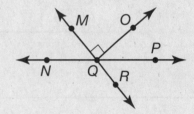

5. ∠OQP and ∠PQR are complementary. The two angles are equal. Which equation can be used to find the measure of each angle?

   A. $2 + a = 90$
   B. $2a = 90$
   C. $2 + a = 180$
   D. $2a = 180$

6. Which is the measure of ∠NQO?

   A. 45°
   B. 90°
   C. 135°
   D. 180°

7. What is the value of x?

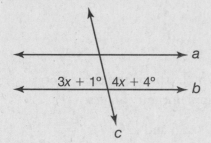

A. $x = 25$

B. $x = 28$

C. $x = 76$

D. $x = 104$

8. Two angles are complementary. One angle measure is 4 times the measure of the other angle. What is the measure of the lesser angle?

A. 18°

B. 22.5°

C. 36°

D. 45°

9. Two angles are vertical angles. One angle measure is 68°. What is the measure of the other angle?

A. 22°

B. 68°

C. 90°

D. 112°

10. A series of angles is shown below.

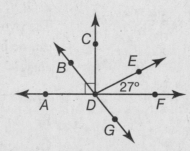

A. What is the measure of $\angle CDE$?

_____

B. The measure of $\angle BDC$ is 32°. What is the measure of $\angle EDG$?

_____

C. What is the measure of $\angle ADG$?

_____

11. Select True or False for each statement.

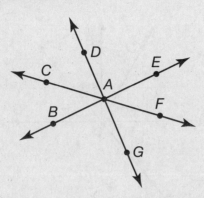

A. $\angle GAF$ and $\angle FAD$ are adjacent angles.	○ True ○ False
B. $\angle DAC$ and $\angle EAF$ are adjacent angles.	○ True ○ False
C. $\angle BAF$ and $\angle CAE$ are vertical angles.	○ True ○ False
D. $\angle CAB$ and $\angle EAF$ are vertical angles.	○ True ○ False

12. $\angle C$ and $\angle D$ are complementary. The measure of $\angle D$ is 48°. Circle the number that makes the statement true.

The measure of $\angle C$ is
> 41
>
> 42
>
> 47
>
> 48

°.

13. Select True or False for each statement.

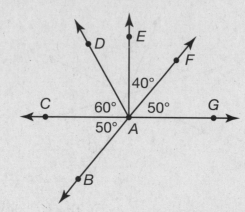

A. m∠*DAE* is 30°.	○ True ○ False
B. m∠*DAE* is 40°.	○ True ○ False
C. ∠*GAF* and ∠*FAE* are supplementary angles.	○ True ○ False
D. ∠*CAE* and ∠*EAG* are supplementary angles.	○ True ○ False
E. ∠*BAD* and ∠*DAF* are supplementary angles.	○ True ○ False

14. In the figure below, m∠*ROT* = 90°. Draw a line from each angle type to its angle pair.

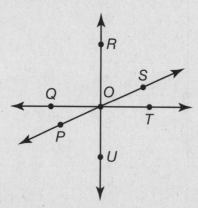

A. acute angles	•	• ∠*QOP* and ∠*SOT*
B. right angles	•	• ∠*ROT* and ∠*ROQ*
C. obtuse angles	•	• ∠*POR* and ∠*POT*
D. vertical angles	•	• ∠*SOT* and ∠*ROS*

Area

Getting the Idea

The **area** of a figure is the number of **square units** inside the figure.

Below are some formulas that can be used to find the areas of common polygons.

Formula	Diagram
Triangle $A = \frac{1}{2}bh$, where b represents the base length and h represents the height.	
Parallelogram $A = bh$, where b represents the base length and h represents the height.	
Rectangle $A = lw$, where l represents the length and w represents the width.	
Square $A = s^2$, where s represents the length of a side.	
Trapezoid $A = \frac{1}{2}(b_1 + b_2)h$, where b_1 and b_2 represent the base lengths and h represents the height.	

Example 1

What is the area of this trapezoid?

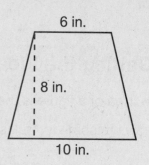

Strategy   **Use the formula for the area of a trapezoid.**

Step 1   Write the formula for the area of a trapezoid.

$$A = \frac{1}{2}(b_1 + b_2)h$$

Step 2   Substitute the known values in the formula and simplify.

Let $b_1 = 10$ in. and let $b_2 = 6$ in.

$$A = \frac{1}{2}(10 \text{ in.} + 6 \text{ in.}) \times 8 \text{ in.}$$

$$= \frac{1}{2}(16 \text{ in.}) \times 8 \text{ in.}$$

$$= 8 \text{ in.} \times 8 \text{ in.} = 64 \text{ in.}^2$$

Solution   **The area of the trapezoid is 64 in.^{2}**

Example 2

Phillip drew the figure on the right to represent the design of his new garage. What is the area of the figure?

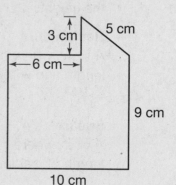

Strategy   **Divide the figure into smaller, familiar figures. Find the area of each figure. Then add to find the total area.**

Step 1   Divide the figure into familiar figures.

The figure is divided into a triangle and a rectangle.

Step 2   Find the area of the triangle.

The height, h, of the triangle is 3 cm.

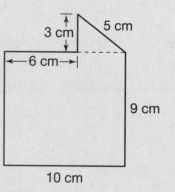

To determine the base length, subtract the two known horizontal lengths: 10 cm − 6 cm = 4.

So, the base, b, of the triangle is 4 cm.

A of triangle $= \frac{1}{2}bh$

$$= \frac{1}{2} \times 4 \times 3 = 6 \text{ cm}^2$$

Step 3   Find the area of the rectangle.

The length, l, is 10 cm, and the width, w, is 9 cm.

A of rectangle $= lw$

$$= 10 \times 9 = 90 \text{ cm}^2$$

Step 4   Add those areas to find the total area of the figure.

A of composite figure = 6 + 90 = 96 cm^2

Solution   **The area of the figure is 96 square centimeters.**

Example 3

Jen is making a bracelet and needs beading for the front as shown in the diagram below. Jen has enough beads for 10 square inches. Is that enough?

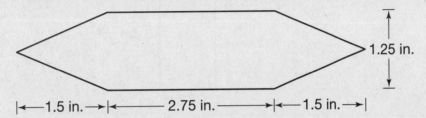

|←—1.5 in.—→|←———— 2.75 in. ————→|←—1.5 in.—→| 1.25 in.

Strategy   **Divide the figure into shapes whose area formulas you know.**

Step 1   Divide the figure into 1 rectangle and 2 triangles.

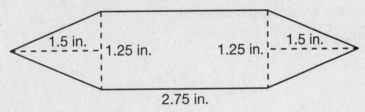

Step 2   Find the area of the rectangle.

$A = lw$

$A = 2.75 \times 1.25$

$= 3.4375$ in.^{2}

Step 3   Find the area of the 2 triangles.

$A = \frac{1}{2}bh$

$A = \frac{1}{2} \times 1.25 \times 1.5$

$= 0.9375$ in.^{2}

There are 2 triangles: 2×0.9375 in.^{2} = 1.875 in.^{2}

Step 4   Add to find the total area of the figure.

3.4375 in.^{2} + 1.875 in.^{2} = 5.3125 in.^{2}

5.3125 < 10

Solution   **Jen has enough beads for 10 square inches.**

Coached Example

Aster made a sticker in the shape shown below.

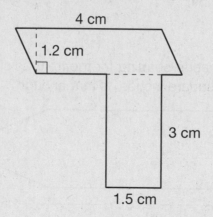

4 cm

1.2 cm

3 cm

1.5 cm

What is the area of the sticker?

A parallelogram and a _____ are combined to form the sticker.

What is the formula for the area of a parallelogram? _____

Find the area of the parallelogram.

What is the formula for the area of a rectangle? _____

Find the area of the rectangle.

Add to find the total area of the figure.

The area of the sticker is _____.

Lesson Practice • Part 1

Choose the correct answer.

1. A rectangular playground is 85 feet long and 60 feet wide. What is the area of the playground?

A. 290 ft^2 **C.** 2,550 ft^2

B. 510 ft^2 **D.** 5,100 ft^2

2. A banner is shaped like the triangle shown below.

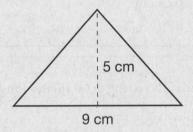

What is the area of the banner?

A. 14 cm^2 **C.** 28 cm^2

B. 22.5 cm^2 **D.** 45 cm^2

3. A window is shaped like the trapezoid shown below.

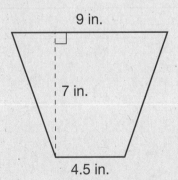

What is the area of the window?

A. 47.25 in.^{2} **C.** 141.75 in.^{2}

B. 63 in.^{2} **D.** 283.5 in.^{2}

4. Which of the figures below have the same area?

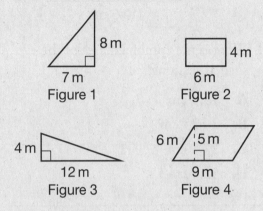

A. figures 1 and 2

B. figures 2 and 3

C. figures 2 and 4

D. figures 3 and 4

5. What is the area of a parallelogram with a base length of 12 yd and a height of 9 yd?

A. 60 yd^2

B. 90 yd^2

C. 108 yd^2

D. 120 yd^2

6. Which figure has the least area?

A. square with a side length of 9 cm

B. parallelogram with a base of 12 cm and a height of 6 cm

C. triangle with a base of 18 cm and a height of 6 cm

D. rectangle with a width of 7 cm and a length of 8 cm

7. Carl cut two triangular boards from the corners of a rectangular board as shown by the shaded sections below.

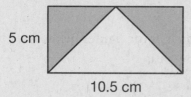

5 cm

10.5 cm

What is the combined area of the shaded sections?

A. 15.5 cm^2

B. 26.25 cm^2

C. 27.5 cm^2

D. 52.5 cm^2

8. What is the area of the figure below?

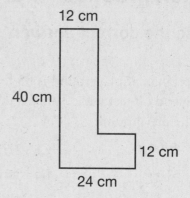

12 cm

40 cm

12 cm

24 cm

A. 960 cm^2

B. 768 cm^2

C. 624 cm^2

D. 480 cm^2

9. Ross uses nylon string as a border around a square picture. The string is 60 inches long.

A. What is the area of the picture in square inches? Show your work.

_____

_____

B. Ross doubles the length of each side of the picture. What is the area of the new square picture in square inches? Show your work.

_____

_____

_____

Lesson Practice • Part 2

Choose the correct answer.

1. What is the area of this figure?

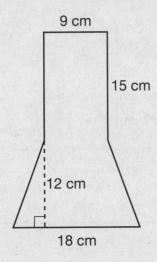

9 cm

15 cm

12 cm

18 cm

  A. 243 cm^2

  B. 297 cm^2

  C. 351 cm^2

  D. 486 cm^2

2. What is the area of this figure?

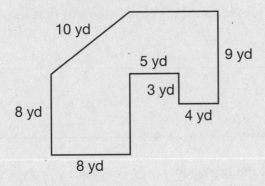

10 yd

5 yd

9 yd

3 yd

8 yd

4 yd

8 yd

  A. 210 yd^2

  B. 184 yd^2

  C. 142 yd^2

  D. 135 yd^2

3. What is the area of the figure below?

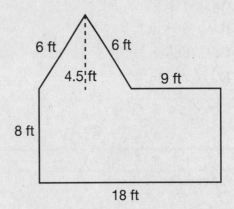

6 ft   6 ft

4.5 ft

9 ft

8 ft

18 ft

  A. 164.25 ft^2 **C.** 180 ft^2

  B. 171 ft^2 **D.** 225 ft^2

4. What is the area of the figure below?

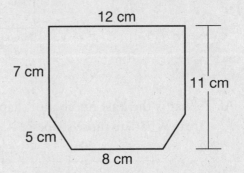

12 cm

7 cm

11 cm

5 cm

8 cm

  A. 112 cm^2 **C.** 132 cm^2

  B. 124 cm^2 **D.** 134 cm^2

5. Three rectangular tables that are each 6 feet long and 4 feet wide are placed end-to-end to form one long table. What is the area of the long table?

  A. 24 ft^2 **C.** 144 ft^2

  B. 72 ft^2 **D.** 216 ft^2

6. A rectangular poster is 32 inches long by 24 inches wide. It will be put into a rectangular frame that is 2 inches wide on all sides. What is the area of the poster when it is inside the frame?

A. 768 in.^{2}

B. 864 in.^{2}

C. 884 in.^{2}

D. 1,008 in.^{2}

7. Which is the area of this pentagon?

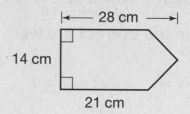

A. 245 cm^2

B. 294 cm^2

C. 343 cm^2

D. 392 cm^2

8. A heptagon is shown.

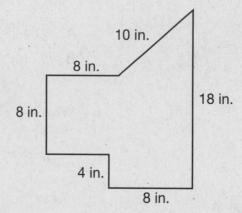

A. What is the least number of shapes that you can decompose the heptagon to find the area? What are those shapes?

_____

B. What is the area of the heptagon?

_____

C. Explain the steps you used to find the area of the heptagon.

_____

_____

_____

9. Which figure has an area of 144 square inches? Circle all that apply.

    A. triangle with base 12 inches and height 24 inches

    B. parallelogram with base 24 inches and height 6 inches

    C. rectangle with length 18 inches and width 9 inches

    D. square with side 12 inches

    E. trapezoid with bases 8 inches and 10 inches and height 8 inches

10. Use numbers from the box to make each statement true.

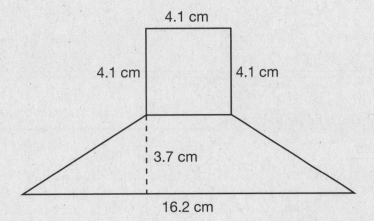

The area of the square is _____ square centimeters.

The area of the trapezoid is _____ square centimeters.

The area of the composite figure is _____ square centimeters.

16.4	37.555
16.81	39.9
54.365	56.3

11. Find the area of each polygon. Write each polygon in the correct box.

Triangle $b = 10$ m $h = 6$ m	Parallelogram $b = 14$ m $h = 10$ m	Rectangle $l = 2$ m $w = 9$ m	Square $s = 8$ m	Trapezoid $b_1 = 6$ m $b_2 = 12$ m $h = 10$ m

Area is a Multiple of 4.	Area is a Multiple of 6.

12. Draw a line from each figure to its area.

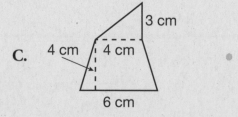

A.

●   ● 24 cm^2

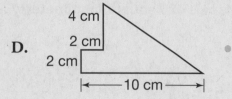

B.

●   ● 26 cm^2

C.

●   ● 27 cm^2

D.

●   ● 28 cm^2

Surface Area

Getting the Idea

The **surface area**, measured in square units, of a solid figure is the sum of the areas of all the surfaces of the figure. You can calculate the surface area of a figure by finding the areas of all of its faces and then adding them.

Looking at a two-dimensional representation, called a **net**, of a solid figure may help you do this.

If the net below is folded along the dotted lines, a rectangular prism is formed.

The surface area of the rectangular prism is the total area of the 6 rectangular faces. The formula for the surface area of a rectangular prism is SA = 2*lw* + 2*lh* + 2*wh*, where *l* is length, *w* is width, and *h* is height.

Example 1

What is the surface area of this rectangular prism?

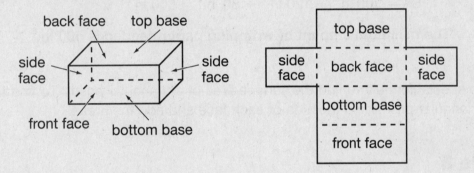

Strategy   Use the formula for the surface area of a rectangular prism.

SA = 2*lw* + 2*lh* + 2*wh*

SA = (2 × 12 cm × 9 cm) + (2 × 12 cm × 5 cm) + (2 × 9 cm × 5 cm)

SA = 216 cm^2 + 120 cm^2 + 90 cm^2 = 426 cm^2

Solution   **The surface area of the rectangular prism is 426 square centimeters.**

Example 2

Mary Jane is going to wrap a box in the shape of rectangular prism that has a length of 15 inches, a width of 10 inches, and a height of 4 inches.

What is the minimum amount of wrapping paper she will need to cover the box?

Strategy   **Find the surface area of a rectangular prism.**

Step 1   Substitute the values for the length, width, and height.

$$SA = 2lw + 2lh + 2wh$$

$$SA = (2 \times 15 \text{ in.} \times 10 \text{ in.}) + (2 \times 15 \text{ in.} \times 4 \text{ in.}) + (2 \times 10 \text{ in.} \times 4 \text{ in.})$$

Step 2   Multiply and add to find the surface area.

$$SA = 300 \text{ in.}^2 + 120 \text{ in.}^2 + 80 \text{ in.}^2 = 500 \text{ in.}^2$$

Solution   **The minimum amount of wrapping paper needed is 500 in.^{2}**

There is no special formula to find the surface area of a triangular prism. To find the surface area of a triangular prism, find the area of each face and add the areas.

Example 3

What is the surface area of this triangular prism?

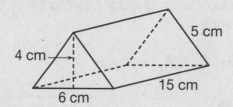

Strategy   **Use a net to find the area of each of the faces. Then add the areas.**

Step 1   Make a net of the triangular prism.

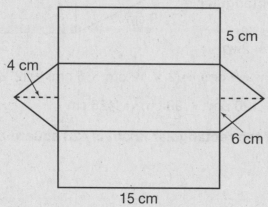

Step 2   Find the area of each of the triangles using the formula $A = \frac{1}{2}bh$.

$A = \frac{1}{2} \times 6 \text{ cm} \times 4 \text{ cm} = 12 \text{ cm}^2$

There are two triangles, so the area of the triangles is $2 \times 12 \text{ cm}^2 = 24 \text{ cm}^2$.

Step 3   Find the area of each of the rectangles using the formula $A = lw$.

Top: $A = 15 \text{ cm} \times 5 \text{ cm} = 75 \text{ cm}^2$

Middle: $A = 15 \text{ cm} \times 6 \text{ cm} = 90 \text{ cm}^2$

Bottom: $A = 15 \text{ cm} \times 5 \text{ cm} = 75 \text{ cm}^2$

Step 4   Add the areas.

$24 \text{ cm}^2 + 75 \text{ cm}^2 + 90 \text{ cm}^2 + 75 \text{ cm}^2 = 264 \text{ cm}^2$

Solution   **The surface area of the triangular prism is 264 square centimeters.**

Coached Example

A toymaker will paint four sides of this toy chest. He will not paint the bottom or top surface. How many square feet of the chest will the toymaker paint?

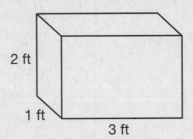

2 ft

1 ft

3 ft

You only need to find the areas of the surfaces that will be painted.

The front and back faces are rectangles that are 3 ft long and _____ ft high.

   A of front face $= lw = 3 \times$ _____ $=$ _____ ft^2

   The area of the back face is also _____ ft^2.

The left and right side faces are rectangles that are 1 ft long and _____ ft high.

   A of left side face $= lw = 1 \times$ _____ $=$ _____

   The area of the right side face is also _____ ft^2.

Add the areas of all four faces: _____ + _____ + _____ + _____ = _____

The toymaker will paint _____ square feet of the toy chest.

Lesson Practice • Part 1

Choose the correct answer.

1. Hermione made a jewelry box shaped like the rectangular prism below. What is the surface area of the jewelry box?

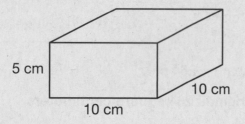

5 cm

10 cm

10 cm

A. 400 cm^2

B. 300 cm^2

C. 200 cm^2

D. 100 cm^2

2. What is the surface area of a cube with 1-inch sides?

A. 36 in.^{2}

B. 24 in.^{2}

C. 6 in.^{2}

D. 4 in.^{2}

3. What is the surface area of the rectangular prism below?

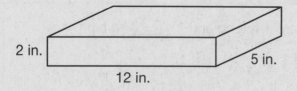

2 in.

5 in.

12 in.

A. 68 in.^{2}

B. 94 in.^{2}

C. 188 in.^{2}

D. 376 in.^{2}

4. What is the surface area of the cube below?

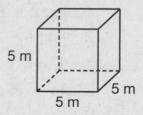

5 m

5 m

5 m

A. 30 m^2

B. 75 m^2

C. 125 m^2

D. 150 m^2

5. Alexis is designing a storage chest shaped like a rectangular prism. The storage chest is 6 feet long, 2 feet wide, and 3 feet high. What is the surface area of the storage chest?

A. 18 ft^2 C. 36 ft^2

B. 24 ft^2 D. 72 ft^2

6. What is the surface area of this triangular prism?

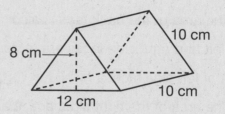

8 cm

10 cm

12 cm

10 cm

A. 416 cm^2

B. 368 cm^2

C. 296 cm^2

D. 208 cm^2

7. Davindra made a paper box that is 8 in. long, 5 in. wide, and 1 in. high. It is shaped like a rectangular prism. What is the surface area of the box?

A. 120 in.^{2}

B. 106 in.^{2}

C. 80 in.^{2}

D. 44 in.^{2}

8. A cube has a surface area of 24 ft^2. What is the length of one edge of the cube?

A. 6 ft

B. 4 ft

C. 2 ft

D. 1 ft

9. Ronnie wants to wrap the boxes below with wrapping paper.

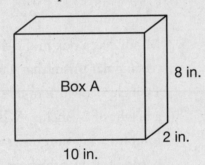
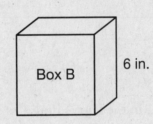

A. What is the surface area of Box A? Show your work.

_____

_____

_____

B. What is the surface area of Box B, which is a cube? Show your work.

_____

_____

_____

Lesson Practice • Part 2

Choose the correct answer.

1. A fish tank in the shape of a rectangular prism has a length of $3\frac{1}{2}$ feet, a width of 2 feet and a height of $2\frac{1}{2}$ feet. What is the surface area of the fish tank?

   A. $17\frac{1}{2}$ ft^2

   B. $20\frac{1}{4}$ ft^2

   C. 35 ft^2

   D. $41\frac{1}{2}$ ft^2

2. The basement in the Petry's house is shaped like a rectangular prism that is 28 feet long, 16 feet wide, and 8 feet high. They are going to paint everything but the floor. What is the area that will need to be painted?

   A. 1,152 ft^2 **C.** 1,472 ft^2

   B. 1,376 ft^2 **D.** 1,600 ft^2

3. What is the surface area of the triangular prism below?

   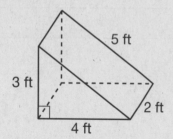

   A. 30 ft^2 **C.** 48 ft^2

   B. 36 ft^2 **D.** 60 ft^2

4. What is the surface area of a cube that has edges that measure 15 centimeters?

   A. 225 cm^2

   B. 675 cm^2

   C. 1,350 cm^2

   D. 3,375 cm^2

5. Mindy has a box in the shape of a rectangular prism that has a length of 14 inches, a width of 8 inches, and a height of $2\frac{1}{2}$ inches. What is the minimum amount of wrapping paper needed to cover the box?

   A. 167 in.^{2}

   B. 280 in.^{2}

   C. 334 in.^{2}

   D. 560 in.^{2}

6. What is the surface area of this triangular prism?

   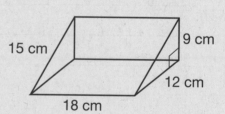

   A. 864 cm^2

   B. 756 cm^2

   C. 666 cm^2

   D. 594 cm^2

7. A closet in the shape of a rectangular prism is $6\frac{1}{2}$ feet long, 3 feet wide, and 8 feet high. There is paneling that needs to be removed from the closet. There is no paneling on the ceiling or floor. How much paneling needs to be removed?

A. 152 ft^2 **C.** $171\frac{1}{2}$ ft^2

B. 156 ft^2 **D.** 191 ft^2

8. A cube has edges of 16 centimeters. The cube is cut vertically into equal halves. What is the surface area of each half?

A. 256 cm^2

B. 384 cm^2

C. 768 cm^2

D. 1,536 cm^2

9. A composite figure is shown.

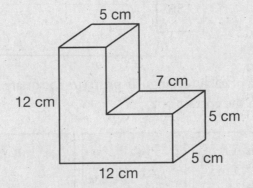

5 cm

7 cm

12 cm

5 cm

5 cm

12 cm

A. What is the surface area of the composite figure?

_____

B. Explain the steps you used to find the surface area of the composite figure.

_____

_____

_____

10. Falak has a ramp that is in the shape of a triangular prism as shown below. Circle the number that makes the statement true.

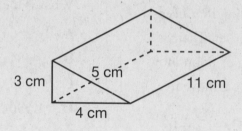

The surface area of this ramp is | 133 / 144 / 156 | square centimeters.

11. Compare the surface area of each rectangular prism to 75 square meters. Write the name of each rectangular prism in the correct box.

Prism A	Prism B	Prism C	Prism D	Prism E
$l = 2$ m	$l = 3$ m	$l = 3$ m	$l = 2$ m	$l = 6$ m
$w = 4$ m	$w = 4$ m	$w = 5$ m	$w = 2$ m	$w = 2$ m
$h = 5$ m	$h = 4$ m	$h = 3$ m	$h = 7$ m	$h = 3$ m

Surface Area < 75 m²	Surface Area > 75 m²

12. Which figure has a surface area greater than 240 meters? Circle all that apply.

   A. cube with side 8 meters

   B. rectangular prism with length 9 meters, width 3 meters, and height 8 meters

   C. rectangular prism with length 9 meters, width 4 meters, and height 6 meters

   D. cube with side 6 meters

   E. rectangular prism with length 10 meters, width 3 meters, and height 7 meters

13. Look at each description of a rectangular prism and a cube. Is the surface area of the rectangular prism greater than the surface area of the cube? Select Yes or No.

   A. rectangular prism: $l = 5$ meters, $w = 9$ meters,   ◯ Yes ◯ No
      $h = 8$ meters;
      cube: $s = 7$ meters

   B. rectangular prism: $l = 7$ meters, $w = 6$ meters,   ◯ Yes ◯ No
      $h = 5$ meters;
      cube: $s = 6$ meters

   C. rectangular prism: $l = 4$ meters, $w = 6$ meters,   ◯ Yes ◯ No
      $h = 4$ meters;
      cube: $s = 5$ meters

   D. rectangular prism: $l = 3$ meters, $w = 5$ meters,   ◯ Yes ◯ No
      $h = 6$ meters;
      cube: $s = 4$ meters

14. Use numbers from the box to make each statement true.

The surface area of a rectangular prism with length
2 centimeters, width 2 centimeters, and height 1 centimeter
is _____ square centimeters.

The surface area of a rectangular prism with length
2 centimeters, width 2 centimeters, and height 3 centimeters
is _____ square centimeters.

16	40
24	48
32	56

The surface area of a rectangular prism with length
2 centimeters, width 2 centimeters, and height 6 centimeters
is _____ square centimeters.

Volume

Getting the Idea

The **volume** of a solid figure is the number of **cubic units** that fit inside it. The formulas below can be used to calculate the volume of a rectangular prism and a cube.

> **Rectangular Prism**
> $V = lwh$, where l is the length, w is the width, and h is the height.
>
> **Cube**
> $V = e^3$, where e is the length of an edge

Example 1

A department store uses the box below for shirts.

What is the volume of the box?

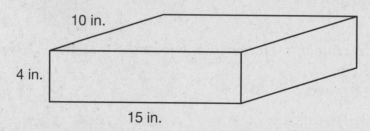

Strategy   **Use the formula for the volume of a rectangular prism.**

Step 1   The box is a rectangular prism. Write the formula for the volume.

$V = lwh$, where l is the length, w is the width, and h is the height.

Step 2   Identify the values for the variables.

The length is 15 in., the width is 10 in., and the height is 4 in.

So $l = 15$ in., $w = 10$ in., and $h = 4$ in.

Step 3   Substitute the values for the variables. Then multiply.

$V = lwh$

$V = 15$ in. $\times 10$ in. $\times 4$ in. $= 600$ in.^{3}

Solution   **The volume of the box is 600 cubic inches.**

To find the volume of a triangular prism, use the formula $V = Bh$, where B is the area of the base.

Example 2

What is the volume of this triangular prism?

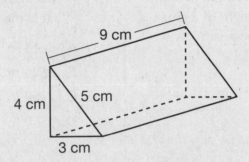

Strategy   **Use the formula for the volume of a triangular prism: $V = Bh$.**

Step 1   Find the area of the base, which is the triangle.

Use $A = \frac{1}{2}bh$.

$A = \frac{1}{2} \times 4 \text{ ft} \times 3 \text{ ft} = 6 \text{ ft}^2$

Step 2   Multiply the area of the base times the height.

$V = 6 \text{ ft}^2 \times 9 \text{ ft} = 54 \text{ ft}^3$

Solution   **The volume of the triangular prism is 54 cubic feet.**

Coached Example

Carol has a planter box that is in the shape of a cube. Each edge of the planter box measures 20 inches. What is the volume of Carol's planter box?

The formula for the volume of a cube is $V = \underline{\hspace{1.5cm}}$.

Substitute the values for the variables.

$V = \underline{\hspace{1.5cm}} \times \underline{\hspace{1.5cm}} \times \underline{\hspace{1.5cm}}$

Multiply.

$V = \underline{\hspace{1.5cm}} \text{ in.}^3$

The planter box has a volume of \underline{\hspace{3cm}} cubic inches.

Lesson Practice • Part 1

Choose the correct answer.

1. A rectangular prism has a length of 3 cm, a width of 7 cm, and a height of 2 cm. What is the volume of the prism?

   A. 21 cm^3

   B. 30 cm^3

   C. 42 cm^3

   D. 45 cm^3

2. A jewelry box is shaped like a cube. Each edge of the jewelry box measures 8 inches. What is the volume of the jewelry box?

   A. 64 cubic inches

   B. 384 cubic inches

   C. 484 cubic inches

   D. 512 cubic inches

3. What is the volume of this triangular prism?

   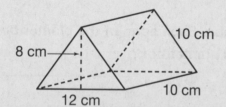

   A. 240 cm^3

   B. 320 cm^3

   C. 480 cm^3

   D. 960 cm^3

4. A cube has edge lengths of 5 meters. What is the volume of the cube?

   A. 15 m^3

   B. 125 m^3

   C. 150 m^3

   D. 750 m^3

5. Which is the volume of the fish tank below?

   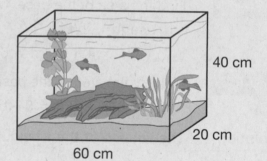

   A. 48,000 cm^3

   B. 40,000 cm^3

   C. 36,000 cm^3

   D. 18,000 cm^3

6. A salt shaker is in the shape of a cube and has edge lengths of 4 centimeters. What is the volume of the salt shaker?

   A. 8 cm^3

   B. 16 cm^3

   C. 32 cm^3

   D. 64 cm^3

7. A sandbox in the shape of a rectangular prism is 5.5 feet long, 3 feet wide, and 2 feet high. What is the volume of the sandbox?

   A. 35 ft^3

   B. 33 ft^3

   C. 30 ft^3

   D. 27 ft^3

8. A cube has a volume of 1,000 cubic inches. What is the length of an edge of the cube?

   A. 5 in.

   B. 10 in.

   C. 20 in.

   D. 100 in.

9. Jake is designing his bedroom in the shape of a rectangular prism.

His model for the bedroom is shown below.

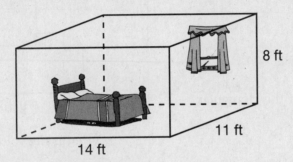

8 ft

11 ft

14 ft

   A. What will be the total volume of his bedroom? Show your work.

   B. If Jake decides to increase the width of his bedroom by 3 feet, what will be the new volume? Show your work.

Lesson Practice • Part 2

Choose the correct answer.

1. A trunk in the shape of a rectangular prism has a length of $2\frac{1}{2}$ feet, a width of $1\frac{1}{2}$ feet, and a height of 2 feet. What is the volume of the trunk?

   A. $4\frac{1}{4}$ ft^3

   B. $7\frac{1}{2}$ ft^3

   C. $11\frac{3}{4}$ ft^3

   D. $23\frac{1}{2}$ ft^3

2. What is the volume of this triangular prism?

   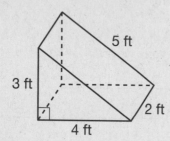

   A. 12 ft^3

   B. 24 ft^3

   C. 30 ft^3

   D. 60 ft^3

3. The dimensions of a cube have been doubled. How many times has the volume increased?

   A. 2   C. 6

   B. 3   D. 8

4. A glass display case shown below consists of three rectangular prisms. The top prism is a cube, and the middle prism is 3 inches longer than the top cube. All the prisms have the same width and height.

   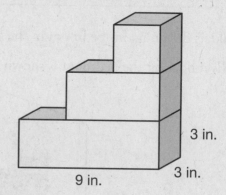

   What is the volume of the display case?

   A. 54 in.^{3}

   B. 162 in.^{3}

   C. 243 in.^{3}

   D. 324 in.^{3}

5. What is the volume of this figure?

   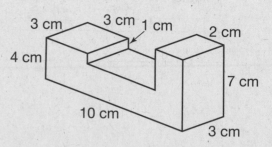

   A. 143 cm^3

   B. 132 cm^3

   C. 123 cm^3

   D. 113 cm^3

6. A cube has a volume of 512 cubic inches. What is the length of each edge?

    A. 5 in.   **C.** 7 in.

    B. 6 in.   **D.** 8 in.

7. What is the volume of this triangular prism?

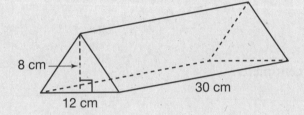

    A. 1,440 cm^3 **C.** 2,880 cm^3

    B. 1,490 cm^3 **D.** 2,980 cm^3

8. How many 2-centimeter cubes can fit inside this rectangular prism?

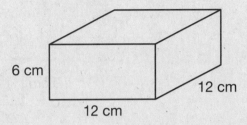

    A. 108

    B. 216

    C. 432

    D. 864

9. A composite figure is shown.

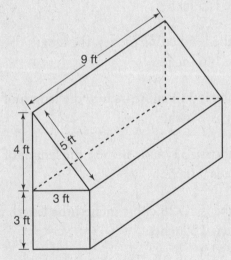

    A. What is the volume of the composite figure?

       _____

    B. Explain the steps you used to find the volume of the composite figure.

       _____

       _____

       _____

10. Hee Sun has a box that is in the shape of a triangular prism as shown below. Circle the number that makes the statement true.

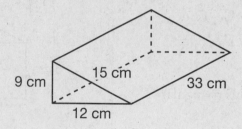

The volume of this box is
| 1,782 |
| 2,227.5 |
| 3,564 |
cubic centimeters.

11. Select True or False for each statement.

A. If the volume of a cube is 125 cubic inches, the length of each edge of the cube is 5 inches. ○ True ○ False

B. If the volume of a cube is 64 cubic inches, the length of each edge of the cube is 6 inches. ○ True ○ False

C. If the volume of a cube is 343 cubic inches, the length of each edge of the cube is 7 inches. ○ True ○ False

D. If the volume of a cube is 731 cubic inches, the length of each edge of the cube is 9 inches. ○ True ○ False

E. If the volume of a cube is 1,728 cubic inches, the length of each edge of the cube is 12 inches. ○ True ○ False

12. Which figure has a volume of 216 cubic meters? Circle all that apply.

A. rectangular prism with length 10 meters, width 3 meters, and height 7 meters

B. rectangular prism with length 9 meters, width 4 meters, and height 6 meters

C. rectangular prism with length 9 meters, width 3 meters, and height 8 meters

D. cube with edge 8 meters

E. cube with edge 6 meters

13. Use numbers from the box to make each statement true.

The volume of a rectangular prism with length
12 centimeters, width 14 centimeters, and height 3 centimeters
is _____ cubic centimeters.

The volume of a rectangular prism with length
20 centimeters, width 2 centimeters, and height 6 centimeters
is _____ cubic centimeters.

The volume of a rectangular prism with length
33 centimeters, width 16 centimeters, and height 9 centimeters
is _____ cubic centimeters.

468	2,080
504	2,400
1,872	2,880

14. Compare the volume of each rectangular prism to 40 cubic meters. Write the name of each rectangular prism in the correct box.

Prism A	Prism B	Prism C	Prism D	Prism E
$l = 6$ m	$l = 3$ m	$l = 2$ m	$l = 2$ m	$l = 3$ m
$w = 2$ m	$w = 4$ m	$w = 4$ m	$w = 2$ m	$w = 5$ m
$h = 3$ m	$h = 4$ m	$h = 5$ m	$h = 7$ m	$h = 3$ m

Volume < 40 m^3	Volume ≥ 40 m^3

Domain 4: Cumulative Assessment for Lessons 20–27

1. A pole that is 12 feet tall casts a shadow that is 9 feet long. At the same time of day, how long is the shadow cast by a tree that is 45 feet tall?

   A. 27 ft

   B. 29.25 ft

   C. 31.5 ft

   D. 33.75 ft

2. A box in the shape of a rectangular prism has a length of 9 inches, a width of 8 inches, and a height 4 inches. What is the least amount of wrapping paper needed to wrap the box?

   A. 288 in.^{2}

   B. 280 in.^{2}

   C. 144 in.^{2}

   D. 140 in.^{2}

3. Carson wants to construct a triangle with side lengths of 4 inches, 7 inches, and 12 inches. Which best describes a triangle with those side lengths?

   A. a unique, right triangle

   B. a unique, acute triangle

   C. nonexistent

   D. ambiguously defined

4. A rectangular prism is sliced by a plane that is perpendicular to its base, as shown. What is the shape of the cross section formed?

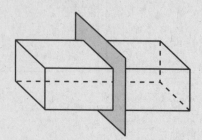

   A. trapezoid

   B. square

   C. rectangle (not a square)

   D. parallelogram (not a rectangle)

5. A circular clock has a radius of 8.5 centimeters. Which is closest to the circumference of the clock? Use 3.14 for π.

   A. 14.13 cm

   B. 26.69 cm

   C. 53.38 cm

   D. 226.87 cm

6. If m∠1 is 55° in the parallelogram below, what is the measure of its supplementary angle?

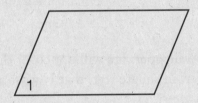

   A. 35°

   B. 45°

   C. 115°

   D. 125°

7. Brook made a scatter guard for her ferret's cage. The drawing below shows the shape of the scatter guard.

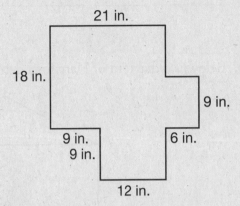

   What is the area of the scatter guard?

   A. 486 in.^{2}

   B. 540 in.^{2}

   C. 567 in.^{2}

   D. 729 in.^{2}

8. A rectangular prism has length 9 centimeters, width 6 centimeters, and height 8 centimeters. What is the volume of the rectangular prism?

   A. 432 cm^3

   B. 328 cm^3

   C. 216 cm^3

   D. 164 cm^3

9. A circular rug has a diameter of 30 inches. What is the area of the rug? Use 3.14 for π and round your answer to the nearest tenth.

_____

10. Below is a diagram of Harrison's den.

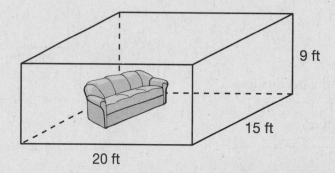

A. Harrison will cover all four walls in his den with wallpaper. He will not cover the ceiling or the floor. What is the least amount of wallpaper, in square feet, that Harrison needs? Show your work.

_____

_____

_____

B. What is the volume of the den? Show your work.

_____

_____

_____

Domain 5 Statistics and Probability

Domain 5: Diagnostic Assessment for Lessons 28–35

Domain 5: Cumulative Assessment for Lessons 28–35

Domain 5: Diagnostic Assessment for Lessons 28–35

1. Kerri conducted an experiment with a number cube. The table shows the number of times that each number landed.

Times Landed

Number	Number of Tosses
1	8
2	10
3	7
4	6
5	9
6	8

For which number below did the experimental probability equal the theoretical probability?

A. 1   **C.** 4

B. 3   **D.** 5

2. Jules wants to know which professional baseball player is most popular among the 300 students at his school. Which is the most representative and reasonable sample for him to survey?

A. data collected from a census of every student at his school

B. data collected from a sample of every student in his math class

C. data collected from a sample of every 20th student who arrives at school one day

D. data collected from a sample of every student on a school sports team

3. The box plot shows the heights of children who attend a library story time.

Children's Heights (in inches)

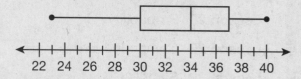

Which statement is **not** true about the data?

A. The range of the heights is 17 inches.

B. The interquartile range of the heights is 4 inches.

C. The median height of the children is 34 inches.

D. About 25% of the children are 30 inches or shorter.

4. The dot plot shows the number of miles Delia ran per week for 10 weeks. The data are a representative sample of the number of miles Delia runs throughout the year.

Number of Miles

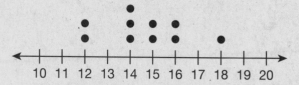

Which best represents the mean number of miles Delia runs per week throughout the year?

A. 14

B. 14.5

C. 14.6

D. 15

5. The stem-and-leaf plots show the number of DVDs sold at two different stores during one month.

Store A

Stem	Leaves
2	0 6 7 8 8 9 9
3	2 2 3 5 7 8 9
4	1 3 5 5 5 8

Key: 2 | 0 = 20 DVDs

Store B

Stem	Leaves
2	0 1 3 5 6 6
3	1 3 3 4 8 9 9
4	2 5 5 6 7 8 9

Key: 2 | 0 = 20 DVDs

Which of the following statements about the median number of DVDs sold is true?

A. The median for Store A is the same as the median for Store B.

B. The median for Store A is 1 more than the median for Store B.

C. The median for Store A is 2 less than the median for Store B.

D. The median for Store A is 3 less than the median for Store B.

---

6. Mark will roll two number cubes. What is the probability that he will roll a sum of 6?

A. $\frac{1}{36}$ **C.** $\frac{1}{6}$

B. $\frac{5}{36}$ **D.** $\frac{5}{6}$

7. Gemma practiced the piano 5 days last week. The list below shows the number of minutes she practiced each day.

20, 25, 30, 20, 30

What is the mean absolute deviation in Gemma's practice times?

A. 4 minutes

B. 8 minutes

C. 12 minutes

D. 25 minutes

8. The table shows the results of two surveys Adam took to find out how many hours of sleep seventh-grade students at his school get on a typical school night.

Sample	Data
A	5, 6, 7, 8, 8, 8, 8, 8, 9, 9
B	7, 7, 7, 7, 8, 8, 8, 8, 10, 10

Based on the sample data, which of the following is most likely to be closest to the mean number of hours of sleep seventh-grade students at Adam's school get?

A. 7 hours

B. 7.75 hours

C. 8 hours

D. 8.25 hours

9. The heights, in feet, of four trees in a citrus grove are 8, 12, 10, and 14. What is the mean absolute deviation of the heights?

_____

10. Middle school students in a school district volunteer in their community every month. The table shows the number of hours that students at one middle school volunteered for five months.

Community Hours

Month	Number of Hours
January	30
February	20
March	25
April	40
May	20

A. What is a reasonable prediction of the mean number of hours that students at the school will volunteer each month throughout the school year? Explain your thinking.

_____

_____

_____

_____

_____

B. What is a reasonable prediction of the median number of hours that students at each middle school in the school district will volunteer each month throughout the school year? Explain your thinking.

_____

_____

_____

_____

_____

Probability

Getting the Idea

Probability measures the chance of an event happening based on the number of the **possible outcomes**. Probability can be expressed as a fraction or a decimal from 0 to 1. A probability of 0 means that an event is impossible and a probability of 1 means that an event is certain. A probability close to 0 means an event is unlikely. A probability close to 1 means an event is very likely. A probability close to $\frac{1}{2}$ or 0.5 means an event is neither unlikely nor likely. You can also express a probability as a percent.

The **theoretical probability** of an event is the ratio of the number of ways the event can occur **(favorable outcome)** to the number of possible outcomes. The probability, P, of an event, A, is:

$$P(A) = \frac{\text{number of favorable outcomes}}{\text{number of possible outcomes}}.$$

Example 1

Josh is going to choose a random card from 13 cards. The cards are numbered from 1 to 13. What is the probability that he will choose a card with a number less than 4? Determine if the event is likely, unlikely, or neither.

Strategy   **Find the theoretical probability.**

Step 1   Count the number of favorable outcomes.

There are 3 cards (1, 2, 3) with a number <u>less</u> than 5.

Step 2   Count the number of possible outcomes.

There are a total of 13 cards, each with the same chance of being drawn.

Step 3   Find the theoretical probability.

$P(\text{card with a number less than 4}) = \frac{\text{number of favorable outcomes}}{\text{number of possible outcomes}} = \frac{3}{13}$

Step 4   Determine if the event is likely or unlikely.

$\frac{3}{13}$ is closer to 0 than it is to 1, and it is less than $\frac{1}{2}$. So, the event is unlikely.

Solution   **The probability of choosing a card with a number less than 4 is $\frac{3}{13}$. The event is unlikely.**

You can use theoretical probability to make a prediction. Multiply the theoretical probability by the number of **trials**, or times the experiment is performed, to predict the number of favorable outcomes.

Example 2

Peter will roll a number cube, labeled 1 through 6, a total of 90 times. What is a good prediction for the number of times that the number cube will land on 5?

Strategy **Find the number of possible outcomes and favorable outcomes.**

Step 1 Find the number of possible outcomes.

There are 6 possible outcomes for the number cube.

Step 2 Find the number of favorable outcomes.

There is one 5 on the number cube.

Step 3 Write the theoretical probability in simplest form.

$$P(\text{rolling a 5}) = \frac{\text{number of favorable outcomes}}{\text{number of possible outcomes}} = \frac{1}{6}$$

Step 4 Multiply the probability by the number of trials.

$$\frac{1}{6} \times 90 = 90 \div 6 = 15$$

Solution **A good prediction is that Peter will roll a 5 about fifteen times.**

Experimental probability is the ratio of the total number of times the favorable outcome happens to the total number of trials, or times the experiment is performed. The experimental probability, P_e, of event A is:

$$P_e(A) = \frac{\text{number of favorable outcomes}}{\text{total number of trials}}.$$

Experimental probability is useful when you need to make predictions about an event. As the number of trials increases, the experimental probability gets closer to the theoretical probability.

Example 3

Minnie conducted an experiment with a spinner. The results are shown in the table.

Number	1	2	3	4	5	6
Times Landed	10	7	6	8	5	6

Based on the data, what is the probability that the spinner will land on 2 on the next spin?

Strategy **Find the experimental probability.**

Step 1 Find the number of trials.

$$10 + 7 + 6 + 8 + 5 + 6 = 42$$

Step 2 Find the number of favorable outcomes.

The spinner landed on 2 a total of 7 times.

Step 3 Write the experimental probability as a fraction in simplest form.

$$\frac{7}{42} = \frac{1}{6}$$

Solution **The experimental probability of the spinner landing on 2 on the next spin is $\frac{1}{6}$.**

Example 4

Gavin rolls a number cube, labeled 1 to 6, a total of 40 times. The number 4 is rolled 8 times. What is the experimental probability of rolling a 4? What is the theoretical probability? Describe the difference between the two.

Strategy **Use the formulas for experimental probability and theoretical probability.**

Step 1 Find the experimental probability.

The total number of trials is 40.

The number 4 is rolled 8 times, so the number of favorable outcomes is 8.

$$P_e(4) = \frac{\text{number of favorable outcomes}}{\text{total number of trials}} = \frac{8}{40} = \frac{1}{5}$$

Step 2 Find the theoretical probability.

The number of possible outcomes is 6.

There is only one 4 on a number cube, so the number of favorable outcomes is 1.

$$P_e(4) = \frac{\text{number of favorable outcomes}}{\text{number of possible outcomes}} = \frac{1}{6}$$

Step 3 Compare the experimental probability and the theoretical probability.

The experimental probability is $\frac{1}{5}$, and the theoretical probability is $\frac{1}{6}$.

The theoretical probability shows the outcome you would expect.

The experimental probability shows the outcome that actually occurred during the experiment.

Solution **The experimental probability of rolling a 4 is $\frac{1}{5}$. This is greater than the theoretical probability of $\frac{1}{6}$.**

Coached Example

The Skate Pro Company manufactures skateboards. They found 12 defective skateboards in a batch of 400. How many defective skateboards might they find in a batch of 1,200?

Find the experimental probability of a defective skateboard in simplest form.

There were ___12___ defective skateboards in a batch of ___400___.

Write the probability and express it in simplest form.

P(defective skateboard) = $\dfrac{12}{400}$ = $\dfrac{3}{100}$

Express the probability as a decimal. ___0.03___

Multiply the probability by 1,200.

1,200 × ___0.03___ = ___36___

The Skate Pro Company might expect to find ___36___ defective skateboards in a batch of 1,200.

Lesson Practice • Part 1

Choose the correct answer.

Use the following event for questions 1 and 2.

Dan rolled a number cube 20 times. The cube landed on the number 3 six times.

1. What is the experimental probability that Dan will roll a number 3 the next time he rolls the number cube?

   A. $\frac{3}{10}$

   B. $\frac{2}{5}$

   C. $\frac{3}{5}$

   D. $\frac{7}{10}$

2. Which best describes what would likely happen if Dan rolled the number cube another 80 times?

   A. There would be no change.

   B. The experimental probability would get farther from the theoretical probability.

   C. The experimental probability would exactly match the theoretical probability.

   D. The experimental probability would get closer to the theoretical probability.

3. Sonya wrote each letter of LEDBETTER on a separate index card and put the cards in a box. She picked one letter at random, put the card back, and then repeated the experiment. If she performed this experiment 90 times, which is the best prediction for the number of times that Sonya would pick a T?

   A. 10

   B. 20

   C. 25

   D. 30

4. A lightbulb manufacturer found that out of 200 lightbulbs, 15 were defective. How many lightbulbs should the manufacturer expect to be defective out of 2,400 lightbulbs?

   A. 40

   B. 80

   C. 120

   D. 180

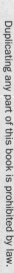

5. Shia conducted an experiment with a spinner. The results are shown in the table below.

Number	1	2	3	4
Times Landed	8	4	5	3

Based on this data, how many times can Shia expect to spin a 1 in the next 20 spins?

A. 8

B. 7

C. 5

D. 3

6. There are 12 girls and 8 boys in Ms. Sander's class. Each day, she randomly asks one student to take attendance. In 180 school days, which is the best prediction for the number of times that the student will be a girl?

A. 72

B. 90

C. 99

D. 108

7. Blake tossed a coin 80 times. The coin landed on heads 60 times.

A. What is the experimental probability that Blake will toss heads? Show your work.

_____

_____

B. Is the experimental probability greater than or less than the theoretical probability? Explain your thinking.

_____

_____

_____

Lesson Practice • Part 2

Choose the correct answer.

1. Which describes the probability of tossing a number less than 6 on a number cube with faces labeled 1–6?

   A. impossible   C. likely

   B. unlikely   D. certain

2. There are 12 boys and 15 girls in Mr. Fraioli's math class. He will randomly call on one person to answer the problem of the day. What is the probability that he will choose a girl?

   A. $\frac{1}{5}$ C. $\frac{5}{9}$

   B. $\frac{4}{9}$ D. $\frac{4}{5}$

3. Katie and Drew are going to play a game of luck 5 times. Which best represents how to find who will win more games before they start playing?

   A. toss a coin once and let heads represent Katie and tails represent Drew

   B. toss a number cube with faces labeled 1–6 and let the prime numbers represent Katie and the composite numbers represent Drew

   C. use a spinner divided into fifths labeled 1–5 and let the even numbers represent Katie and the odd numbers represent Drew

   D. toss a coin five times and let heads represent Katie and tails represent Drew

Use this information for questions 4 and 5.

Murray has tossed a coin 120 times. The coin landed on heads 54 times.

4. What is the theoretical probability that the coin will land on heads on the next toss?

   A. $\frac{9}{20}$

   B. $\frac{1}{2}$

   C. $\frac{11}{20}$

   D. $\frac{3}{4}$

5. What is the experimental probability that the coin will land on heads on the next toss?

   A. $\frac{9}{20}$

   B. $\frac{1}{2}$

   C. $\frac{11}{20}$

   D. $\frac{3}{4}$

6. In a spot check of cartons of eggs, Matilda found that 6 out of 200 eggs were cracked. If the store has 3,000 eggs for sale, how many can expect to be cracked?

   A. 60   C. 600

   B. 90   D. 900

7. Mya practiced her penalty kicks with her brother as the goalie. The table shows the results of Mya's attempts.

Penalty Kick Attempts

Result	Frequency
Goal	22
Goalie Save	8
Missed Wide	6
Overshot Goal	4

Based on this data, how many goals can Mya expect to score if she takes 200 penalty kicks?

A. 90   **C.** 110

B. 100   **D.** 120

8. Eva tossed a number cube with faces labeled 1–6 a total of 150 times. The number 6 landed 22 times. Which sentence is true?

A. The experimental probability exceeded the theoretical probability.

B. The number 6 landed less often than any of the other numbers.

C. The number 6 landed more often than any of the other numbers.

D. The theoretical probability exceeded the experimental probability.

9. Yesica conducted an experiment with a spinner.

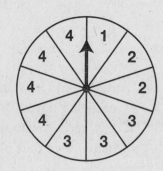

A. What is the theoretical probability of the spinner landing on 3? Write your answer as a fraction in simplest form.

_____

B. If Yesica were to spin the spinner 80 times, how many times can she expect 2 to land? Explain your thinking.

_____

_____

_____

C. Suppose Yesica spun the spinner 80 times and 4 landed 40 times. Is the experimental probability greater than or less than the theoretical probability? Explain your thinking.

_____

_____

10. A random card is chosen from cards that are numbered from 1 to 20. Which probability is unlikely? Circle all that apply.

   A. the card chosen is 1

   B. the card chosen is a composite number

   C. the card chosen is an even number

   D. the card chosen is a multiple of 7

   E. the card chosen is divisible by 6

11. Evelyn rolls a number cube, labeled 1 through 6. Write each probability of an event in the correct box.

P(rolling a 1)	P(rolling a prime number)	P(rolling a number > 1)	P(rolling a number > 5)	P(rolling an even number)

Unlikely	**Neither Unlikely Nor Likely**	**Likely**

12. William wrote each letter of INSTITUTION on a separate index card and put the cards in a box. He picked one letter at random, put the card back, and then repeated the experiment. Circle the number that makes the statement true.

If William performed this experiment 110 times, the best prediction for the number of times that he would pick an I is

11
30
33

.

13. Sam conducted an experiment with a spinner. The results are shown in the table. Draw a line from each experimental probability to its value.

Color	Red	White	Blue	Green	Yellow	Orange
Times Landed	24	30	23	25	21	27

A. P(land on Red) •

• $\dfrac{1}{5}$

B. P(land on Yellow) •

• $\dfrac{9}{50}$

C. P(land on Orange) •

• $\dfrac{7}{50}$

D. P(land on White) •

• $\dfrac{4}{25}$

14. A ping-pong ball manufacturer found that out of 400 ping-pong balls, 25 were defective. Should the manufacturer expect each number of defective ping-pong balls given the number made? Select Yes or No.

A. 5 defective out of 80 made   ○ Yes   ○ No

B. 15 defective out of 250 made   ○ Yes   ○ No

C. 35 defective out of 600 made   ○ Yes   ○ No

D. 45 defective out of 720 made   ○ Yes   ○ No

E. 60 defective out of 960 made   ○ Yes   ○ No

15. Courtney rolled a number cube, labeled 1 to 6, a total of 80 times. The number 2 was rolled 18 times. Use an item from the box to make each statement true.

The experimental probability of rolling 2 was _____.

The theoretical probability of rolling 2 was _____.

The experimental probability was _____ than the theoretical probability.

$\dfrac{1}{7}$ $\dfrac{7}{120}$

$\dfrac{1}{6}$ less

$\dfrac{9}{40}$ greater

Compound Events

Getting the Idea

A **compound event** is a combination of two or more events. Compound events can be dependent or independent. **Independent events** are two events in which the occurrence of the first event does not affect the probability of the occurrence of the second event. **Dependent events** are when the first event affects the outcome of the second event.

To find the probability of two independent events, multiply the probability of the first event by the probability of the second event.

P(two independent events) = P(first event) × P(second event)

Example 1

Adriana tosses a number cube with faces numbered 1 through 6 and spins the spinner shown below at the same time.

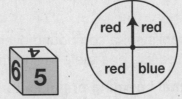

What is the probability of tossing a number greater than 2 on the cube and spinning red on the spinner?

Strategy   **Find the probability of each event and multiply them together.**

Step 1   Find the probability of the number cube landing on a number greater than 2.

A number cube has 6 possible outcomes.

Four outcomes (3, 4, 5, 6) are greater than 2.

$P(>2) = \dfrac{\text{number of favorable outcomes}}{\text{number of possible outcomes}} = \dfrac{4}{6} = \dfrac{2}{3}$

Step 2   Find the probability of spinning red on the spinner.

Three of the 4 sections are labeled "red."

$P(\text{red}) = \dfrac{\text{number of favorable outcomes}}{\text{number of possible outcomes}} = \dfrac{3}{4}$

Step 3   Multiply the two probabilities.

$\dfrac{2}{3} \times \dfrac{3}{4} = \dfrac{6}{12} = \dfrac{1}{2}$

Solution   **The probability of the cube landing on a number greater than 2 and the spinner landing on red is $\frac{1}{2}$.**

Example 2

Carlos has 3 comedies, 2 dramas, 2 concerts, and 1 horror movie in a DVD booklet. He will pick two DVDs from the booklet to play. What is the probability of Carlos picking a comedy DVD and then a drama DVD?

Strategy   **Find the probability of each event and multiply.**

Step 1   Find the probability of picking a comedy DVD.

$$P(\text{comedy}) = \frac{3}{3 + 2 + 2 + 1} = \frac{3}{8}$$

Step 2   Find the probability of picking a drama DVD second.

There is now 1 less DVD to pick.

$$P(\text{drama}) = \frac{2}{7}$$

Step 3   Multiply the probabilities.

$$\frac{3}{\overset{}{\underset{4}{8}}} \times \frac{\overset{1}{2}}{7} = \frac{3}{28}$$

Solution   **The probability of picking a comedy DVD and then a drama DVD is $\frac{3}{28}$.**

When you need to find the probability of a compound event, sometimes it is necessary to make a tree diagram, an organized list, or a table to find the number of possible outcomes.

You can also use the **fundamental counting principle** to find the number of possible outcomes. If event A can occur in m ways and event B can occur in n ways, then events A and B can occur in $m \times n$ ways.

Example 3

Cara is are going to order the lunch special that consists of a sandwich, soup, and dessert for Emma and herself. The choices are shown below.

Sandwich	Soup	Dessert
Grilled Cheese	Split Pea	Ice Cream
Roast Beef	Chicken Noodle	Fruit
Turkey		

Emma does not like chicken and turkey, but Cara does not know that. What is the probability that Emma will avoid turkey and chicken in her lunch?

Strategy   **Make an organized list of the possible outcomes.**

Step 1   List the possible outcomes. Represent each food or beverage by using its first letter.

G-S-I, G-S-F, G-C-I, G-C-F

R-S-I, R-S-F, R-C-I, R-C-F

T-S-I, T-S-F, T-C-I, T-C-F

Step 2   Use the fundamental counting principle to check the number of possible outcomes.

$3 \times 2 \times 2 = 12$

Step 3   Find the combinations that do not include turkey (T) or chicken noodle soup (C).

G-S-I, G-S-F, G-C-I, G-C-F

R-S-I, R-S-F, R-C-I, R-C-F

T-S-I, T-S-F, T-C-I, T-C-F

Step 4   Write the probability.

$\frac{4}{12} = \frac{1}{3}$

Solution   **The probability of Emma avoiding chicken and turkey in her lunch is $\frac{1}{3}$.**

A **simulation** is a way of acting out a problem by conducting experiments. The outcomes of a simulation are comparable to, but not the same as, what the actual outcomes would be. One way to conduct a simulation is to use random numbers. Random numbers can be generated by a computer or a random number table.

Example 4

Marco his shooting 70% at the free throw line. Conduct a simulation to find the probability that he will make at least one of his next two free throws.

Strategy	**Use a random number table.**

Step 1 Set up your rules.

Since Marco is a 70% free throw shooter let 7 of the digits represent a made shot and 3 of the digits a missed shot.

Let 0-6 represent a made shot and 7–9 represent a missed shot.

Step 2 Use a random number generator. Try the first 20 digits.

46398803548565510177

Step 3 Break the random digits into twos.

If at least one of the two numbers is less than 7, then Marco made at least one of his shots.

46 39 88 **03 54 85 65 51 01** 77

In $\frac{8}{10}$ of the sets, Marco made at least one of the two free throws.

Solution **The simulation states the probability of Marco making at least one of his next two free throws is $\frac{4}{5}$ or 80%.**

Coached Example

Chris tosses two number cubes labeled 1 to 6. What is the probability of rolling double 4s?

Use the fundamental counting principle to find the number of outcomes.

How many faces does a number cube have? _____

How many possible outcomes are there for a number cube to land? _____

To find the number of possible outcomes, multiply _____ × _____ = _____.

There are _____ possible outcomes.

How many different ways are there to toss doubles 4s? _____

What is the probability of rolling double 4s? _____

The probability of rolling double 4s is _____.

Lesson Practice • Part 1

Choose the correct answer.

Use the spinners below for questions 1 and 2.

 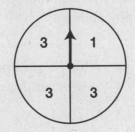

1. What is the probability of spinning a 3 on both of the spinners?

   A. 0.25

   B. 0.3

   C. 0.35

   D. 0.4

2. What is the probability of spinning a sum of 4 when spinning both spinners at the same time?

   A. 20%

   B. 25%

   C. 30%

   D. 35%

3. Gabriel is doing a probability experiment. He is tossing a coin and spinning a spinner with 4 equal sections numbered from 1 through 4. How many possible outcomes are there?

   A. 2

   B. 4

   C. 6

   D. 8

4. There are 4 boys and 2 girls from the seventh grade and 3 boys and 5 girls from the eighth grade on the soccer team. Coach Hart will pick one captain from each grade. What is the probability that both captains will be girls?

   A. $\frac{5}{24}$

   B. $\frac{1}{4}$

   C. $\frac{3}{10}$

   D. $\frac{1}{2}$

Use this information for questions 5 and 6.

There are 6 forwards and 4 guards on the Tigers girls basketball team. Coach Briggs will randomly choose two captains for the next game.

5. What is the probability that both captains will be forwards?

    A. $\frac{1}{3}$

    B. $\frac{9}{25}$

    C. $\frac{5}{9}$

    D. $\frac{3}{5}$

6. What is the probability that a guard and a forward will be captains?

    A. $\frac{1}{4}$ C. $\frac{6}{25}$

    B. $\frac{4}{15}$ D. $\frac{1}{2}$

Use this information for questions 7 and 8.

Jimmy wins 60% of his air hockey games against his brother. Jimmy wants to run a simulation to determine the probability of him winning the next two games. He will use a random number table to determine the probability.

7. Which digits from 0–9 should Jimmy use to represent him winning?

    A. 0–4   C. 0–6

    B. 0–5   D. 0–7

8. These random numbers were generated.

    54 96 21 43 79 10 55 95 09 40

    Based on the simulation, what is the probability that Jimmy will win both games?

    A. 40%   C. 60%

    B. 50%   D. 70%

9. Patrick tosses a penny and a number cube, with faces numbered 1 through 6, at the same time.

    A. Are the events dependent or independent? Explain your thinking.

    _____

    _____

    B. What is the probability that the penny will land on heads and the number cube will land on a multiple of 3? Show your work.

    _____

    _____

Lesson Practice • Part 2

Choose the correct answer.

Use this information for questions 1–3.

Dilson is going to toss two number cubes each with faces labeled 1–6.

1. What is the probability of tossing a sum of 6?

   A. $\frac{1}{12}$ C. $\frac{5}{36}$

   B. $\frac{1}{9}$ D. $\frac{1}{6}$

2. What is the probability of one number cube landing on a number less than 3 and the other landing on a number greater than 5?

   A. $\frac{1}{6}$

   B. $\frac{1}{9}$

   C. $\frac{1}{12}$

   D. $\frac{1}{18}$

3. What is the probability that one number cube will land on a prime number and the other number cube will land on a composite number?

   A. $\frac{1}{6}$

   B. $\frac{1}{4}$

   C. $\frac{1}{2}$

   D. $\frac{5}{6}$

Use this information for questions 4–6.

There are 6 pop songs, 4 rock songs, 4 country songs, and 2 rap songs on Jasmine's playlist. She will randomly play a song and then randomly play another. She will not play the same song twice.

4. What is the probability of a rock song being played followed by a rap song?

   A. $\frac{1}{32}$ C. $\frac{1}{16}$

   B. $\frac{1}{30}$ D. $\frac{3}{8}$

5. What is the probability of the first two songs being pop songs?

   A. $\frac{3}{8}$ C. $\frac{1}{8}$

   B. $\frac{9}{64}$ D. $\frac{3}{32}$

6. What is the probability of picking a country song followed by a rock song?

   A. $\frac{1}{16}$

   B. $\frac{1}{15}$

   C. $\frac{1}{8}$

   D. $\frac{1}{4}$

Use this information for questions 7 and 8.

Samantha has an on base percentage of .400 on her softball team. She wants to run a simulation to determine the probability of her getting on base versus outs. She will use a random number table to determine the probability.

7. Which digits from 0–9 should Samantha use to represent her getting on base?

   A. 0–2

   B. 0–3

   C. 0–4

   D. 0–5

8. These random numbers were generated.

   3120 1810 2057 4982 4759

   2587 1510 1246 2853 7033

   Based on the simulation, what is the probability that Samantha will get on base at least twice in her next four plate appearances?

   A. 40%

   B. 50%

   C. 60%

   D. 70%

9. A bag has 4 red marbles, 4 blue marbles, and 2 green marbles. Jessie will randomly pick a marble.

   A. If Jessie randomly picks a marble, replaces the marble and then randomly picks a second marble, what is the probability that she picks a blue marble and then a green marble? Write your answer as a fraction in simplest form. Show your work.

   B. If Jessie randomly picks a marble, keeps it, and then randomly picks a second marble, what is the probability that she picks a red marble and then a blue marble? Write your answer as a fraction in simplest form. Show your work.

   C. Jessie wants to run a simulation of 10 trials to determine the probability of her picking at least one green marble in her next two picks. She will replace the marble after the first pick. Explain how Jessie can conduct a simulation using random digits from 0–9.

10. Tao wrote the letters of Washington's state nickname on a set of same-size cards and placed the cards into two bags as shown below. She will choose one card from each bag without looking. Select True or False for each statement.

A. The events of drawing a letter from Bag 1 and drawing a letter from Bag 2 are independent. ○ True ○ False

B. The probability of drawing an R from Bag 1 is $\frac{2}{9}$. ○ True ○ False

C. The probability of drawing a T from Bag 2 is 0.2. ○ True ○ False

D. The probability of drawing an R from Bag 1 and a T from Bag 2 is $\frac{4}{9}$. ○ True ○ False

E. The probability of drawing an E from Bag 1 and a T from Bag 2 is $\frac{8}{45}$. ○ True ○ False

11. Brian tossed 4 pennies. Circle the number that makes the statement true.

The probability that all 4 pennies landed on tails is
$$\frac{1}{16}$$
$$\frac{1}{8}$$
$$\frac{1}{4}$$
$$\frac{1}{2}$$
.

12. Is the number of possible outcomes for each experiment correct? Select Yes or No.

A. tossing two coins and a number cube labeled 1 through 6; number of possible outcomes = 24 ○ Yes ○ No

B. tossing three number cubes labeled 1 through 6; number of possible outcomes = 216 ○ Yes ○ No

C. tossing two coins and two number cubes labeled 1 through 6; number of possible outcomes = 144 ○ Yes ○ No

D. tossing a coin and spinning a spinner with 3 equal sections numbered 1 through 3; number of possible outcomes = 9 ○ Yes ○ No

E. tossing three coins; number of possible outcomes = 16 ○ Yes ○ No

13. Find P(2 on both spinners) for each set of spinners. Draw a line from each set of spinners to its value.

A. • • $\dfrac{9}{20}$

B. 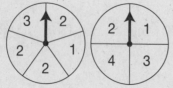 • • $\dfrac{3}{20}$

C. 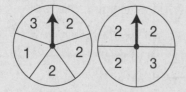 • • $\dfrac{2}{5}$

D. 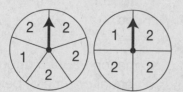 • • $\dfrac{3}{5}$

Samples

Getting the Idea

Statistics can be used to make generalizations about a population. A **population** is the group of interest. It is usually not possible to gather data from each member of a population, so the generalizations are often based upon a sample. A **sample** is a smaller group taken from the population.

Samples allow researchers to save time and money when gathering information. Samples are only useful if they are representative of the population. A **representative sample** is a portion of the population that is similar to the entire population. A **biased sample** is one in which some members of the population have a greater chance of being selected for the sample than other members. Because of bias, the sample does not fairly represent the population.

One way to gather information is by surveying the members of the sample. A **survey** is a question or set of questions used to gather **data**, or pieces of information. A survey can also be biased.

Example 1

Reggie thinks that more students in his school are right-handed than left-handed. He surveys the students in his class and finds that 23 of the 27 students are right-handed. Do the results of Reggie's survey support his inference that more students in his school are right-handed than left-handed?

Strategy   **Use the definition of a representative sample to evaluate Reggie's sample.**

A sample should be representative of the population.

The population being studied is the students in Reggie's school.

The students in Reggie's class are representative of all students in his school.

More students in his class are right-handed than left-handed.

The results of the survey support his inference.

Solution   **The results of Reggie's survey support his inference that more students in his school are right-handed than left-handed.**

Random samples are usually preferred when gathering information about a population. In a random sample, each individual in the population has an equal chance of being part of the sample.

Example 2

Collin asked every eighth student entering the school which of four subjects was his or her favorite. Can the results of Collin's survey be used to draw inferences about students' favorite subjects at the school?

Strategy   **Decide if the sample is representative and the survey is unbiased.**

Step 1   Decide if the sample is a random sample.

In a random sample, each individual in the population has the same chance of being part of the sample. Each student entering the school has the same chance of being one of every eight students entering the school.

Step 2   Decide if the sample is representative of the population.

The students in the school are the population.

The random sample is representative of the school population.

Step 3   Decide if the survey is biased.

The results are only representative of the four subjects included in the survey. It is biased toward these four subjects since other subjects are not included. The results can only be used to draw inferences about student preferences for the four subjects included in the survey.

Solution   **The results of Collin's survey can be used to draw inferences about student preferences for the four subjects included in the survey.**

You can use the results of a survey to make predictions about a population.

Example 3

The table below shows the results of Collin's survey from Example 2.

Favorite Subject

Subject	Number of Students
Math	15
Science	20
Language Arts	10
Social Studies	5

There are 400 students at Collin's school. How many students would you predict prefer language arts?

Strategy   **Write and solve a proportion.**

Step 1   Add to find the total number of students Collin surveyed.

15 + 20 + 10 + 5 = 50

Step 2   Write a proportion.

Have each ratio show the number of students who prefer language arts to the total number of students. Let x represent all of the students at the school who prefer language arts.

$$\frac{10}{50} = \frac{x}{400}$$

Step 3   Cross multiply and solve for x.

$$\frac{10}{50} = \frac{x}{400}$$
$$10 \times 400 = 50 \times x$$
$$4{,}000 = 50x$$
$$x = 80$$

Solution   **Out of 400 students, 80 students would probably say they prefer language arts.**

Example 4

Which two of the following samples are **not** good samples? Explain why.

    A. Every third shopper at a clothing store is asked whether he or she owns a pet.

    B. Every third shopper at a pet store is asked whether he or she owns a pet.

    C. At the beach in the summer, 150 people are asked to name their favorite vacation spot.

    D. A survey is mailed to 50 homes in a neighborhood, asking residents to name their favorite vacation spot.

Strategy   **Read each sample description and decide whether it is random or biased.**

Step 1   In sample A, people shopping for clothes are chosen randomly to answer a question about pets, so this is a representative sample.

Step 2   Sample B is a biased sample. It is likely that most people who enter a pet store go there to purchase something for their pet.

Step 3   Sample C is biased since these people are probably already at a vacation spot.

Step 4   For sample D, the survey is randomly mailed to people in the neighborhood. The random sample is representative of the people in the neighborhood.

Solution   **Samples B and C are not good samples because each sample is biased.**

The greater the number of participants in a survey, the closer the predictions will be to the actual choices of the population.

Example 5

Tory and Flavia each surveyed students in their school about how they would vote for the student council representative from the seventh grade. Tory surveyed the students in her homeroom. Flavia randomly surveyed 10 students from each of the five seventh-grade homeroom classes. Their results are shown in the tables below.

Tory's Results

Candidate	Number of Students
Timothy	8
Andrew	9
Lea	7

Flavia's Results

Candidate	Number of Students
Timothy	14
Andrew	21
Lea	15

Use their results to predict the winner of the election.

Step 1 Identify the population.

The population is the seventh graders at the school.

Step 2 Decide if the samples are representative samples.

Both samples appear to be representative samples.

Step 3 Compare the data in the tables.

In both tables, Andrew has the greatest number of votes.

Step 4 Use the results to predict the winner.

It appears likely that Andrew will win the election.

Notice that Andrew has a bigger lead in Flavia's table than in Tory's.

Since Flavia's sample size is greater than Tory's, her results make it seem more likely that Andrew will win than Tory's table. Her results also predict that Andrew will win by a larger margin than Tory's results.

Solution **From the survey results, Andrew is the predicted winner.**

Coached Example

Victoria randomly surveyed every tenth student who came to school on Monday. She asked each student to name his or her least favorite vegetable. The table below shows the results of her survey.

Least Favorite Vegetable

Vegetable	Number of Students
Broccoli	3
Asparagus	5
Spinach	12
Turnips	5

In a survey of 100 students at her school, how many students would you predict to choose spinach as their least favorite vegetable?

Victoria surveyed a total of _____25_____ students.

Write a proportion in which each ratio shows the number of students who chose __Spinach__ as their least favorite vegetable to the ___total___ number of students.

Let s equal the number of students out of 100 who would choose spinach.

Cross multiply and solve for s.

$$\frac{12}{25} = \frac{x}{100}$$

$$25x = 1200$$

$$x = 48$$

$s =$ ___48___

In a survey of 100 students, ___48___ students would probably choose spinach as their least favorite vegetable.

Lesson Practice • Part 1

Choose the correct answer.

1. Martha is planning to survey people at a water park to determine the most popular water slide at the park. Which would be the best sample for her survey to draw a valid inference?

   A. children at the park between the ages of 3 and 5

   B. children at the park between the ages of 6 and 10

   C. adults at the park between the ages of 20 and 30

   D. adults and children of all ages at the park

2. A newspaper is conducting a survey to determine which American professional baseball team is most popular. How would it most likely get a random sample that is representative of the population?

   A. by asking people at a Miami Marlins game

   B. by calling people from around the country

   C. by asking every fifth person entering the stadium at a Red Sox game

   D. by asking people at a Cincinnati Reds game

Use the information below for questions 3 and 4.

Mr. Callahan just opened a flower shop. He took a random survey of shoppers to find out their favorite flowers and recorded the results in the table below.

Favorite Flower

Type	Shoppers
Daffodil	14
Lily	10
Rose	24
Daisy	12

3. What is the size of the sample?

   A. 4

   B. 50

   C. 60

   D. 64

4. If Mr. Callahan expects to sell 150 bunches of flowers next week, which is the best prediction of how many bunches of daffodils he should have in his shop?

   A. 28

   B. 35 $\dfrac{7}{30} = \dfrac{x}{150}$

   C. 42

   D. 60

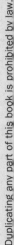

5. Which of these is **not** a random sample that would be valid to determine the favorite food of students in your school?

A. five students at a local pizza parlor

B. every sixth student on the school roster

C. every tenth student entering school in the morning

D. three students from each table in the lunchroom

6. Miko took a survey of the students in her grade to see how many are likely to join a book club if she starts one. She surveyed 48 students, and ten said they would join. If there are 240 students in her grade, how many students might Miko expect to join the club?

A. 28

B. 38

C. 48

D. 50

$$\frac{10}{48} = \frac{x}{240}$$

7. A survey asked students at a middle school which of four after-school sports they would most like to have at their school. The students who participated in the survey were randomly selected during their lunch period. The results are shown in the table below.

After-School Sports

Sport	Number of Students
Track	22
Cross-Country	15
Lacrosse	48
Tennis	15

A. Identify the population and the sample. Is the sample representative of the population? Explain your thinking.

The population is the students at the middle school, and the sample is representative of the population, since no student is more likely to get selected than any other, and the students were not in a position that would make the students any more likely to pick one of the sports.

B. If you assume that the sample is representative of the population, how many students would you predict to choose lacrosse in a school of 750 students? Is the prediction a good prediction? Explain.

I would predict 360 students would choose lacrosse, since of the 100 kids surveyed, 48 of them said they would choose lacrosse, 48%. Therefore, 48% of 750, 360, is my prediction, a good prediction since it was based on a large, unbiased, sample.

Lesson Practice • Part 2

Choose the correct answer.

Use the table for questions 1 and 2.

Students were asked in a survey whom they would vote for class president in the upcoming class elections. The table below shows the results of a randomly sampled survey of seventh-grade students.

Candidate	Room 1	Room 2	Room 3
Wallace	3	2	6
Casey	5	2	1
Whitney	2	4	2
Lisle	3	4	1

1. Based on the survey, which is the best prediction of the winner?

   A. Wallace

   B. Casey

   C. Whitney

   D. Lisle

   $\dfrac{11}{35}$

2. If there are 420 seventh-grade students at the school, how many can be expected to vote for Whitney?

   A. 24

   B. 48

   C. 72

   D. 96

   $\dfrac{8}{35} = \dfrac{x}{420}$

   $35x = 3360$

   $x = 96$

3. A news station is conducting a survey to determine the favorite summer movie of teens in its city. Which method would most likely get a random sample that is representative of the population?

   A. by asking every fifth person at a city movie theater to name his or her favorite movie

   B. by asking random teens from city schools to name their favorite movie

   C. by asking all the teens attending a current movie to name their favorite movie

   D. by calling random teens from around the country

4. Which would be the best sample for determining the favorite sport of students at Harrison Middle School?

   A. ten students at a movie theater

   B. every tenth student entering the school in the morning

   C. five students from each of the school's sports teams

   D. the first ten students in the cafeteria at lunchtime

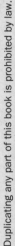

5. The seventh-grade spring class trip will either be to a zoo or an art museum. Which survey method is most likely to provide a biased sample?

   A. survey all of the seventh-grade students

   B. survey every fifth seventh-grade student that arrives at school

   C. survey 50 seventh-grade students whose names are chosen from an alphabetical list

   D. survey those seventh-grade students who participated in this year's art fair

6. Sean randomly surveyed 10 students and found that 7 would like for the school to have a science fair this year. Nikki randomly surveyed 100 students and found that 68 would like the school to have a science fair this year. Which sentence is true?

   A. Sean's survey is more valid than Nikki's because a greater percent of students in his survey wanted to have a science fair.

   B. Sean's survey is more valid than Nikki's because his was more selective of who participated.

   C. Nikki's survey is more valid than Sean's because she surveyed more people than Sean.

   D. Nikki's survey is more valid than Sean's because a lesser percent of students in her survey wanted to have a science fair.

7. Hannah surveyed 50 of the 450 students at her school to determine ownership of cats and dogs. Her results are shown in the table.

   Pet Ownership

Pet Owned	Frequency
Cat only	8
Dog only	12
Cat and dog	10
No pet	20

   A. Identify the population and the sample.

   The population is the 450 students attending her school. The sample is the 50 students Hannah surveyed.

   B. Is it likely that the sample is representative of the population? Explain your thinking.

   It is likely Hannah's sample is representative of the population, since the students surveyed were a part of the population, however, depending on how Hannah took her survey, it may or may not be biased.

   C. Based on the table, how many of the students in Hannah's school would you predict own at least one cat or dog? Explain your reasoning.

   I would predict that 180 people own at least one cat or dog since 20 people out of 50 owned at least one cat or dog, 40%. 40% of 450 is 180, therefore, I think 180 people will own at least one cat or dog.

8. Carson is going to survey students in his school to determine how many students use social media. Is each a good sampling method? Select Yes or No.

A. Carson will survey random students in the computer club.   ○ Yes ● No

B. Carson will survey three random students from each homeroom.   ● Yes ○ No

C. Carson will survey every third student leaving school in the afternoon.   ● Yes ○ No

D. Carson will survey all of his friends.   ○ Yes ● No

9. George took a survey of students in his grade to see how many are likely to go to the championship basketball game. He surveyed 52 students, and 32 said they would go to the game. Circle the number that makes the statement true.

$$\frac{32}{52} = \frac{x}{260} \qquad 52x = 8320$$
$$x = 160$$

Based on George's survey, if there are 260 students in his grade, he might expect | (160) 165 170 175 | of them to go to the game.

10. Teresa plans to survey people to determine their favorite type of movie. Is each a good sampling method? Select True or False.

A. Survey every fifth person in line for the opening of an action movie.   ○ True ● False

B. Survey every fifth person entering supermarket in the morning.   ● True ○ False

C. Survey every tenth person in the phone book.   ● True ○ False

D. Survey four students from each table in the lunch room.   ○ True ● False

E. Survey every third person entering the science fiction club meeting.   ○ True ● False

11. Which sample is **not** a good sample? Circle all that apply.

    A. Every fourth student coming out of a college cafeteria is asked about his or her favorite college.

    B. Every fourth person in line at an airport in New York City is asked about his or her favorite college.

    C. Every fourth person at a grocery store is asked about his or her favorite college.

    D. Every fourth person in a college dormitory is asked about his or her favorite college.

12. Stacey took a survey of students in her grade to estimate the number of students who have cell phones. She surveyed 70 students, and 45 said they have cell phones. Circle the number that makes the statement true.

    $$\frac{45}{70} = \frac{x}{300} \qquad 70x = 13500$$
    $$x = 193$$

    Based on Stacey's survey, if there are 300 students in her grade, she might expect about _____ of them have cell phones.

45
120
183
(193)

13. Kenesha surveyed random students in her school about their choice for the prom queen. The results are shown in the table below. Is each a good prediction based on the survey results? Select Yes or No.

    Prom Queen

Candidate	Number of Students
Hana	9
Cindy	11
Mavis	18
Bala	7
Diane	5

    50 students total

    A. If 120 vote for prom queen, Mavis would get approximately 43 votes. ● Yes ○ No

    B. If 80 vote for prom queen, Diane would get approximately 8 votes. ● Yes ○ No

    C. If 150 vote for prom queen, Bala would get approximately 21 votes. ● Yes ○ No

    D. If 180 vote for prom queen, Hana would get approximately 18 votes. ○ Yes ● No

    E. If 210 vote for prom queen, Cindy would get approximately 26 votes. ○ Yes ● No

Measures of Central Tendency

Getting the Idea

Measures of central tendency help to describe and interpret a data set. They are used to interpret the "average item" of a data set. The table below shows the measures of central tendency for this data set: 5, 1, 1, 6, and 7.

Measure of Central Tendency	Example
The **mean** is equal to the sum of the terms in a data set divided by the number of terms in the data set.	$\text{mean} = \dfrac{\text{sum of terms}}{\text{number of terms}}$ $\text{mean} = \dfrac{5 + 1 + 1 + 6 + 7}{5} = \dfrac{20}{5} = 4$
The **median** is the middle term in a data set ordered from least to greatest. If there is an even number of terms in a data set, the median is the mean of the two middle numbers.	The data ordered from least to greatest are: 1, 1, 5, 6, 7. The middle term, 5, is the median.
The **mode** is the term or terms that appear most often in a data set. A data set may have no mode, one mode, or more than one mode.	5, 1, 1, 6, 7 The number 1 appears twice in the data set. Every other number appears only once. So, 1 is the mode.

Example 1

The scores on a science quiz are: 7, 7, 9, 7, 10, 8, 6, 9, 10, and 7.

What are the mean, median, and mode of the science quiz scores?

Strategy   Calculate each measure of central tendency.

> **Step 1**   Find the mean.
>
> Add the values and then divide the sum by the number of values.
>
> 7 + 7 + 9 + 7 + 10 + 8 + 6 + 9 + 10 + 7 = 80
>
> 80 ÷ 10 = 8

> **Step 2**   Find the median.
>
> Order the values from least to greatest.
>
> 6, 7, 7, 7, 7, 8, 9, 9, 10, 10
>
> There is an even number of terms.
>
> The two middle values are 7 and 8.
>
> Find the mean of the two middle values.
>
> (7 + 8) ÷ 2 = 15 ÷ 2 = 7.5

| Step 3 | Find the mode.

The value that occurs most frequently is 7.

Solution   **The mean is 8, the median is 7.5, and the mode is 7.**

To choose which measure of central tendency is most appropriate for a situation, look at the distribution of the ordered data from a sample. If there is a value that is much less or much greater than the other values in the set of data, the median or mode better represents the sample data than the mean. If the mode occurs at either extreme of the data, the mean or the median are better choices to represent the sample data.

Some data sets are shown on a **dot plot**, which is a display that uses a number line and dots to show data.

Example 2

Karen randomly surveyed some classmates to see how many books each of them read over the summer. The results of her survey are shown in the dot plot.

Number of Books Read

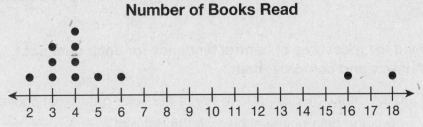

How does the mode compare to the median number of books read?

| Strategy | Find the median and the mode. Compare the measures.

| Step 1 | Find the median.

Use the data points shown on the dot plot.

Median: 2, 3, 3, 3, 4, **4**, **4**, 4, 5, 6, 16, 18

The two middle values are 4.

The median is 4.

| Step 2 | Find the mode.

Mode: 2, 3, 3, 3, **4, 4, 4, 4**, 5, 6, 16, 18

The mode is 4.

| Step 3 | Compare the measures.

The median and the mode are the same.

Solution   **The median and the mode are both 4.**

You can use measures of central tendency to make inferences about two populations.

Example 3

The dot plots show the test scores of students in Mr. Coen's sixth- and seventh-grade English classes.

Sixth-Grade Test Scores

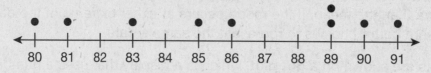

Seventh-Grade Test Scores

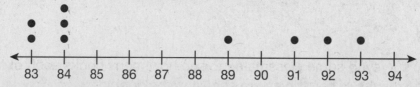

Are the test scores of the seventh graders generally higher than the test scores of the sixth graders?

Strategy   **Find the measures of central tendency for each data set. Analyze and compare them.**

Step 1   Find the mean, median, and mode of the sixth-grade test scores.

Use the data points shown on the dot plot.

Mean: $\dfrac{80 + 81 + 83 + 85 + 86 + 89 + 89 + 90 + 91}{9} = \dfrac{774}{9} = 86$

The mean is 86.

Median: 80, 81, 83, 85, **86**, 89, 89, 90, 91

The median is 86.

Mode: 80, 81, 83, 85, 86, **89, 89**, 90, 91

The mode is 89.

Step 2   Find the mean, median, and mode of the seventh-grade test scores.

Mean: $\dfrac{83 + 83 + 84 + 84 + 84 + 89 + 91 + 92 + 93}{9} = \dfrac{783}{9} = 87$

The mean is 87.

Median: 83, 83, 84, 84, **84**, 89, 91, 92, 93

The median is 84.

Mode: 83, 83, **84, 84, 84**, 89, 91, 92, 93

The mode is 84.

Step 3   Compare the measures of central tendency.

The sixth-grade mean is 86, and the seventh-grade mean is 87.

The seventh-grade mean is one point higher than the sixth-grade mean.

The sixth-grade median is 86, and the seventh-grade median is 84.

The sixth-grade median is two points higher than the seventh-grade median.

The sixth-grade mode is 89, and the seventh-grade mode is 84.

The sixth-grade mode is four points higher than the seventh-grade mode.

Step 4   Analyze the data.

All the data points are close together in both grades.

The mean, median, and mode for each data set are close to most of the data points.

The question does not ask for the most common test scores, so the mode is not the best measure to use to compare the data sets.

The sixth-grade median is slightly higher than the seventh-grade median, while the seventh-grade mean is slightly higher than the sixth-grade mean. The "average" test scores are close for both classes.

Solution   **The test scores of the seventh graders are not generally higher than the test scores of the sixth graders.**

Example 4

Students in Mrs. Becker's class and Mr. Roland's class sold boxes of popcorn for a school fund-raiser. The tables below show the number of boxes that each student sold.

Popcorn Boxes Sold

Mrs. Becker's Class

5	8	76	15
16	84	7	12
17	11	13	

Mr. Roland's Class

9	10	12	20
8	34	6	27
14	10	3	51

How does the average number of boxes sold by each class compare?

Strategy   **Find the measures of central tendency for each data set. Analyze and compare them.**

Step 1   Find the mean, median, and mode of Mrs. Becker's class.

Mean: $\dfrac{5 + 8 + 76 + 15 + 16 + 84 + 7 + 12 + 17 + 11 + 13}{11} = \dfrac{264}{11} = 24$

Median: 5, 7, 8, 11, 12, **13**, 15, 16, 17, 76, 84

The median is 13.

There is no mode since no value appears more than once.

Step 2   Find the mean, median, and mode of Mr. Roland's class.

Mean: $\dfrac{9 + 10 + 12 + 20 + 8 + 34 + 6 + 27 + 14 + 10 + 3 + 51}{12} = \dfrac{204}{12} = 17$

Median: 3, 6, 8, 9, 10, **10**, **12**, 14, 20, 27, 34, 51

Find the mean of the two middle values, 10 and 12.

$(10 + 12) \div 2 = 22 \div 2 = 11$

The median is 11.

Mode: 3, 6, 8, 9, **10**, **10**, 12, 14, 20, 27, 34, 51

The mode is 10.

Step 3   Compare the measures of central tendency.

The mean for Mrs. Becker's class is greater than the mean for Mr. Roland's class.

The median for Mrs. Becker's class is greater than the median for Mr. Roland's class.

There is only one mode, so you cannot compare them.

Solution   **The average number of boxes sold by Mrs. Becker's students was greater than the average number sold by Mr. Roland's students.**

Coached Example

The dot plots show the number of books read by fifth graders and by seventh graders during one month.

Books Read by Fifth Graders

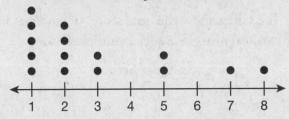

Books Read by Seventh Graders

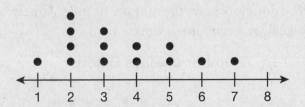

How does the average number of books read by the fifth graders compare to the average number of books read by the seventh graders?

Find the mean number of books read by fifth graders to the nearest tenth:

The mean is __2.9__.

Find the median number of books read by fifth graders:

The median is __2__.

Find the mean number of books read by seventh graders to the nearest tenth:

The mean is __3.5__.

Find the median number of books read by seventh graders:

The median is __3__.

The mean number of books read by the fifth graders is __2.9__, while the mean number of books read by the seventh graders is __3.5__.

The median number of books read by the fifth graders is __2__, while the median number of books read by the seventh graders is __3__.

The seventh graders read about an average of __1 more__ book than the fifth graders.

Lesson Practice • Part 1

Choose the correct answer.

Use the dot plot for questions 1–3.

The dot plot shows the number of miles Jamal biked per week for ten weeks.

Number of Miles Biked

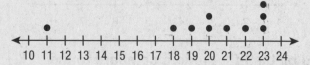

1. What is the mean number of miles that Jamal biked per week?

    A. 20 miles

    B. 20.5 miles

    C. 21 miles

    D. 23 miles

2. What is the median number of miles that Jamal biked per week?

    A. 19 miles

    B. 20 miles

    C. 20.5 miles

    D. 21 miles

3. Which measure of central tendency best represents the average number of miles that Jamal biked per week?

    A. mean or mode

    B. mean or median

    C. median or mode

    D. mean, median, or mode

Use the tables for questions 4 and 5.

The tables show the quiz scores of students in two seventh-grade social studies classes.

Quiz Scores

Class A

9	8	8	9
10	9	8	10
9	9	10	

Mean: 9

Class B

9	10	8	10
10	9	10	6
5	7	8	10

Mean: 8.5

4. Which best describes the comparison between the mode quiz scores?

    A. The modes are the same.

    B. The mode score for Class A is 2 points higher than for Class B.

    C. The mode score for Class A is 1 point higher than for Class B.

    D. The mode score for Class A is 1 point lower than for Class B.

5. Which best describes the comparison between the mean quiz scores?

    A. The means are the same.

    B. The mean score for Class A is 0.5 point higher than for Class B.

    C. The mean score for Class A is 1 point higher than for Class B.

    D. The mean score for Class A is 1 point lower than for Class B.

6. The dot plots show the number of miles hiked by Fatima and by Paula over one week.

Miles Hiked by Fatima

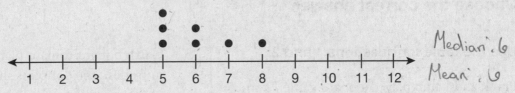

Median: 6
Mean: 6

Miles Hiked by Paula

Median: 4
Mean: 5

A. How does the median number of miles hiked by Fatima compare to the median number of miles hiked by Paula? Show your work.

The median miles hiked by Fatima is larger than the median miles hiked by Paula, indicating Fatima generally hiked more than Paula. Her median number was 6, while paula's was 4.

B. How does the mean number of miles hiked by Fatima compare to the mean number of miles hiked by Paula? Show your work.

The mean number of miles hiked by Fatima is larger than the mean number of miles hiked by Paula. The mean number of miles hiked by Fatima was 6, while paula's mean was 5.

Lesson Practice • Part 2

Choose the correct answer.

Use the table for questions 1 and 2.

Frank and Laura played a board game 7 times. Their scores are shown below.

Game Scores

Game	Frank	Laura
1 L	236	284
2 W	290	276
3 W	320	288
4 L	292	305
5 W	320	284
6 L	247	311
7 L	286	292

1. Which sentence about the medians is true?

   A. Frank had the greater median by 2 points.

   B. Frank had the greater median by 36 points.

   C. Laura had the greater median by 7 points.

   D. Laura had the greater median by 13 points.

2. Which sentence about the data is true?

   A. Frank had the greater mean and mode and won most of the games.

   B. Frank had the greater mode and won most of the games.

   C. Laura had the greater mean and mode and won most of the games.

   D. Laura had the greater mean and won most of the games.

3. Garth bought tomato plants from two nurseries. The dot plots show the heights of the plants from each nursery after a month.

Plant Heights (in centimeters)

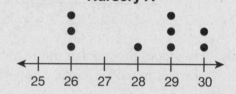

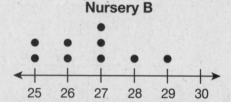

Which best describes how the median heights of the plants from Nursery A compare to the median heights of the plants from Nursery B?

   A. The median of Nursery B is greater by 2 centimeters.

   B. The medians are equal.

   C. The median of Nursery A is greater by 1 centimeter.

   D. The median of Nursery A is greater by 2 centimeters.

4. The table shows the mean monthly temperatures in Los Angeles and San Francisco.

Mean Monthly Temperatures (in °F)

	J	F	M	A	M	J	J	A	S	O	N	D
LA	58	59	61	63	66	69	73	74	73	69	62	58
SF	50	53	55	57	60	62	64	65	65	62	56	51

   A. Patti said Los Angeles has the greater mode. Jeff said Los Angeles has the lesser mode. Who is correct? Explain.

   _____

   _____

   _____

   B. What is the difference between the medians of the mean monthly temperatures? Explain your answer.

   6 _____

   _____

   C. What is the difference between the means of the mean monthly temperatures? Explain your answer.

   _____

   _____

   _____

5. Find the measures of central tendency for the set of numbers below. Draw a line from each measure of central tendency to its value.

   26, 28, 28, 28, 29, 30, 31, 32

   A. mean •   • 28
   B. median •   • 28.5
   C. mode •   • 29

6. Merida completed math problems from her homework packet each night. Below is a list of the numbers of problems she completed each night. Find the measures of central tendency. Circle each measure of central tendency.

2, 7, 5, 9, 7, 4, 8

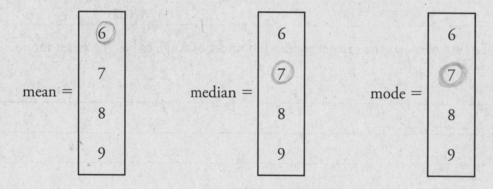

mean = ⑥ 7 8 9

median = 6 ⑦ 8 9

mode = 6 ⑦ 8 9

7. Daniel kept track of the miles he ran each day for 2 weeks. The distances are displayed in the table below.

4	3	4	3	2	4	6
2	4	1	4	4	5	3

Determine whether each number below is a measure of central tendency for the set of data. Write each number in the correct box.

| 2 | 2.5 | 3 | 3.5 | 4 | 4.5 | 5 |

Measure of Central Tendency	Not a Measure of Central Tendency
Mean: 3.5 Median: 4 Mode: 4	LQ: 3 UQ: 4 IQR: 1

8. Which is a measure of central tendency for the dot plot? Circle all that apply.

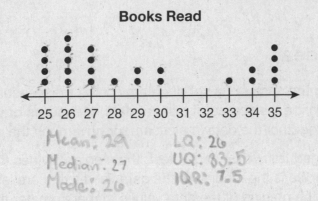

Books Read

A. 26
B. 27
C. 28
D. 29
E. 30
F. 31

Mean: 29   LQ: 26
Median: 27   UQ: 33.5
Mode: 26   IQR: 7.5

9. Seventh-grade students are selling popcorn tins for a fund-raiser. The dot plots below show the number of popcorn tins each student sold in two classes. Compare the two dot plots of data. Select True or False for each statement.

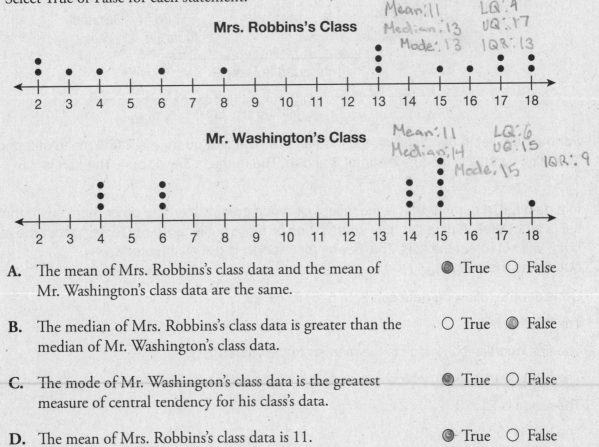

Mrs. Robbins's Class

Mean: 11   LQ: 4
Median: 13   UQ: 17
Mode: 13   IQR: 13

Mr. Washington's Class

Mean: 11   LQ: 6
Median: 14   UQ: 15
Mode: 15   IQR: 9

A. The mean of Mrs. Robbins's class data and the mean of Mr. Washington's class data are the same.   ● True   ○ False

B. The median of Mrs. Robbins's class data is greater than the median of Mr. Washington's class data.   ○ True   ● False

C. The mode of Mr. Washington's class data is the greatest measure of central tendency for his class's data.   ● True   ○ False

D. The mean of Mrs. Robbins's class data is 11.   ● True   ○ False

Measures of Variation

Getting the Idea

Instead of describing the center of a set of data by using the measures of central tendency, you may wish to describe the spread of a set of data. **Measures of variation** show how spread out or close together the data in a set are, or how much the data points vary.

When data are arranged from least to greatest, the median divides the data into two equal halves. The **first quartile** is the median of the data values that are less than the median. The **third quartile** is the median of the data values that are greater than the median. The **quartiles** and the median divide the data into four quarters. The **range** is the difference between the greatest value in a data set and the least value. The **interquartile range (IQR)**, is the difference between the third quartile and the first quartile. The range measures the spread of all the data. The IQR measures the spread of the two middle quarters of the data.

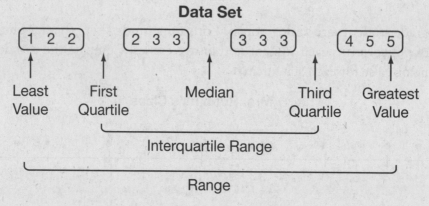

For the data set in the diagram, the median is 3. The first quartile is 2 (the mean of 2 and 2). The third quartile is 3.5 (the mean of 3 and 4). The range is 5 − 1, or 4. The IQR is 3.5 − 2, or 1.5.

In a data set, a number that is much less or much greater than the other numbers in the data set is an **outlier**. A data set may contain one or more outliers. An outlier will affect the range, but it will not affect the IQR. This is why the median is not as affected by outliers as the mean is.

Consider the following data set: 2, 3, 5, 6, 8, 10, 23.

The median is 6.

The first quartile is 3, which is the median of the values 2, 3, 5.

The third quartile is 10, which is the median of the values 8, 10, 23.

The range is 21: 23 − 2 = 21.

The IQR is 7: 10 − 3 = 7.

For this data set, 23 is an outlier. It is much greater than the other numbers in the set. The range is affected by this outlier. It suggests that there is a greater variability in the data, since it shows a greater spread, than the IQR suggests. The data vary by 21 from the least to greatest values, while they only vary by 7 away from the median, or the center of the data.

Example 1

The dot plot below shows the grades students received on a grammar test in Ms. Parsi's class.

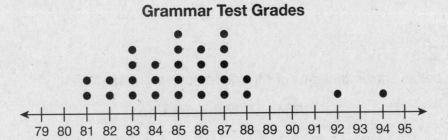

What is the range in the grades? What is the median grade?

Strategy	Use the dot plot.
Step 1	Find the greatest and least test grades. The lowest grade is 81. The highest grade is 94.
Step 2	Find the range. Subtract the lowest grade from the highest grade. range = 94 − 81 = 13
Step 3	Count the total number of test grades. There are 29 grades.
Step 4	Find the median. The median is the middle grade. It is halfway between the lowest and the highest grade. Since there are 29 grades, there are 14 grades below the median and 14 grades above the median. The median is the fifteenth grade in the ordered list of grades. Start at 81 and count the dots until you reach the fifteenth dot. This dot is at the grade of 85. So the median is 85.
Solution	**The range in the grades is 13, and the median is 85.**

A **box plot** is a method of visually displaying a distribution of data values by using the median, quartiles, and extremes (least and greatest values) of the data set. The box shows the middle 50% of the data.

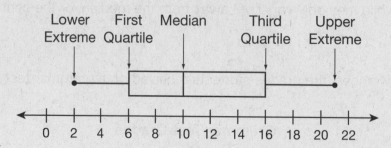

Example 2

The box plot below shows the ages of Mr. Morehouse's grandchildren.

Ages of Grandchildren

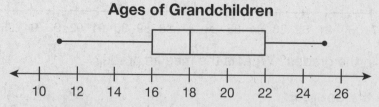

Find the median, first quartile, third quartile, and the IQR of their ages.

Strategy   **Use the box plot.**

Step 1   Find the median.

The median is the middle value. On a box plot, it is represented by the vertical line inside the box.

The vertical line inside the box is above 18. The median is 18.

Step 2   Find the first quartile.

On a box plot, the first quartile is represented by the box's left vertical line.

The left vertical line is above 16. The first quartile is 16.

Step 3   Find the third quartile.

On a box plot, the third quartile is represented by the box's right vertical line.

The right vertical line is above 22. The third quartile is 22.

Step 4   Find the IQR.

IQR = third quartile − first quartile = 22 − 16 = 6

Solution   **The median of the ages is 18. The first quartile is 16. The third quartile is 22. The IQR is 6.**

Example 3

Below are the quiz scores from students in two different class sections.

Section 1: 7, 9, 9, 10, 8, 6, 8, 5, 5, 9, 10, 7, 8, 7, 9

Section 2: 7, 8, 9, 9, 8, 8, 7, 9, 9, 10, 8, 8, 7, 10, 8

Which section has greater variability in the scores?

Strategy	**Compare the ranges and IQRs of the two class sections.**
Step 1	Find the range for Section 1.
	Order the scores from least to greatest.
	5, 5, 6, 7, 7, 7, 8, 8, 8, 9, 9, 9, 9, 10, 10
	The highest score was 10. The lowest score was 5.
	Range = 10 − 5 = 5
Step 2	Find the median and the quartiles for Section 1.
	5, 5, 6, <u>7</u>, 7, 7, 8, <u>8</u>, 8, 9, 9, <u>9</u>, 9, 10, 10
	The median is 8, the first quartile is 7, and the third quartile is 9.
Step 3	Find the IQR for Section 1.
	The IQR is the difference between the third and first quartiles.
	IQR = 9 − 7 = 2
Step 4	Find the range for Section 2.
	Order the scores from least to greatest.
	7, 7, 7, 8, 8, 8, 8, 8, 8, 9, 9, 9, 9, 10, 10
	Range = 10 − 7 = 3
Step 5	Find the median and the quartiles for Section 2.
	7, 7, 7, <u>8</u>, 8, 8, 8, <u>8</u>, 8, 9, 9, <u>9</u>, 9, 10, 10
	The median is 8, the first quartile is 8, and the third quartile is 9.
Step 6	Find the interquartile range for Section 2.
	IQR = 9 − 8 = 1
Step 7	Compare the range and IQR for each section.
	The range for Section 1 is 5, and the IQR is 2.
	The range for Section 2 is 3, and the IQR is 1.
	The range and IQR for Section 1 are greater than for Section 2.
Solution	**Section 1 has greater variability in the quiz scores than Section 2.**

Example 4

The double box plot below shows the number of points scored in games by two basketball players on the same team.

Points Scored in Games

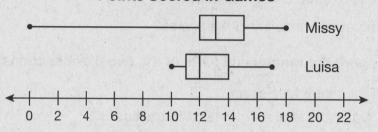

Find the range and the IQR for each player. Who is the more consistent scorer?

Strategy **Compare the range and IQR for each player.**

Step 1 Find the range and the IQR for Missy.

Missy's highest score was 18. Her lowest score was 0.

Range = 18 − 0 = 18

IQR = 15 − 12 = 3

Step 2 Find the range and the IQR for Luisa.

Luisa's highest score was 17. Her lowest score was 10.

Range = 17 − 10 = 7

The third quartile score for Luisa is 14, and the first quartile score is 11.

IQR = 14 − 11 = 3

Step 3 Who is the more consistent scorer?

Missy's scores per game show a much greater range than Luisa's.

Notice that Missy's scores have an outlier. She scored 0 points during one game.

The outlier affects the range of her scores.

The IQR for both players is the same.

Solution **Luisa may be a slightly more consistent scorer. Since the IQRs for Luisa and Missy are the same, it is likely that Missy is about as consistent a scorer as Luisa.**

Coached Example

The double box plot below shows the weights, in pounds, of Labrador retrievers and cocker spaniels from a veterinarian's office.

Dog Weights (in pounds)

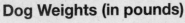
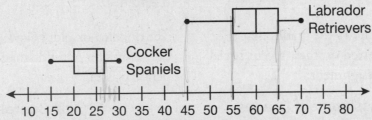

Which type of dog shows greater variability in weight?

The least weight for the cocker spaniels is ___15___ pounds.

The greatest weight for the cocker spaniels is ___30___ pounds.

Find the range of the cocker spaniels' weights: ___30___ – ___15___ = ___15___.

The range of the weights of the cocker spaniels is ___15___ pounds.

The third quartile weight for the cocker spaniels is ___27___ pounds.

The first quartile weight for the cocker spaniels is ___20___ pounds.

Find the IQR for the cocker spaniels' weights: 27 – ___20___ = ___7___.

The IQR for the weights of the cocker spaniels is ___7___ pounds.

The least weight for the Labrador retrievers is ___45___ pounds.

The greatest weight for the Labrador retrievers is ___70___ pounds.

Find the range of the Labrador retrievers' weights: ___70___ – ___45___ = ___25___.

The range of the weights of the Labrador retrievers is ___25___ pounds.

The third quartile weight for the Labrador retrievers is ___65___ pounds.

The first quartile weight for the Labrador retrievers is ___55___ pounds.

Find the IQR for the Labrador retrievers' weights: ___65___ – ___55___ = ___10___.

The IQR for the weights of the Labrador retrievers is ___10___ pounds.

The range and the IQR for cocker spaniels are ___less___ than for Labrador retrievers.

___Labrador Retrievers___ **have greater variability in weight**
than ___Cocker spaniels___.

Lesson Practice • Part 1

Choose the correct answer.

Use the dot plot below for questions 1 and 2.

The dot plot below shows the grades that a class of students received on their recent social studies homework assignment.

Homework Assignment Grades

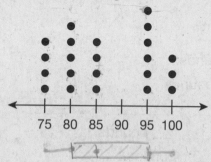

1. What is the first quartile grade?

   A. 75
   B. 80
   C. 85
   D. 90

2. What is the third quartile grade?

   A. 85
   B. 90
   C. 95
   D. 100

Use the double box plot for questions 3 and 4.

The double box plot below shows the vocabulary quiz scores for Mr. Edelman's first and second period classes.

Quiz Scores

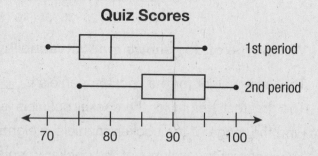

3. What is the IQR of the first period quiz scores?

   A. 5
   B. 10
   C. 15
   D. 20

4. Which statement about the quiz scores is true?

   A. The range of the scores was the same for both classes.
   B. The IQR of the scores was the same for both classes.
   C. The mean score was the same for both classes.
   D. About 25% of the students in both classes scored 95 or higher on the quiz.

5. The box plot shows the number of miles run per week by the members of a running club.

Miles Run Per Week

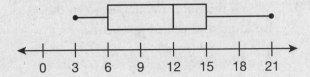

What is the range of the data?

A. 9 miles

B. 12 miles

C. 15 miles

D. 18 miles

6. The box plot shows the ages of the participants in a park clean-up.

Ages of Clean-Up Participants (in years)

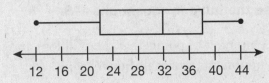

What is the IQR of the ages, in years?

A. 12

B. 16

C. 20

D. 32

7. The double box plot below shows the heights, in millimeters, of plants that Jerand and Marsha grew for a science project.

Plant Heights (in millimeters)

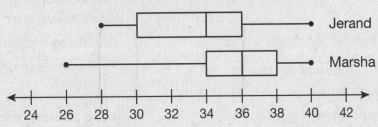

A. How do the range and the IQR for Jerand's plants compare to the range and the IQR for Marsha's plants? Show your work.

_____

_____

_____

B. Whose plants show greater variability in height? Explain your thinking.

_____

_____

_____

Lesson Practice • Part 2

Choose the correct answer.

Use the table for questions 1–5.

The number of points that the Bulldogs and its opponents scored is shown below.

Bulldogs Season

Bulldogs	Opponents
48	40
57	51
44	56
60	48
42	36
40	48
51	45

1. Which sentence about the ranges is true?

   A. The ranges of the Bulldogs and its opponents are equal.

   B. The Bulldogs' opponents have the greater range by 2 points.

   C. The Bulldogs' opponents have the greater range by 4 points.

   D. The Bulldogs have the greater range by 4 points.

   Bull range: 20   O range 20

2. What is the IQR for the Bulldogs?

   A. 3

   B. 8

   C. 15

   D. 20

3. Which measure is equal between the Bulldogs and their opponents?

   A. first quartile

   B. median

   C. third quartile

   D. IQR

4. Which sentence about the quartiles is true?

   A. The Bulldogs' opponents have the greater first quartile.

   B. The Bulldogs have the greater median.

   C. The Bulldogs' opponents have the greater third quartile.

   D. The Bulldogs have the greater interquartile range.

5. Which sentence is true?

   A. The Bulldogs score of 60 is an outlier.

   B. The Bulldogs' opponents score of 36 is an outlier.

   C. The Bulldogs' opponents score of 56 is an outlier.

   D. There is no outlier in this data.

6. The normal monthly precipitation for Miami and New Orleans is shown.

Normal Monthly Precipitation (in inches)

	J	F	M	A	M	J	J	A	S	O	N	D
Miami	1.6	2.3	3.0	3.1	5.3	9.7	6.5	8.9	9.9	6.3	3.3	2.0
NO	5.2	5.3	4.6	4.6	4.6	8.1	5.9	6.0	5.1	3.6	4.5	5.3

Which sentence is true?

A. Miami has the greater first quartile and IQR.

B. Miami has the greater third quartile and IQR.

C. New Orleans has the greater median and IQR.

D. New Orleans has the greater third quartile and IQR.

7. The double box plot shows the number of miles cycled by Lana and Beryl while they were training for a summer race.

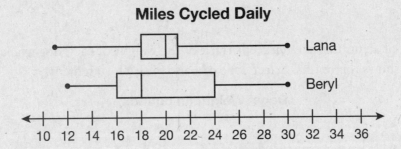

A. Who has the greater median of miles cycled? By how much?

_____

_____

B. Who has the greater IQR? By how much?

_____

C. Who has the greater variability in number of miles cycled? Explain your reasoning.

_____

_____

_____

8. Pooja kept track of the number of miles she biked each day for a month. Her results are shown in the box plot shown below. Find the measures of central tendency and the measures of variation. Draw a line from each measure to its value.

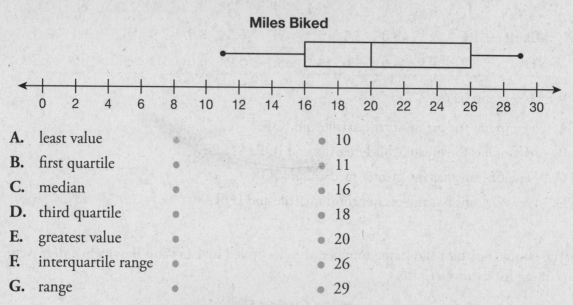

A. least value   •   • 10

B. first quartile   •   • 11

C. median   •   • 16

D. third quartile   •   • 18

E. greatest value   •   • 20

F. interquartile range •   • 26

G. range   •   • 29

9. The manager of an animal shelter keeps track of the weight of each dog available for adoption. The dot plot shows the results. Select True or False for each statement.

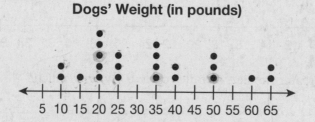

A. The values of the IQR and the first quartile are equivalent.   ○ True   ○ False

B. The range of the dogs' weights is 55 pounds.   ○ True   ○ False

C. The third quartile of the data is 20 pounds.   ○ True   ○ False

D. The median weight of the dogs is 35 pounds.   ○ True   ○ False

10. Elena and Charlie are in the Student Leaders Club. They kept track of the number of service hours they completed each month. The results are shown in the box plots shown below. Which is a true statement? Circle all that apply.

Service Hours Completed

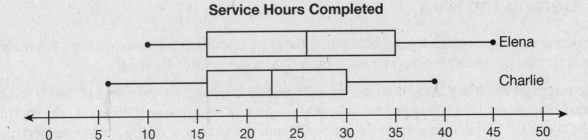

A. Elena's IQR is greater than Charlie's IQR.

B. The medians of both sets of data are equal.

C. Charlie's range is less than Elena's range.

D. Elena's greatest number of service hours is less than Charlie's greatest number of service hours.

11. Compare the two box plots of data. Find the values for the first quartiles, third quartiles, and interquartile ranges. Write each value in the correct box.

Money Saved (in dollars)

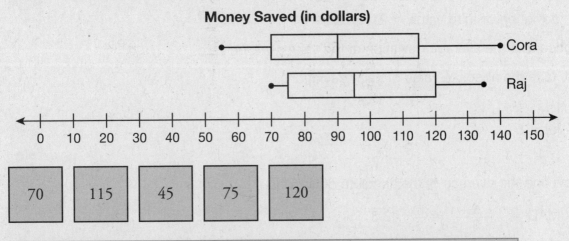

| 70 | 115 | 45 | 75 | 120 |

First Quartile	Third Quartile	Interquartile Range
70 75	115 120	45

Mean Absolute Deviation

Getting the Idea

Another way to measure the variability of a data set is to measure variation from the mean. You do this by measuring how far each individual value is from the mean.

To measure variability away from the mean, first find the mean of the data set. Next, find the absolute value of the difference between the mean and each value of the data set. This gives the deviation of each value from the mean. Then find the sum of all the deviations and divide the sum by the number of values in the data set. The average of the absolute deviations from the mean is called the **mean absolute deviation (MAD)**.

Suppose the heights, in inches, of three plants, are: 18, 27, and 21.

Find the mean of the heights, in inches.

$$\text{mean} = \frac{18 + 27 + 21}{3} = \frac{66}{3} = 22$$

Find how each height differs from the mean height. This is the deviation from the mean.

deviation of first value = 18 − 22 = −4

deviation of second value = 27 − 22 = 5

deviation of third value = 21 − 22 = −1

Notice that the average deviation of the values will be zero.

So, take the absolute value of each deviation.

$|-4| = 4$

$|5| = 5$

$|-1| = 1$

Now find the average of the absolute deviations.

$$\text{MAD} = \frac{4 + 5 + 1}{3} = \frac{10}{3} = 3.\overline{3}$$

So, the plant heights vary by an average of $3.\overline{3}$ inches from the mean.

When the MAD is small, it means the data is bunched closely together. For the plant heights, the MAD is $3.\overline{3}$, which is relatively small. This makes sense since the plant heights are not very different. So, there is not much variability in the plant heights.

If the MAD is large, it means the data is spread out and has greater variability.

Example 1

Find the MAD for the following quiz scores: 6, 9, 6, 9, 8, and 10. The mean score on the quizzes is 8.

Strategy **Find the deviation of each score from the mean score. Then find the absolute deviations to get the MAD.**

Step 1 Find the deviation of each score from the mean score.

Subtract each score from the mean score to find the deviations.

$6 - 8 = -2$

$9 - 8 = 1$

$6 - 8 = -2$

$9 - 8 = 1$

$8 - 8 = 0$

$10 - 8 = 2$

Step 2 Find the absolute deviations, the absolute value of each deviation.

$|-2| = 2$

$|1| = 1$

$|-2| = 2$

$|1| = 1$

$|0| = 0$

$|2| = 2$

Step 3 Find the MAD.

Add the absolute deviations: $2 + 1 + 2 + 1 + 0 + 2 = 8$

There are 6 quiz scores in the set.

$MAD = \frac{8}{6} = 1.\overline{3}$

Solution **The MAD is $1.\overline{3}$.**

You can use the MAD to compare two populations.

Two sets with similar variability may overlap. To determine the level of overlap between two data sets, find the difference of the means divided by the quotient of the MAD.

If two sets of data have the same MAD, a quotient near 0 will mean that there is much or almost complete overlap. The greater the quotient the less overlap exists between the two sets.

Example 2

The heights of players on two volleyball teams are shown on the dot plots below.

Players' Heights (in inches)

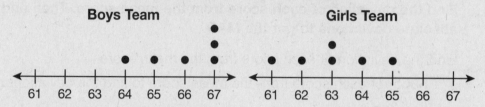

Find the difference of the means divided by the quotient of the MADs to find the overlap.

Strategy   **Find the MAD of each team's heights.**

Step 1   Find the mean of each team's heights in inches.

Boys: $\dfrac{64 + 65 + 66 + 67 + 67 + 67}{6} = \dfrac{396}{6} = 66$

Girls: $\dfrac{61 + 62 + 63 + 63 + 64 + 65}{6} = \dfrac{378}{6} = 63$

Step 2   Find the absolute deviation of each team.

For the boys, find the absolute value of the difference between each value and 66. For the girls find the absolute value of the difference between each value and 63.

Since you are finding the absolute values, the order of the subtraction does not matter.

Boys	Girls
$|64 - 66| = 2$	$|61 - 63| = 2$
$|65 - 66| = 1$	$|62 - 63| = 1$
$|66 - 66| = 0$	$|63 - 63| = 0$
$|67 - 66| = 1$	$|63 - 63| = 0$
$|67 - 66| = 1$	$|64 - 63| = 1$
$|67 - 66| = 1$	$|65 - 63| = 2$

Step 3   Find the MAD for each team.

Boys: $\dfrac{2 + 1 + 0 + 1 + 1 + 1}{6} = \dfrac{6}{6} = 1$

Girls: $\dfrac{2 + 1 + 0 + 0 + 1 + 2}{6} = \dfrac{6}{6} = 1$

The MADs are the same.

Step 4   Divide the difference of the means by the quotient of the MAD.

$$\frac{66 - 63}{1} = 3$$

There will be some overlap.

Step 5   Combine the dot plots to check your answer.

Players' Heights (in inches)

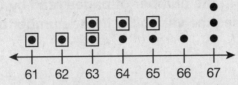

Let the dots inside squares represent the girls.

Solution   **There is some overlap between the sets of data.**

Example 3

The numbers of pages in books read by sixth- and seventh-grade students during one semester are shown below.

   Sixth grade: 125, 132, 150, 137

   Seventh grade: 198, 174, 208, 120

Compare the variability in the mean number of pages read by students in each grade.

Strategy   **Find the MADs of the pages read by each grade.**

Step 1   Find the MAD of the pages read by sixth graders.

$$\text{mean} = \frac{125 + 132 + 150 + 137}{4} = \frac{544}{4} = 136$$

Find the absolute deviations.

$|125 - 136| = |-11| = 11$ $|150 - 136| = |14| = 14$

$|132 - 136| = |-4| = 4$ $|137 - 136| = |1| = 1$

Find the MAD.

$$\text{MAD} = \frac{11 + 4 + 14 + 1}{4} = \frac{30}{4} = 7.5$$

Step 2   Find the MAD of the pages read by seventh graders.

$$\text{mean} = \frac{198 + 174 + 208 + 120}{4} = \frac{700}{4} = 175$$

Find the absolute deviations.

$|198 - 175| = |23| = 23$ $|208 - 175| = |33| = 33$

$|174 - 175| = |-1| = 1$ $|120 - 175| = |-55| = 55$

Find the MAD.

$$\text{mean absolute deviation} = \frac{23 + 1 + 33 + 55}{4} = \frac{112}{4} = 28$$

Step 3 Compare the MADs.

$7.5 < 28$

The MAD in the number of pages read by the sixth graders is much less than the MAD for the seventh graders. 28 is almost 4 times 7.5.

Solution **The variability in the number of pages read by the seventh graders is almost 4 times the variability in the number of pages read by the sixth graders.**

Coached Example

The weights, in pounds, of the dogs that boarded at a veterinarian's clinic over the weekend were: 43, 87, 12, 15, and 23.
Find the MAD of the weights of the dogs that boarded at the clinic.

Find the mean weight of the dogs that boarded at the clinic.

_____36_____

To find the deviations, ___Subtract___ each weight from the mean weight.

$43 - \underline{36} = \underline{7}$ $\quad$ $87 - \underline{36} = \underline{51}$ $\quad$ $12 - \underline{36} = \underline{-24}$

$15 - \underline{36} = \underline{-21}$ $\quad$ $23 - \underline{36} = \underline{-13}$

To find the absolute deviations, find the ___absolute value___ of each deviation.

$|\underline{7}| = \underline{7}$ $\qquad$ $|\underline{51}| = \underline{51}$ $\qquad$ $|\underline{-24}| = \underline{24}$

$|\underline{-21}| = \underline{21}$ $\qquad$ $|\underline{-13}| = \underline{13}$

Add the absolute deviations.

_____116_____

Find the average of the absolute deviations.

mean absolute deviation $= \dfrac{\qquad}{\qquad} = \underline{\qquad}$

The MAD of the weights of the dogs is __23.2__ pounds.

Lesson Practice • Part 1

Choose the correct answer.

Use the following information for questions 1 and 2.

Paula's grades on her history tests this semester are 79, 93, 92, 86, and 90.

1. Which shows the deviation of each of her grades from her mean grade?

   A. $-9, 5, 4, -2, 2$

   B. $-8, 6, 3, -3, 2$

   C. $-11, 6, 5, -4, 4$

   D. $-14, 9, 5, -3, 2$

2. What is the MAD of Paula's history grades?

   A. 0

   B. 4.2

   C. 4.4

   D. 22

3. What is the affect of an outlier on the MAD of a data set?

   A. An outlier does not change the MAD.

   B. An outlier always increases the MAD.

   C. An outlier always decreases the MAD.

   D. An outlier can either decrease or increase the MAD.

Use the following information for questions 4–6.

The lengths, in seconds, of four folk songs are 128, 165, 182, and 141.

The lengths, in seconds, of four pop songs are 90, 98, 102, and 94.

4. What is the MAD, in seconds, of the folk songs?

   A. 18   C. 19.5

   B. 18.25   D. 19.75

5. What is the MAD, in seconds, of the pop songs?

   A. 2   C. 6

   B. 4   D. 8

6. Which of the following statements is true?

   A. The variability in the times of the folk songs is about half that of the pop songs.

   B. The variability in the times of the folk songs is about twice that of the pop songs.

   C. The variability in the times of the folk songs is about 3 times that of the pop songs.

   D. The variability in the times of the folk songs is about 4 times that of the pop songs.

Use the following information for questions 7 and 8.

The ages of volunteers at a hydration station during a marathon are 16, 27, 31, 24, 19, and 63.
The ages of volunteers at the finish line during a marathon are 32, 28, 25, 20, 40, and 35.

7. What is the MAD, in years, of the ages of
    the volunteers at the hydration station?

    A. $11.\overline{3}$
    B. $11.\overline{6}$
    C. $12.\overline{3}$
    D. $12.\overline{6}$

8. What is the MAD, in years, of the ages of
    the volunteers at the finish line?

    A. $4.\overline{3}$
    B. $5.\overline{6}$
    C. $6.\overline{3}$
    D. $6.\overline{6}$

9. The lengths, in minutes, of the school band and orchestra practices are shown on the dot
    plots below.

Length of Practice (in minutes)

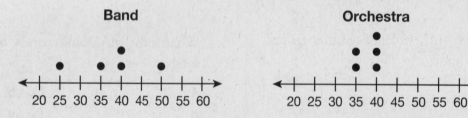

A. What is the MAD, in minutes, of the length of each group's practice?
    Show your work.

    _____

    _____

    _____

B. How does the variability in the length of band practice compare to the variability in the
    length of orchestra practice? Explain your thinking.

    _____

    _____

    _____

Lesson Practice • Part 2

Choose the correct answer.

Use the data for questions 1–3.

The numbers of pages read in books by fourth-grade students and seventh-grade students are shown below.

Fourth grade: 287, 295, 276, 348, 304

Seventh grade: 383, 387, 404, 415, 396

1. What is the MAD of the number of pages read by fourth-grade students?

   A. $15.\overline{3}$

   B. 19.2

   C. 24

   D. 46

2. What is the MAD of the number of pages read by seventh-grade students?

   A. 10

   B. 12.5

   C. 14

   D. 18

3. Which statement about the comparison of the variability of the pages read by the fourth-grade students and the variability of the pages read by the seventh-grade students is true?

   A. The variability of the number of pages read by the fourth-grade students is slightly greater.

   B. The variability of the number of pages read by the fourth-grade students is about double.

   C. The variability of the number of pages read by the seventh-grade students is slightly greater.

   D. The variability of the number of pages read by the seventh-grade students is about double.

Use this information for questions 4–6.

The number of customers that Eat Here and Dan's Diner had each morning for breakfast is shown.

Eat Here: 54, 59, 55, 70, 64, 72, 67

Dan's Diner: 50, 60, 56, 64, 62, 60, 68

4. What is the MAD of the number of breakfast customers for Eat Here?

   A. 6
   B. 8
   C. 12
   D. 18

5. What is the MAD of the number of breakfast customers for Dan's Diner?

   A. 14
   B. 10
   C. 8
   D. 4

6. If you were to plot the data on a double dot plot, which describes the amount of overlap that there would be between the data?

   A. no overlap
   B. some overlap
   C. much overlap
   D. all would overlap

7. Two samples are shown.

   Sample A: mean = 60, MAD = 10

   Sample B: mean = 65, MAD = 10

   Which describes how much the two data sets will overlap when graphed?

   A. They will not overlap at all.
   B. There will be some overlap.
   C. There will be much but not complete overlap.
   D. There will be complete overlap.

8. Two samples are shown.

   Sample C: mean = 120, MAD = 10

   Sample D: mean = 180, MAD = 10

   Which describes how much the two data sets will overlap when graphed?

   A. They will not overlap at all.
   B. There will be some overlap.
   C. There will be much but not complete overlap.
   D. There will be complete overlap.

9. The scores from a science quiz last week and this week for a group of 8 friends are shown.

Last week: 76, 80, 80, 80, 84, 88, 92, 92

This week: 80, 84, 84, 84, 88, 92, 96, 96

A. What is the mean of each set of quizzes?

_____

B. Explain how to find the MAD of each group. Include the MAD from each group in your explanation.

_____

_____

_____

C. If the data were graphed, how much overlap would there be? Explain your answer.

_____

_____

_____

10. The dot plot shows the distances jumped at the long jump competition in the city championships. Find each deviation from the mean. Write each number in the correct box.

Distances Jumped (in inches)

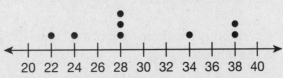

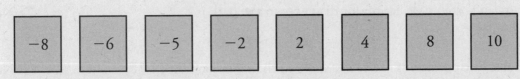

Deviation from Mean	Not a Deviation from Mean

11. Tim kept track of the number of points he scored in each game during a tournament. Circle the absolute deviation for each data point.

Points Scored

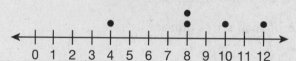

A. 1.6

B. 3.4

C. 4.4

D. 6.6

E. 1.4

F. 0.4

G. 3.6

12. Five friends determined the distances, in miles, from each of their houses to the school and to the park. Is each statement true? Select Yes or No.

Distance to School (in miles)   **Distance to Park (in miles)**

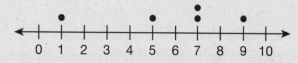   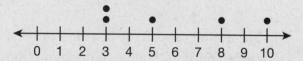

A. The means of both sets of data are equal.   ◯ Yes   ◯ No

B. The mean absolute deviation is greater for the distances to the park   ◯ Yes   ◯ No
    than the distances to the school.

C. The mean absolute deviation for distances to the park is   ◯ Yes   ◯ No
    2.56 miles.

D. The absolute deviations of the distances to the school are 5.8, 1.16,   ◯ Yes   ◯ No
    0.83, 0.83, and 0.64.

Make Predictions Using Data

Getting the Idea

You can use the data from a sample to make predictions about the population. It is important that the sample be representative of the population for the predictions to be reasonable.

Example 1

There are 60 students who take band classes at Mr. Tempo's school. Mr. Tempo surveyed 10 of those students to find out how long they practice their instruments each day. The survey was randomly distributed and anonymous. The results of the survey are shown below. The times are in minutes.

40, 25, 30, 40, 20, 15, 25, 30, 20, 25

Find the mean practice time for the sample. Predict the mean practice time of all the students who take band classes. Is the prediction reasonable?

Strategy   **Use the mean from the sample data to predict the mean for the population.**

Step 1   Identify the sample and the population.

The students surveyed are the sample.

The population is all the students who take band classes.

Step 2   Find the mean for the sample data.

$40 + 25 + 30 + 40 + 20 + 15 + 25 + 30 + 20 + 25 = 270$

$270 \div 10 = 27$

The mean practice time is 27 minutes.

Step 3   Predict the mean for the population.

The mean practice time for the sample is 27 minutes.

The mean for the population should be about 27 minutes.

Step 4   Decide if the prediction is reasonable.

The sample was a random sample.

The size of the sample (10) is fairly large compared to the population (60).

The prediction is reasonable.

Solution   **The mean practice time for the sample is 27 minutes. The sample mean provides a reasonable prediction of the population's mean practice time.**

Example 2

Mindy is the captain of the dance team at her school. She is running in a class election for class president. April surveyed the students on the dance team to see whom they planned to vote for in the election. The results of her survey are shown below.

Student	Number of votes
Mindy	18
Tobey	6
Roland	7

Based on the survey, predict who will win the class election. Is the prediction reasonable?

Strategy   **Use the data to make a prediction. Evaluate the data to decide if the prediction is reasonable.**

Step 1   Use the data to make a prediction.

From the data in the table, the student with the greatest number of votes is Mindy.

Based on the data, Mindy should win the election.

Step 2   Evaluate the data to decide if the prediction is reasonable.

Mindy has quite a few more votes than either of the other students in the table.

However, Mindy is the captain of the dance team. All of the students who were surveyed are on the dance team. This suggests that they might be biased toward Mindy.

The prediction that Mindy will win does not seem reasonable.

Solution   **Although the results of the survey suggest that Mindy will win, the survey is biased. The prediction that Mindy will win is not reasonable.**

Coached Example

There are 70 students taking a biology class. Eight of the students took a test one day early because they had to go to a track meet on the day of the test. Their test scores are shown below.

87, 84, 89, 91, 95, 73, 90, 87

The students are a representative sample of all the students taking biology. Predict the mean test score for all the students taking biology. Is the prediction reasonable?

What is the sample? _____

What is the population? _____

Find the mean of the sample to predict the mean of the _____.

Find the sum of the test scores. _____

Divide the sum by the number of scores in the sample. _____

The mean of the sample test scores is _____.

Based on the mean test score from the sample, the mean test score for the population should be about _____.

Is the prediction reasonable? _____

Explain. _____

_____

The mean test score for all students taking biology should be about _____.

The sample mean provides a _____ prediction of the population test scores.

Lesson Practice • Part 1

Choose the correct answer.

1. The heights of five pepper plants, in centimeters, selected at random from a greenhouse with 50 pepper plants are shown below.

   20, 24, 18, 23, 26

   Which is a reasonable prediction of the mean height of all the pepper plants in the nursery?

   A. 19 cm   **C.** 25 cm

   B. 22 cm   **D.** 26 cm

2. A city is having a clean-up day for the 25 parks in the city. The list below shows the ages of volunteers participating in the clean-up project at one of the parks.

   17, 18, 15, 16, 24, 20, 16

   Which is a reasonable prediction of the mean age of all the participants in the clean-up project?

   A. 16 years old

   B. 17 years old

   C. 18 years old

   D. 19 years old

3. Ines read the following number of pages each day last week: 76, 123, 84, 110, 36, 20, and 90. Which is a reasonable prediction of the mean number of pages she reads each day throughout the year?

   A. 75   **C.** 95

   B. 85   **D.** 100

4. Vincent stood by the log flume at an amusement park and asked 120 people exiting the ride to name their favorite ride. The table below shows the results of his survey.

   Favorite Ride

Ride	Number of People
Roller coaster	25
Ferris wheel	22
Log flume	58
Carousel	15

   Which of the following is the most reasonable prediction based on the survey?

   A. The results of the survey that show the log flume is the favorite ride are biased results because only log flume riders were surveyed.

   B. The results of the survey that show the log flume is the favorite ride are reasonable results.

   C. The results of the survey that show the log flume is the favorite ride are unreasonable because the number of people surveyed was so small.

   D. The results of the survey that show the roller coaster is the favorite ride are unbiased results.

5. Carla runs for exercise several days each week. The number of miles she ran each week for the last 6 weeks is shown below.

   10, 9, 8, 14, 9, 12

   Which is a reasonable prediction of the mean number of miles Carla runs each week throughout the year?

   A. 14   **C.** 12

   B. 13   **D.** 10

6. Middle school students in a school district are collecting books to share with sister schools in Africa. The table shows the number of books that students at Lincoln Middle School collected for five months.

   Books Collected

Month	Number of Books
August	60
September	50
October	30
November	40
December	70

   A. What is a reasonable prediction of the mean number of books that students at Lincoln Middle School will collect each month throughout the school year? Explain your thinking.

   _____

   _____

   _____

   B. What is a reasonable prediction of the mean number of books collected each month by the students at each middle school in the school district? Explain your thinking.

   _____

   _____

   _____

Lesson Practice • Part 2

Choose the correct answer.

1. The table shows the results of two surveys that a teacher took to find out how many minutes her students spend on homework each night.

Sample	Data
A	20, 25, 30, 15, 20, 15, 25, 15
B	10, 10, 25, 20, 25, 25, 20, 10

Based on the sample data, which of the following is most likely to be closest to the median number of minutes that her students spend on homework each night?

A. 10 minutes

B. 15 minutes

C. 20 minutes

D. 25 minutes

2. The number of miles that Mr. Petty drove for work each week during the last 8 weeks is shown.

180, 170, 190, 200,
170, 200, 180, 210

Which is a reasonable prediction for the mean number of miles per week that Mr. Petty drives throughout the year?

A. 170 miles

B. 190 miles

C. 200 miles

D. 210 miles

3. Caroline surveyed 150 people at an NFL game and asked them to name their favorite professional sport to attend. The table below shows the results of her survey.

Favorite Sport to Attend

Sport	Number of People
Baseball	15
Basketball	28
Football	82
Hockey	14
Soccer	11

Which is the most reasonable prediction based on the survey?

A. The results showing football as the most popular professional sport is reasonable.

B. The results showing football as the most popular professional sport is biased because too many people were surveyed.

C. The results showing football as the most popular professional sport is biased because too few people were surveyed.

D. The results showing football as the most popular professional sport is biased since the only people who were surveyed paid to see a football game.

4. The number of minutes that Ella spent writing in her journal each week for the last 8 weeks is shown below.

    150, 120, 150, 140, 120, 140, 135, 145

    Which is a reasonable prediction for the mean number of minutes that Ella writes in her journal each week?

    A. 120 minutes

    B. 140 minutes

    C. 145 minutes

    D. 150 minutes

5. Eric surveyed people in front of a music store that sells a wide variety of musical instruments and asked them to name the instrument they like to play most. Eric's data is in the table.

    Favorite Instrument to Play

Instrument	Number of People
Bass	12
Drums	23
Guitar	36
Organ	12
Piano	17

    A. What is a reasonable prediction for the percent of musicians who like to play the guitar? Explain your reasoning.

    _____

    _____

    _____

    B. Does Eric surveying people in front of a music store make the survey biased? Explain your reasoning.

    _____

    _____

    _____

6. Mr. Dorsey teaches 80 math students. He surveyed 15 of those students to find out how many hours they studied over seven days. The survey was randomly distributed and anonymous. The results of the survey are shown below. Is each statement true? Select Yes or No.

9, 12, 16, 18, 10, 12, 11, 13, 8, 18, 14, 14, 15, 16, 17

A. The sample is representative of the population.   ○ Yes ○ No

B. The mean of the sample data is 15.   ○ Yes ○ No

C. The predicted mean for the population is about 13.5.   ○ Yes ○ No

D. The prediction that the mean of the population is about 13.5 is reasonable.   ○ Yes ○ No

7. Hamid stood outside Cooper's department store and asked random people as they exited to name their favorite department store. The table below shows the results of the survey. Which is a true statement? Circle all that apply.

Favorite Department Store

Store	Cooper's	Santo's	Green's	Wong's
Number of People	28	16	22	14

A. The number of people surveyed was 75.

B. Thirty-five percent of the people said Cooper's was their favorite department store.

C. The results of the survey were biased.

D. The results of the survey that show Cooper's was the favorite department store are not reasonable.

8. Mrs. Sakata teaches math. She surveyed students about their favorite subject. The results are shown in the table. Select True or False for each statement.

Favorite Subjects

Subject	English	Math	Science	History	Art
Number of Students	4	12	5	4	5

A. Twelve percent of the students chose math as their favorite subject.　　　○ True　○ False

B. The same number of students picked science and art.　　　○ True　○ False

C. Less than one-half of the students did **not** pick math.　　　○ True　○ False

D. The prediction that math would be the favorite subject in the school is reasonable.　　　○ True　○ False

9. Mr. Reed is a librarian. He kept track of the number of people who came to the library last week. The results are shown in the table below. Is each statement true? Select Yes or No.

Library Attendance

Day	Monday	Tuesday	Wednesday	Thursday	Friday	Saturday
Number of People	224	210	208	225	215	212

A. The total number of people who went to the library last week was 1,294.　　　○ Yes　○ No

B. The mean number of people who go to the library each day is about 250.　　　○ Yes　○ No

C. A reasonable prediction of the mean number of people who will go to the library each day throughout the year is 216.　　　○ Yes　○ No

D. Mr. Reed's prediction is biased.　　　○ Yes　○ No

Compare Data Sets

Getting the Idea

You can compare the means, medians, modes, ranges, and interquartile ranges of two different data sets to draw conclusions about the data.

A **stem-and-leaf plot** is an arrangement that shows groups of data arranged by place value. The stems represent multiples of 10 and the leaves represent the ones place. If a value occurs more than once, it is listed each time it occurs. For example the number 64 would have a stem of 6 and a leaf of 4.

Example 1

Students at two middle schools sold reusable bags to raise money for Earth Day. Nellie surveyed a sample of ten students from each school to find out how many bags each student sold. Her data is shown in the stem-and-leaf plots.

Roosevelt Middle School	
Stem	**Leaves**
1	0 3 7 9
2	0 1 4 4
3	5
4	2

Key: 1 | 0 = 10 bags

Madison Middle School	
Stem	**Leaves**
1	2 4
2	1 3 6 8 9
3	0 0 4
4	

Key: 1 | 2 = 12 bags

Compare the measures of central tendency for the two schools.

What conclusions can you draw from the comparisons?

Strategy   **Find the mean, median, and mode of each data set. Then compare.**

Step 1   Find the mean number of bags for Roosevelt Middle School.

The numbers of bags that students sold are listed below.

10, 13, 17, 19, 20, 21, 24, 24, 35, 42

$$\text{mean} = \frac{10 + 13 + 17 + 19 + 20 + 21 + 24 + 24 + 35 + 42}{10} = \frac{225}{10} = 22.5$$

Step 2 Find the median number of bags for Roosevelt Middle School.

The median is the middle number.

There are 10 values, so the median is the mean of the two middle values.

Find the mean of the fifth and sixth entries in the stem-and-leaf plot.

$$\text{median} = \frac{20 + 21}{2} = \frac{41}{2} = 20.5$$

Step 3 Find the mode number of bags for Roosevelt Middle School.

The mode is the value that occurs most often.

The mode is 24.

Step 4 Find the mean number of bags for Madison Middle School.

The numbers of bags that students sold are listed below.

12, 14, 21, 23, 26, 28, 29, 30, 30, 34

$$\text{mean} = \frac{12 + 14 + 21 + 23 + 26 + 28 + 29 + 30 + 30 + 34}{10} = \frac{247}{10} = 24.7$$

Step 5 Find the median number of bags for Madison Middle School.

Find the mean of the fifth and sixth entries in the stem-and-leaf plot.

$$\text{median} = \frac{26 + 28}{2} = \frac{54}{2} = 27$$

Step 6 Find the mode number of bags for Madison Middle School.

The mode is 30.

Step 7 Compare the measures of central tendency.

Compare the means: $24.7 - 22.5 = 2.2$

Compare the medians: $27 - 20.5 = 6.5$

Compare the modes: $30 - 24 = 6$

Solution **Students at Madison Middle School sold an average of about 2 to 6 more bags than the students at Roosevelt Middle School.**

Example 2

The dot plots show the weights of 8 packages that are waiting to be shipped from two stores owned by a large shipping company.

Weights of Packages (in pounds)

 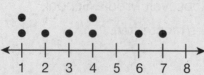

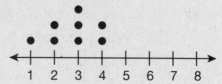

Compare the measures of central tendency for the two stores. What conclusions can you draw from the comparisons? What conclusions can you draw from the dot plots?

Strategy   **Find the mean, median, and mode of each data set. Then compare.**

Step 1   Find the mean, median, and mode for Store A.

The weights of the packages at Store A are 1, 1, 2, 3, 4, 4, 6, and 7.

$$\text{mean} = \frac{1 + 1 + 2 + 3 + 4 + 4 + 6 + 7}{8} = \frac{28}{8} = 3.5$$

$$\text{median} = \frac{3 + 4}{2} = \frac{7}{2} = 3.5$$

$$\text{modes} = 1 \text{ and } 4$$

Step 2   Find the mean, median and mode for Store B.

The weights of the packages at Store B are 1, 2, 2, 3, 3, 3, 4, 4.

$$\text{mean} = \frac{1 + 2 + 2 + 3 + 3 + 3 + 4 + 4}{8} = \frac{22}{8} = 2.75$$

$$\text{median} = \frac{3 + 3}{2} = \frac{6}{2} = 3$$

$$\text{mode} = 3$$

Step 3   Compare the measures of central tendency.

Compare the means: $3.5 - 2.75 = 0.75$

Compare the medians: $3.5 - 3 = 0.5$

Compare the modes: You cannot compare the modes since one set of data has 1 mode and the other set has 2 modes.

The mean and median weights of the packages are 0.5 to 0.75 pound heavier at Store A than at Store B.

Step 4   Compare the dot plots.

From the dot plots, you can see that the weights of the packages at Store A are more spread out than at Store B. At Store B, the package weights are more closely clustered together.

Solution   **The mean and median weights of the packages are greater at Store A than at Store B. There is a greater variability in the weights of the packages at Store A than at Store B.**

Example 3

The dot plots show the heights of sunflowers grown in two different plots on a farm.

Height of Sunflowers (in inches)

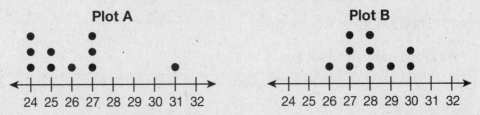

Make a visual comparison of the dot plots. What do they tell you about the average heights of the sunflowers on the two farms?

Compare the mean heights and the mean absolute deviations of the two plots. What conclusions can you draw about the variability of the heights?

Strategy   **Examine and compare the two dot plots. Then, find the mean height and mean absolute deviation for each plot and compare these to your visual findings.**

Step 1   Look at the dot plots and compare them visually.

Notice that the scale on both plots is the same; they both show numbers from 24 to 32.

In Plot A, the dots are all toward the left side of the plot, except for one value. They form a cluster from 24 to 27 inches and have a single outlier of 31 inches.

In Plot B, the dots are all in the middle, with the highest columns of dots on 27 and 28 inches.

In general, the heights appear to be higher in Plot B, and more variable in Plot A.

Step 2   Find the mean for Plot A.

The heights of the sunflowers in Plot A are 24, 24, 24, 25, 25, 26, 27, 27, 27, 31.

$$\text{mean} = \frac{24 + 24 + 24 + 25 + 25 + 26 + 27 + 27 + 27 + 31}{10} = \frac{260}{10} = 26$$

Step 3   Find the MAD for Plot A.

Subtract to find the deviations.

$24 - 26 = -2$ $24 - 26 = -2$ $24 - 26 = -2$

$25 - 26 = -1$ $25 - 26 = -1$ $26 - 26 = 0$

$27 - 26 = 1$ $27 - 26 = 1$ $27 - 26 = 1$ $31 - 26 = 5$

Add the absolute deviations: $2 + 2 + 2 + 1 + 1 + 0 + 1 + 1 + 1 + 5 = 16$

Find the MAD.

$$\text{MAD} = \frac{16}{10} = 1.6$$

Step 4   Find the mean for Plot B.

The heights of the sunflowers in Plot B are: 26, 27, 27, 27, 28, 28, 28, 29, 30, 30.

$$\text{mean} = \frac{26 + 27 + 27 + 27 + 28 + 28 + 28 + 29 + 30 + 30}{10} = \frac{280}{10} = 28$$

Step 5   Find the MAD for Plot B.

Subtract to find the deviations.

$26 - 28 = -2$ $27 - 28 = -1$ $27 - 28 = -1$ $27 - 28 = -1$

$28 - 28 = 0$ $28 - 28 = 0$ $28 - 28 = 0$

$29 - 28 = 1$ $30 - 28 = 2$ $30 - 28 = 2$

Add the absolute deviations: $2 + 1 + 1 + 1 + 0 + 0 + 0 + 1 + 2 + 2 = 10$

Find the MAD.

$$\text{MAD} = \frac{10}{10} = 1$$

Step 6   Compare the means and MADs to your visual findings for the dot plots.

The mean height of the sunflowers in Plot B is greater than the mean height of the sunflowers in Plot A. The deviation from the mean is greater in Plot A than in Plot B. These results support the conclusions that you drew in Step 1 from a visual comparison of the two dot plots.

Solution   **The mean height of the sunflowers in Plot B is greater than the mean height of the sunflowers in Plot A. There is a greater variability in the heights in Plot A than in Plot B.**

Coached Example

The dot plots show the grades of students who took the same ten-question science quiz in two different classes.

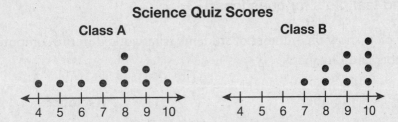

Science Quiz Scores

Compare the measures of central tendency for each class. What conclusions can you draw from the comparisons?

What are the measures of central tendency? _____

What are the quiz scores for Class A? _____

What is the mean for Class A? _____

What is the median for Class A? _____

What is the mode for Class A? _____

What are the quiz scores for Class B? _____

What is the mean for Class B? _____

What is the median for Class B? _____

What is the mode for Class B? _____

Subtract to compare the means. _____

The mean score of Class A is about _____ than the mean score of Class B.

Subtract to compare the medians. _____

The median score of Class A is about _____ than the median score of Class B.

Subtract to compare the modes. _____

The mode score of Class A is about _____ than the mode score of Class B.

Look at the dot plots.

How does the variability of the scores from Class A compare to the variability of the scores from Class B? _____

The mean, median, and mode scores of Class A are _____ than those of Class B.

The variability of the scores from Class A _____ the variability of the scores from Class B.

Lesson Practice • Part 1

Choose the correct answer.

Use the stem-and-leaf plots for questions 1–3.

The stem-and-leaf plots show the number of students who worked in the computer lab during the months of September and October.

September			October		
Stem	Leaves		Stem	Leaves	
1	0 3 6 7 8		1	1 4 5 5 7 8 8 9	
2	1 2 3 4 4 7		2	0 0 0 2 5 6	
3	2 2 2 9		3	1	

Key: 1 | 0 = 10 students   Key: 1 | 1 = 11 students

1. Which statement about the median number of students in the computer lab is true?

    A. The median for September is the same as the median for October.

    B. The median for September is 4 more than the median for October.

    C. The median for September is 3 less than the median for October.

    D. The median for September is 2 more than the median for October.

2. Which statement about the mode number of students in the computer lab is true?

    A. The mode for September is the same as the mode for October.

    B. The mode for September is 4 less than the mode for October.

    C. The mode for September is 8 more than the mode for October.

    D. The mode for September is 12 more than the mode for October.

3. Which statement about the range of the number of students in the computer lab is true?

    A. The range for September is the same as the range for October.

    B. The range for September is 12 more than the range for October.

    C. The range for September is 9 more than the range for October.

    D. The range for September is 2 less than the range for October.

4. The dot plots show the heights of students on the basketball team and the lacrosse team.

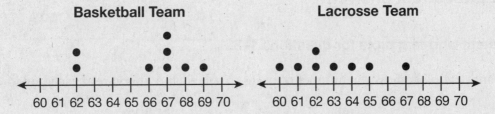

Which statement about the mean heights is true?

A. The mean height on the basketball team is 3 inches more than the mean height on the lacrosse team.

B. The mean height on the basketball team is 5 inches more than the mean height on the lacrosse team.

C. The mean height on the basketball team is 7 inches more than the mean height on the lacrosse team.

D. The mean height on the basketball team is the same as the mean height on the lacrosse team.

5. The double box plot below shows the math quiz scores for Ms. Lindsey's first and second period classes.

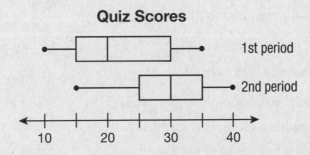

A. Find the median, range, and IQR for each class period.

_____

_____

_____

B. What conclusions can you draw from the comparisons? Explain your thinking.

_____

_____

_____

Lesson Practice • Part 2

Choose the correct answer.

Use the stem-and-leaf plots for questions 1–3.

The stem-and-leaf plots show the number of pages that Neil and Sheryl read each day for 2 weeks.

Neil

Stem	Leaves
0	0 8 9
1	6 7 9
2	3 4 5 7
3	
4	2 4 8 8

Key: 1 | 2 = 12 pages

Sheryl

Stem	Leaves
0	
1	5 7 8
2	2 6 6 7 9
3	0 2 3 6 9
4	2

Key: 1 | 5 = 15 pages

1. Which statement about the mean pages read is true?

   A. The mean for Sheryl is 1.5 more than for Neil.

   B. The mean for Sheryl is 3 more than for Neil.

   C. The mean for Sheryl is 42 more than for Neil.

   D. The mean for Neil is 22 more than for Sheryl.

2. Which statement about the IQR is true?

   A. The IQR for Sheryl is 4.5 more than for Neil.

   B. The IQR for Sheryl is 6 more than for Neil.

   C. The IQR for Neil is 9 more than for Sheryl.

   D. The IQR for Neil is 15 more than for Sheryl.

3. Which statement about the variability of the data is true?

   A. The data for Neil has significantly more variability than the data for Sheryl.

   B. The data for Neil has slightly more variability than the data for Sheryl.

   C. The data for Sheryl has significantly more variability than the data for Neil.

   D. The data for Sheryl has slightly more variability than the data for Neil.

4. The dot plots show the number of runs the Panthers softball team scored and allowed.

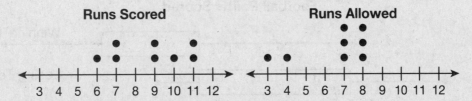

Runs Scored and Allowed

Which statement about the variability of the data is true?

A. The data for runs scored has a greater IQR and MAD.

B. The data for runs scored has a greater IQR and the data for runs allowed has a greater MAD.

C. The data for runs allowed has a greater IQR and the data for runs scored has a greater MAD.

D. The data for runs allowed has a greater IQR and MAD.

5. Martina is going to make a double box plot. This is the information she has.

- Set B has the least value.

- Set A has a greater first quartile.

- Set B has a greater third quartile.

- Set B has the greatest value.

- The means and medians are equal.

A. Which data set has the greater IQR? Explain your reasoning.

_____

_____

B. Which data set has the greater MAD? Explain your reasoning.

_____

_____

C. If the data were graphed on a dot plot, how much overlap would there be? Explain your answer.

_____

_____

_____

6. The box plot compares the points scored by the winning and losing football teams in a league. Use numbers from the box to make each statement true.

Football Points Scored

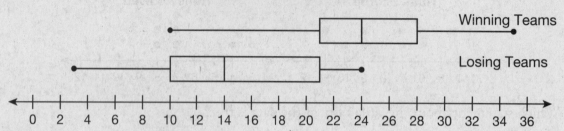

The median for the winning teams was _____.

The median for the losing teams was _____.

The range for the winning teams was _____.

The range for the losing teams was _____.

The IQR for the winning teams was _____.

The IQR for the losing teams was _____.

3	14	25
7	21	28
11	24	35

7. Richard surveyed a sample of waitresses from two restaurants to find out how much money they make in tips on a weekday evening. The results are shown in the dot plots below. Which is a true statement? Circle all that apply.

Waitress Tips (in dollars)

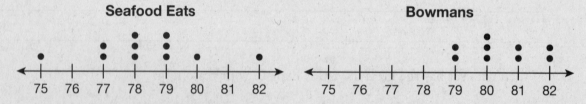

A. On average, the waitresses at Bowmans generally make about $2 more per day in tips than the waitresses at Seafood Eats.

B. The median daily tip total at Bowmans is $2 more than the median daily tip total at Seafood Eats.

C. The mode daily tip total at Seafood Eats is $78 and $79.

D. The range of daily tip totals at Seafood Eats is $4.

E. The range of daily tip totals at Bowmans is $7.

8. The ages of workers at two companies are shown in the stem-and-leaf plots below. Write each number in the correct box.

Endo, Inc.			Blanco, Ltd.	
Stem	**Leaves**		**Stem**	**Leaves**
1	8		1	
2	0 3 3 3 7 9		2	2 4 5 8
3	2 6		3	3 5 7 7
4	3		4	6
5			5	2

Key: 1 | 8 = 18 years old   Key: 2 | 2 = 22 years old

23	37	27.4	34	30	25

Mean, Median, Mode of Endo, Inc. Ages	Mean, Median, Mode of Blanco, Ltd. Ages

Domain 5: Cumulative Assessment for Lessons 28–35

1. Reyes conducted an experiment by tossing two number cubes a total of 72 times. He found the sums and recorded the results in the table.

Sum	Frequency
2	2
3	4
4	7
5	7
6	11
7	12
8	9
9	9
10	5
11	5
12	1

Which sum has a greater experimental probability than theoretical probability?

A. 3

B. 5

C. 6

D. 12

2. Isabelle is taking a survey to find the most popular music group of students in her community. Which of these is **not** a way for her to get a representative sample of this information?

A. ask every tenth student she sees at a concert

B. ask every fifth student entering her school in the morning

C. ask every third student she encounters at the mall

D. ask every student at a local movie theater

3. Students on a soccer team sold health bars for a fund-raiser. The box plot shows the number of bars sold by the students on the team.

Health Bar Sales

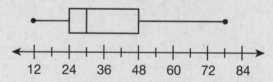

Which statement is **not** true about the data?

A. The range of the sales is 72 bars.

B. The first quartile of the data is 24 bars.

C. The third quartile of the data is 48 bars.

D. The IQR of the data is 24 bars.

4. The dot plot shows the number of skateboards sold at a shop each week over 10 weeks. The data are a representative sample of the number of skateboards sold throughout the year.

Number of Skateboards Sold

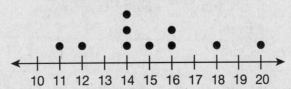

Which best represents the mean number of skateboards sold each week throughout the year?

A. 14

B. 14.5

C. 15

D. 15.5

5. The stem-and-leaf plots show the ages of people who attended a local play on two different nights.

Thursday

Stem	Leaves
1	8 9
2	0 3 5
3	0 1 4 6 7 9 9
4	3 4 7 8
5	2 5 6 8

Key: 1 | 8 = 18 years old

Friday

Stem	Leaves
1	1 2 2 3 4 5 6 6
2	1 2 4 5 6 7
3	0 2 5
4	1 6
5	3

Key: 1 | 1 = 11 years old

Which statement about the median ages is true?

A. The median for Thursday is the same as the median for Friday.

B. The median for Thursday is 15 more than the median for Friday.

C. The median for Thursday is 18 more than the median for Friday.

D. The median for Thursday is 20 more than the median for Friday.

6. Amir rolled two number cubes, labeled 1 to 6, 25 times. His results are shown in the table below.

Amir's Number Cube Results

Sum	Number of Tosses
Even	9
Odd	16

Amir repeats the experiment and rolls the two number cubes 125 times. Based on the experimental probability, which of the following is the most reasonable prediction?

A. The sum of the cubes will be odd 80 times.

B. The sum of the cubes will be even 25 times.

C. The sum of the cubes will be odd 20 times.

D. The sum of the cubes will be even 13 times.

7. The times that Gemma practiced piano last week were 20, 25, 30, 20, and 30 minutes. The times that Arturo practiced piano last week were 50, 15, 30, 35, and 10 minutes. Which of the following statements is true?

A. The variability in Gemma's mean practice times is about half the variability in Arturo's mean practice times.

B. The variability in Gemma's mean practice times is about twice the variability in Arturo's mean practice times.

C. The variability in Gemma's mean practice times is about one-third the variability in Arturo's mean practice times.

D. The variability in Gemma's mean practice times is about one-fourth the variability in Arturo's mean practice times.

8. The table shows the results of two surveys that Melinda took to find out how many minutes students in the all-city band spend practicing their instruments each day.

Sample	Data
A	20, 35, 45, 45, 60
B	25, 45, 50, 50, 60

Based on the sample data, which of the following is most likely to be closest to the mean number of minutes that students in the all-city band spend practicing each day?

A. 41

B. 44

C. 46

D. 48

9. The weights, in pounds, of five pumpkins from a pumpkin patch are 17, 18, 17, 15, and 13. What is the MAD of the weights?

_____

10. Chris sells homemade soap. The table shows the number of bars of soap Chris sold at the Farmer's Market over a five week period.

Soap Sales

Week	Number Sold
1	130
2	180
3	200
4	110
5	140

A. What is a reasonable prediction of the mean number bars of soap Chris will sell each week at the Farmer's Market? Explain your thinking.

_____

_____

_____

_____

_____

B. What is a reasonable prediction of the median number of bars of soap Chris will sell each week if he sells his soap at other craft markets? Explain your thinking.

_____

_____

_____

_____

_____

Glossary

absolute value the distance of a number from 0 (Lesson 2)

acute angle an angle that measures less than 90° (Lessons 21, 24)

acute triangle a triangle with 3 acute angles (Lesson 21)

additive inverse the opposite of a number; the additive inverse of 4 is -4 (Lesson 5)

adjacent angles two angles with a side in common (Lesson 24)

altitude the height of a pyramid (Lesson 22)

angle a geometric figure formed by two rays that have a common endpoint called the vertex (Lesson 24)

area the number of square units inside a figure (Lessons 23, 25)

associative property of addition changing the grouping of the addends does not change the sum: $(a + b) + c = a + (b + c)$ (Lesson 14)

associative property of multiplication changing the grouping of the factors does not change the product: $(a \times b) \times c = a \times (b \times c)$ (Lesson 14)

base a number that is raised to a given power; in 5^3, the base is 5 (Lesson 14)

base a face of a solid figure; the face for which a solid figure is named (Lesson 22)

biased sample a sample in which some members of the population have a greater chance of being selected for the sample than other members (Lesson 30)

box plot a method of displaying a distribution of data values by using the median, quartiles, and extremes of the data set; also known as box-and-whiskers plot (Lesson 32)

center a point such that every point on the circle is an equal distance from it (Lesson 23)

circle the set of all points in a plane that are the same distance from a given point called the center (Lesson 23)

circumference the distance around a circle (Lesson 23)

coefficient the numerical factor of a term containing a variable (Lesson 17)

commutative property of addition changing the order of the addends does not change the sum: $a + b = b + a$ (Lesson 14)

commutative property of multiplication changing the order of the factors does not change the product: $a \times b = b \times a$ (Lesson 14)

complementary angles two angles whose measures have a sum of 90° (Lesson 24)

complex fraction a fraction in which the numerator and/or denominator contains a fraction (Lesson 4)

compound event a combination of two or more events in a probability experiment (Lesson 29)

constant a symbol representing a value that does not change (Lesson 17)

constant of proportionality the constant ratio by which two quantities co-vary in a proportion; also called the unit rate or the constant ratio (Lesson 11)

cross multiplication multiplying the numerator of one ratio by the denominator of the other ratio in a proportion (Lesson 10)

cross section a two-dimensional shape obtained by the slicing of a plane through a three-dimensional figure (Lesson 22)

cube a solid figure with 6 faces that are squares (Lesson 22)

cubic unit a cube with an edge length of 1 of any unit (Lesson 27)

data numerical information (Lesson 30)

decimal a number with a decimal point that names part of a whole or group (Lesson 1)

denominator the bottom number of fraction that tells how many equal parts there are (Lesson 1)

dependent event an event in which the first outcome affects the second outcome (Lesson 29)

diameter the distance across a circle through its center (Lesson 23)

directly proportional an equation that can be written in the form $y = kx$ (Lesson 12)

discount the amount of money that is taken off the original price (Lesson 2)

distributive property over addition When the sum of two numbers is multiplied by a factor, multiply each of the two numbers by the factor, and then add the products: $a(b + c) = ab + ac$. (Lessons 6, 14)

distributive property over subtraction When the difference of two numbers is multiplied by a factor, multiply each of the two numbers by the factor, and then subtract the products: $a(b - c) = ab - ac$. (Lesson 14)

dividend a number to be divided (Lesson 4)

divisor the number by which the dividend is divided (Lesson 4)

dot plot a display that uses a number line and dots to show data (Lesson 31)

equation a mathematical sentence that contains an equal sign (Lesson 16)

existence of additive inverses for every a, there exists $-a$ so that $a + (-a) = (-a) + a = 0$ (Lesson 5)

experimental probability the ratio of the total number of times the favorable outcome occurs to the total number of trials in a probability experiment;
$$P_e = \frac{\text{number of favorable outcomes}}{\text{total number of trials}}$$
(Lesson 28)

exponent tells how many times a number is used as a factor (Lesson 14)

expression a mathematical statement that combines numbers, operational signs, and sometimes variables (Lesson 13)

face a flat surface of a solid figure (Lesson 22)

favorable outcome the desired outcome of a probability experiment (Lesson 28)

first quartile the median of the data values less than the median (Lesson 32)

fraction a rational number that names part of a whole or group (Lesson 1)

fundamental counting principle a method used to find the number of possible outcomes of a given set of events by multiplying the number of possible outcomes of each event (Lesson 29)

greatest common factor (GCF) the greatest factor that is common to two or more numbers (Lesson 1)

improper fraction a fraction with a numerator that is greater than the denominator (Lesson 4)

independent event an event in which the first outcome does not affect the second outcome (Lesson 29)

inequality a mathematical sentence that compares two expressions (Lesson 19)

integers the set of numbers consisting of the counting numbers, their opposites, and zero: ..., -3, -2, -1, 0, 1, 2, 3, ... (Lesson 1)

interest the amount of money you are paid by the bank for its use of the money you have in a savings account, or the amount of money you pay a lender for the use of borrowed money (Lesson 2)

interquartile range (IQR) the difference between the first and third quartiles in a data set (Lesson 32)

inverse operations operations that undo each other, such as addition and subtraction or multiplication and division (Lesson 17)

is greater than (>) a symbol that shows that the first quantity is greater than the second quantity (Lesson 19)

is greater than or equal to (≥) a symbol that shows that the first quantity has a value greater than or equal to the second quantity (Lesson 19)

is less than (<) a symbol that shows that the first quantity is less than the second quantity (Lesson 19)

is less than or equal to (≤) a symbol that shows that the first quantity has a value less than or equal to the second quantity (Lesson 19)

least common denominator (LCD) the least common multiple of the denominators (Lesson 7)

like terms terms that contain the same variable(s) raised to the same power(s) (Lesson 14)

linear relationship a relationship with a constant rate of change; it forms a straight line when graphed (Lesson 12)

mean the sum of the terms in a data set divided by the number of terms in the set (Lesson 31)

mean absolute deviation (MAD) the average of the absolute deviations from the mean (Lesson 33)

measure of central tendency the measures of the mean, median, and mode, which describe the center of a data set (Lesson 31)

measure of variation the measures of the range, interquartile range, and mean absolute deviation, which describe the spread of a data set (Lesson 32)

median the middle term in a data set ordered from least to greatest (Lesson 31)

mixed number a number that has a whole-number part and a fraction part (Lesson 4)

mode the term or terms that appear most often in a data set (Lesson 31)

net the amount that remains after deductions and adjustments have been made (Lesson 7)

net two-dimensional representation of a solid figure that shows each face of the solid (Lesson 26)

numerator the top number in a fraction that tells how many equal parts are being considered (Lesson 1)

obtuse angle an angle that measures greater than 90° and less than 180° (Lessons 21, 24)

obtuse triangle a triangle that has 1 obtuse angle (Lesson 21)

order of operations the agreed-upon sequence for conducting multiple operations (Lesson 14)

origin the point named by (0, 0) on a coordinate grid, where the axes intersect (Lesson 12)

outlier a number that is much less or much greater than the other numbers in the data set (Lesson 32)

parallel two lines or line segments that never meet and remain the same distance apart (Lesson 22)

parallelogram a quadrilateral with 2 sets of parallel sides (Lessons 23, 25)

percent (%) per hundred (Lesson 1)

percent error the difference between an estimate and the actual value, divided by the actual value (Lesson 2)

π (pi) the ratio of the circumference to the diameter of a circle, approximated as 3.14 (Lesson 23)

population the group of interest in a survey (Lesson 30)

possible outcome any of the results that can happen in an experiment (Lesson 28)

power of 10 the number 10 used as a base with an exponent (Lesson 8)

principal an amount of money saved or borrowed (Lesson 2)

prism a solid figure with a pair of bases that are parallel, congruent polygons (Lesson 22)

probability the chance of an event happening (Lesson 28)

product the result of multiplication (Lesson 4)

proportion an equation that shows that two ratios are equivalent (Lesson 10)

pyramid a solid figure with one base that is a polygon and all the other faces are triangles (Lesson 22)

quartile one of the three values that divide the data set into four quarters (Lesson 32)

quotient the result of division (Lesson 3)

radius the distance from the center of a circle to any point on the circle (Lesson 23)

random sample a sample in which each individual in the population has an equal chance of being part of the sample (Lesson 30)

range the difference between the greatest value and the least value in a data set (Lesson 32)

rate a ratio that compares two quantities that have different units of measure (Lesson 9)

ratio a comparison of two numbers (Lesson 9)

rational number a number that can be expressed in the form $\frac{a}{b}$, where a and b are integers and $b \neq 0$; includes integers, fractions, and some decimals (Lesson 1)

reciprocals two numbers whose product is 1; a and $\frac{1}{a}$ are reciprocals (Lesson 4)

rectangle a quadrilateral with 2 sets of parallel sides and 4 right angles (Lesson 25)

rectangular prism a solid figure with 6 faces that are rectangles (Lesson 22)

rectangular pyramid a pyramid with a base that is a rectangle (Lesson 22)

repeating decimal a decimal with one or more digits that repeat without limit (Lesson 3)

representative sample a sample that is similar to the entire population (Lesson 30)

right angle an angle that measures 90° (Lessons 21, 24)

right triangle a triangle that has 1 right angle (Lesson 21)

sale price the cost of an item after a discount has been applied (Lesson 2)

sales tax a tax based on the cost of an item (Lesson 2)

sample a smaller group taken from a population (Lesson 30)

scale the part of a scale drawing that tells how much the actual object has been reduced or enlarged (Lesson 20)

scale drawing a representation of an object that is proportional to the actual object (Lesson 20)

similar figures that have the same shape but may have different sizes; similar figures are proportional (Lesson 21)

simple interest one type of fee paid when money is deposited or loaned (Lesson 2)

simplest form a fraction whose numerator and denominator have only 1 as a common factor (Lesson 1)

simulation a way of acting out a problem by conducting an experiment similar to the problem that needs to be solved (Lesson 29)

slant height the height of a lateral face in a pyramid (Lesson 22)

solid figure a figure that has length, width, and height (Lesson 22)

solution set the solution of an inequality (Lesson 19)

square a quadrilateral with 4 equal sides and 4 right angles (Lesson 25)

square pyramid a pyramid with a base that is a square (Lesson 22)

square unit a square with a side length of 1 of any unit (Lesson 25)

stem-and-leaf plot an arrangement of numerical data that separates the one digits from the other place values (Lesson 35)

subtrahend the number that is being subtracted; in 7 - 3 the subtrahend is 3 (Lesson 5)

supplementary angles two angles whose measures have a sum of 180° (Lesson 24)

surface area the sum of the areas of all the surfaces of a solid figure (Lesson 26)

survey a question or set of questions used to gather data (Lesson 30)

term a number in a ratio (Lesson 9)

terminating decimal a decimal with a finite number of decimal places (Lesson 3)

theoretical probability the ratio of the number of favorable outcomes to the total number of possible outcomes; $P(A) = \dfrac{\text{number of favorable outcomes}}{\text{number of possible outcomes}}$ (Lesson 28)

third quartile the median of the data values greater than the median (Lesson 32)

three-dimensional figure a figure that has length, width, and height (Lesson 22)

trapezoid a quadrilateral with 1 set of parallel sides (Lesson 25)

trial one of the times that an experiment is performed (Lesson 28)

triangle a two-dimensional figure with 3 sides (Lessons 21, 25)

unit rate a rate in which the second quantity in the comparison is 1 unit (Lesson 9)

vertex the point where two rays or line segments meet (Lesson 24)

vertical angles two non-adjacent angles formed by intersecting lines; vertical angles are congruent (Lesson 24)

volume the number of cubic units that fit inside a solid figure (Lesson 27)